SAINT COLUMBA

For my aunt 'Bada', Imelda Harding –
my first history teacher

Brian Lacey

SAINT COLUMBA

HIS LIFE AND LEGACY

the columba press

First published in 2013 by
the columba press
55A Spruce Avenue,
Stillorgan Industrial Park,
Blackrock, County Dublin

Cover by Shaun Gallagher
Origination by The Columba Press
Printed by Bell & Bain Ltd

ISBN 9781 85607 879 5

Contents

Preface

> As I am not worthy myself to obtain what I ask from God, I pray to you Colum Cille to speak to Him as one of his own household, to get grace from Him for me so that I can properly finish this work that I want to do for you, so that it might be to his Honour and the raising up of your name, and to the good of the people who read or listen to it and to the good of my own soul and body, and to the Devil's dishonour and great hurt.
>
> Manus O'Donnell,
> *Betha Colaim Chille* (1532)

Colum Cille (the form in Irish) or Columba (the form in Latin), along with Brigid and Patrick, was honoured throughout the medieval period as one of the three patron saints of Ireland, but he was also greatly honoured in Scotland and further afield. This book sets out to describe why this was so. Among other things he was the founder of the important monastery on Iona which became one of the most influential centres of the Christian religion and cultural activity in these islands in the early medieval period. The memorialisation of the saint also resulted in an enormous cultural legacy. Of the three patron saints of Ireland, Colum Cille could be said to have some little extra claim to our attention. Patrick, of course, was not Irish but British and it is an open question, to say the least, whether or not Brigid ever really existed. Colum Cille, although heavily disguised as a result of the admiration of his later devotees, was a genuine Irish historical person who lived throughout much of the sixth century.

This book is based on a much smaller version, *Colum Cille and the Columban Tradition*, which was published in June 1997 in conjunction with the programme of events intended to commemorate what was then generally understood to be the fourteen-hundredth anniversary of the death of its subject in 597. However, the widespread celebrations in 1997 generated and stimulated a series of lectures, conferences, publications and research programmes that greatly extended our existing knowledge on the subject.

A separate but related event was the thirteen-hundredth anniversary, also in 1997, of the 697 Synod of Birr where the 'Law of Innocents' was promulgated by Adomnán, the ninth abbot of Iona. 'Adomnán's Law' as it was also known was 'guaranteed' by a host of clerical and royal figures from both Ireland and northern Britain, all of them apparently united in various ways by some form of loyalty to the federation of 'Columban' churches (the *familia Columbae*) that was led from Iona. That anniversary also generated its share of conferences, lectures and memorial publications.

The overall result of all of that concentrated scholarly activity – during and in the run-up to 1997 and the following years – was that, subsequently, a much better understanding of the details of the subject became available than had been the case only a relatively few years previously.

Perhaps one of the most important 'structural' breakthroughs in this regard came about from the publication – in print and on the internet – of the researches into the chronology of the Irish annals by Dr Daniel Mc Carthy of Trinity College Dublin. The annals are our basic skeletal guide to events in Ireland and Scotland in the earliest part of the early medieval period. However, the oldest surviving versions of them, embedded in for instance the Annals of Ulster and the Annals of Tigernach, often provide contradictory or multiple dates for a known event at this early period. Dr Mc Carthy's published 'synchronisms' considerably revised (he might prefer to say, 'restored') the dating systems of those annals, giving what is probably a more accurate picture of the real chronology of the period. Where possible in the text below the dates cited have been co-related with his revisions.

Perhaps the greatest impact in this regard in the context of this book was on the revision of the dates of three of the major events in the saint's own life: his birth, his '*navigatio*' or journey to Iona, and his death. Dr Mc Carthy's work would now suggest that those events took place respectively in 520, 562 and 593, rather than in 521, 563 and 597, as was previously generally thought to be the case. Although Dr Mc Carthy was already aware that Columba's death had most probably occurred in the year 593, he sensitively refrained from 'spoiling' the 1997 'party' and did not publish his conclusions widely until some years later. Dr Mc Carthy's work has also allowed a much fuller picture to emerge of the role of the monastery on Iona, and indeed probably of Columba himself as well as some of his successors, in the origination and development of the very idea of the annals themselves.

Other significant developments in Ireland since 1997 include an important paper published in 2000 by Dr Ailbhe Mac Shamhráin, in which the received account of the genealogical connections of king Díarmait mac Cerbaill are questioned. Díarmait was a contemporary and possibly a close relative of Columba and a major actor in the battle of Cúl Dreimne which was one of the alleged significant events of the saint's life. Recent research by the present author on the origins of the various kingdoms of Donegal in the early medieval period – which partly builds on Dr Mac Shamhráin's work – has also required a revision of some of the alleged 'facts' about Columba and his monastery on Iona. For instance, as will be argued below the common assertion that many of the early abbots of Iona were drawn from the founder's own kin cannot be accepted unquestioningly any more – although a Donegal connection does seem likely in most cases.

Relevant research developments have also been taking place in Scotland such as the publication in 2000 of the report of the excavations at the important Dál Riata site at Dunadd in Argyll. Martin Carver's preliminary reports on research at the ancient ecclesiastical site of Portmahomack in northeastern Scotland have also been published. Ian Fisher's study of the *Early Medieval Sculpture in the West Highlands and Islands* which appeared in 2001 allows, among other things, informative comparisons to be made with the similar material from various places in Ireland and elsewhere. Although a very different kind of book, George and Isabel Henderson's, *The Art of the Picts: Sculpture and Metalwork in Early Medieval Scotland*, published in 2004, deals with those areas of the country not specifically covered by Ian Fisher. Most significantly James Fraser's revisionist book *From Caledonia to Pictland: Scotland to 795* appeared in 2009. Fraser shows how much more complex the political situation in northern Britain was in early medieval times than was previously understood, as also the interaction of the various polities there with their counterparts in Ireland. Alex Woolf's companion volume *From Pictland to Alba 789–1070* (2007) gives a totally new interpretation of the emergence of the Scottish kingdom of Alba.

Many other papers and books by British, Irish and other scholars – archaeologists, historians, art historians and philologists – on diverse aspects of the subject of Colum Cille and related issues have also appeared since 1997. One Celtic scholar from Russia, Tatyana Mihailova, even gave a conference paper (somewhat tongue-in-cheek) on the colour of the saint's eyes (!) – at least as reflected in the romantic literature of the medieval period. Attention might be drawn to the 1997 compendium book *Studies in the Cult of Saint Columba* edited by Cormac Bourke, which contains a host of relevant papers that will be referred to time and again below. It might also be worth singling out two papers by Prof. Jean Michel Picard which describe in great detail the spread of the cult of Columba during the early medieval period in various countries in continental Europe. One of those papers was originally given as a Royal Irish Academy, Columban memorial discourse in Derry on 9 June – the saint's feast day – in 1997. The other paper had been delivered at a conference in Cork in April of the same year also organised to commemorate the saint's alleged anniversary. The proceedings of the latter conference – including several other papers that are directly relevant here – were published in 2001 as *Studies in Irish Hagiography: Saints and Scholars*, edited by John Carey, Máire Herbert and Pádraig Ó Riain.

The thirteen-hundredth anniversary in 2004 of the death of Adomnán, Columba's most famous 'biographer' also stimulated a similar range of studies and revisions. Perhaps the most memorable of the related events was the wonderful conference organised by the Centre for the Study of Religion in Celtic Societies of the University of Wales at Lampeter, in association with Historic Scotland, on the island of Iona itself. The papers arising from that conference have been published in *Adomnán of Iona: Theologian, Lawmaker, Peacemaker*, edited by Jonathan Wooding (2010).

As a result of all this new research and interest, a major revision of a book originally written for 1997 – which set out then to digest and synthesize the available information about the life and legacy of Saint Colum Cille, is now timely. The text of that 1997 publication has been thoroughly revised, corrected and extended, and several totally new chapters as well as many new sections and bibliographical notes have also been added. This book is over twice the length of its 1997 exemplar and, in view of all the research carried out since then, it could have been even longer. However, this study cannot deal with every single aspect of a subject that covers over fourteen hundred years of history and cultural achievement; it aims instead at selecting the most important points, at least from the viewpoint of the author.

In offering my sincere thanks to the entire team at Columba Press, I am also extremely grateful to the late Michael Adams and the other members of staff of Four Courts Press for facilitating this new publication. I am particularly indebted to the many scholars – only some of whom have been mentioned above – whose work on these matters I have had the benefit of studying, especially in and since 1997. I would most especially want to thank my colleague and long-term friend Ian Fisher for reading and commenting in detail on an earlier draft of this book and for being my first and best guide to Iona. I also wish to thank my former colleagues in the Discovery Programme for various kindnesses and practical help. The remaining errors and misunderstandings are, of course, my own.

Introduction

> I protest that, for the miraculous deeds and gifts ascribed in this little book to certain servants of God, I claim no other belief than that which is ordinarily given to history resting on mere human authority; and that, in giving the appellation of Saint or Blessed to any person not canonized or beatified by the Church, I only intend to do it according to the usage and opinion of men.
>
> Father William Doherty,
> *Derry Columbkille* (1899)

Columba or Colum Cille, also known by a variety of spellings and pronunciations, has been venerated as a 'saint' for nearly a millennium and a half. In a cultural (although clearly not in a theological) sense, a medieval saint is a social construct, the character of which often grows and changes over time. Below we will see the character attributed to Colum Cille being revised many times. In this regard, as will also be shown below, even the name Colum Cille is part of such a construct. Colum Cille was never officially canonized by the church and much of his special status is derived from long-standing tradition and widespread but often very localised folklore – both in Ireland and Scotland as well as elsewhere. Nevertheless, without much doubt, the original individual must have been a very influential and almost certainly also a 'saintly' man. From shortly after his death at the end of the sixth century his alleged reputation for holiness as well as for other virtues and abilities began to be cultivated and celebrated in literary and other forms. To his successor and distant relative, Adomnán, at the end of the seventh century Colum Cille was unambiguously Saint Columba. He has retained that distinction ever since.

Whether that honorific title is accepted or not and even whether or not it is accepted that there can really be such a thing as a 'saint', Columba stands out as one of the most important figures of the sixth century in Ireland and Scotland and, indeed, of the early history of these islands in general. In this book no judgement is made on the issue of his special religious status – his reputation as a saint. Such a judgement would have to rely on values derived from sources other than 'history'. However, it is still important to have some understanding of what the relevant people of the time may have understood by such a claim. As two recent commentators have noted in connection with Columba:

> It is of vital importance, if we want to understand the early medieval world, to come to terms with saints. It is the belief in saints which separates, more than anything else, the medieval world from the classical world which preceded it, and the modern world which followed it.[1]

Whatever about his importance in the religious sphere, the impact that Columba and his followers made in many other aspects of contemporary culture – such as what we would now call the visual arts, literature, even science and the recording of history, as well as what we would know as international diplomatic and political relations – would be difficult to overestimate. It is little wonder that he – or at least the achievements accumulated in his name – has been so much honoured and remembered over such a long time.

Since Columba died in the last decade of the sixth century, people have been writing in praise of him – both in secular and religious terms and in poetry as well as prose. Despite the vast accumulation of those texts it would still not be possible to write a modern biography of him. Many of the stories and collections of stories told about him are legendary in content and were written down many hundreds of years – in one outstanding case as much as a thousand years – after his death. Some sort of memory of him was also propagated in a variety of artistic and oral forms; not only, as we will see, in Ireland and Scotland but also in several parts of continental Europe as well. A study of Colum Cille is in that sense a study of his legacy; a study of what he left to his successors and what each successive generation in turn has made of that story over the fourteen hundred years or so that have elapsed since he died. Much of what was subsequently told or written about him far from clarifying the events of his own life for us, actually distorts them. However, these later works testify to the enormous affection in which the memory of this man has been held and cultivated down the intervening centuries. The later works often tell us, incidentally, a great deal about the times in which they were composed and about the state of the cult of the saint at those times.

The principal problem in attempting to excavate sixth-century fact from the well-meaning but later elaborations and fictions is that of finding authentic sources from which to reconstruct an accurate picture of the past.

[1] T. Clancy & G. Márkus, *Iona: The earliest Poetry of a Celtic Monastery* (Edinburgh 1995), 116.

We have a vast amount of texts purporting to deal with Colum Cille and his followers. It is not too much of an exaggeration to say that since the saint's day there has been – almost in the manner of modern literary figures such as James Joyce and W.B. Yeats – a Colum Cille 'industry'. However, a fundamental problem remains: how much, if anything, do these subsequent works tell us about events in the sixth century or in the other relevant periods of later time?

Columba is mentioned briefly in the various documents known as the Irish annals. These normally provide us with the skeletal outline of early Irish and Scottish history, but they have their own complicated history and the extent to which we can rely on them as contemporary evidence for the sixth century when Columba was actually living is still the subject of considerable scholarly analysis and debate. Paradoxically as we will see, Columba himself – as well as some of his better known successors on Iona such as Adomnán – appear to have played a pioneering role in the initiation and development of the particular form of chronicle-writing that developed into the annals. In that sense, the concept of the accurate contemporary recording of Scottish and Irish 'history', as distinct from the propagation of legend and myth, can arguably be described as a Columban 'invention'.

We also have some fairly reliable genealogical material that can be used to identify the family connections of Columba and those associated with him. The great Anglo–Saxon scholar and churchman – the Venerable Bede (673–735) mentions Columba (as he usually calls him) and his followers frequently in his important work *Historia Ecclesiastica Gentis Anglorum* ('Ecclesiastical History of the English People') written in 731. There are three so-called 'Lives' of the saint, unfortunately none of which provide us with a straightforwardly acceptable narrative account of his life. Adomnán's *Vita Columbae* was written in Latin on Iona towards the end of the seventh century. Early in the second half of the twelfth century an anonymous author – almost certainly based in Derry – wrote another Life in the Irish language. Finally, in the years leading up to 1532 the soon-to-be chieftain of the O'Donnell lords of Donegal – the flamboyant Manus – collected a huge amount of information about the saint and had a major Life composed, also in the Irish language.

In the intervals between these three seminal works and subsequent to them, other material was written and versions and abridgements of the older texts were circulated and copied – not alone in Ireland and Scotland but in other parts of Britain and on the continent. The figure of Colum Cille also frequently appears in the medieval Lives of other early Irish saints, as well as in some of the secular texts of approximately the same period. Most of this literature was unashamedly propagandistic, written as much in the interest of the institution or place and time of its origin as on behalf of its sixth-century subject. Even Adomnán, the greatest of Columba's 'biographers' – who was closest to him in time, and seemingly in spirituality, was not totally innocent of such a motive.

Adomnán too was clearly a very 'saintly' man and was himself later venerated as a saint. As we will see, he was the author of other written material besides the Life he wrote about his predecessor. But more than anyone else Adomnán was responsible for establishing Columba's reputation as a saint. In reading his *Vita Columbae* it is difficult to separate the ideas of the author from those alleged to have belonged to his subject. While some people may think the parallel a little strained, there is more than a hint in Adomnán's work of a similarity with the sort of relationship that existed about a thousand years previously between the ideas of Socrates and the writings of Plato.

The great English historian of the early Irish church Kathleen Hughes said of Adomnán's method of composition that it was marked by 'the frequent borrowings of words and phrases, sometimes sentences' from older works on the Lives and writings of such earlier saints as Anthony, Martin and Jerome. At least in that respect this work is following in the Columban tradition; it certainly owes a great deal to the authors, ancient as well as modern, who have written about Colum Cille and his followers. Many of the ideas and words used in those various texts have been 'borrowed' and recycled here.

No one has done more in modern times to make our task of understanding the Columban textual inheritance easier than Prof. Máire Herbert. Both in her work on the individual texts and in her general approach, she has taught us, literally, how to 'read' the original Columban material in order to get closer to its true historical meaning. We are indebted also to all those who have provided scholarly and annotated modern translations of the original works, such as Marjorie and the late Alan Anderson and Prof. Richard Sharpe. Those authors as well as countless others have acknowledged their indebtedness to the great nineteenth-century scholar and Church of Ireland ecclesiastic William Reeves, who was working in a supremely academic manner on those texts as much as one hundred and fifty years ago. I long ago gave up trying to remember how many times I thought I had discovered a new idea about this subject only to find that Reeves had published it already in the 1850s.

This work does not claim to be a substitute for any of the accounts mentioned above. Instead it attempts to make a digest of what is now known about Columba and the 'institution' that he founded as it evolved through subsequent history. I also want to describe something about the way the memory and the legacy of the saint were passed on in literature, in art, in folklore, and even in the landscapes of Ireland, Scotland and other places. Of necessity it was essential to be sceptical about some of the best-known stories concerning the saint, but those stories are still included here and related to what the ancient Irish *Liber Hymnorum* calls the *causa*, the reason or cause why they were written or composed – possibly even invented. If there is a critical approach here to the saint's legacy, it is exercised with affection and praise.

The Columban legacy was itself one of praise-poetry and story-telling. Manus O'Donnell attributed the defence of that inheritance to none other than the saint himself. In the fictional accounts of the Convention of Druim Cett – held sometime in the last quarter of the sixth century, Colum Cille was said to have been asked to give his 'judgement' there on whether the kings should continue to support the role of poets and poetry in Ireland. In his reply, Colum Cille claimed no less than the highest possible precedent:

> For know you that God himself bought three-fifties of Psalms of praise from King David ... And on that account it is right for you to buy the poems of the poets and to keep the poets in Ireland. And as all the world is but a fable, it were well for you to buy the more enduring fable rather than the one that is less enduring.
>
> And he then made this quatrain:
>
> If poet's verses be but fables,
> So be food and garments fables,
> So is all the world a fable,
> So is man of dust a fable.[2]

[2] B. Lacey, *The Life of Colum Cille by Manus O'Donnell* (Dublin 1998), 178–9.

Sources

A note on primary sources

All study of Columba has to start with the original texts which purport to describe his life. Adomnán's *Vita Columbae* is available in several modern editions. A.O. and M.O. Anderson, *Adomnán's Life of Columba* (Edinburgh 1961; 2nd edition, Oxford 1991), gives the Latin text as well as a translation and comprehensive explanatory material. Richard Sharpe, *Adomnán of Iona: Life of St Columba* (London 1995, reprinted 2005), gives an English translation as well as copious detailed notes on many aspects of the subject. John Marsden, *The Illustrated Columcille* (London 1991), has a translation and discussion, and contains many marvellous photographs of some of the sites, manuscripts and objects associated with the saint.

Máire Herbert, *Iona, Kells and Derry: the history and hagiography of the monastic familia of Columba* (Oxford 1988; reprinted Dublin 1996), is the most important book on the subject, and also contains an edition and translation of the twelfth-century Middle Irish Life of Colum Cille. Thomas Owen Clancy's and Gilbert Márkus's book, *Iona: The earliest Poetry of a Celtic Monastery* (Edinburgh 1995), contains scholarly editions of the texts with translations of all the important early poems associated with the saint, as well as detailed notes and discussions.

The original Irish language text of one of the manuscripts of Manus O'Donnell's Life of the saint, together with a translation into sixteenth-century English as well as supporting introductory material, is available in A. O'Kelleher and G. Schoepperle, *Betha Colaim Chille: Life of Columcille* (Urbana 1918, reprinted Dublin 1994). A more modern English version with an introduction and some notes can be found in B. Lacey *The Life of Colum Cille by Manus O'Donnell* (Dublin 1998).

The relevant Irish annals are also available in modern printed editions, to varying degrees. The so-called Annals of the Four Masters has been edited by John O'Donovan as: *Annals of the Kingdom of Ireland by the Four Masters,* 7 Vols, (Dublin 1851–6, reprinted Dublin 1998). The Annals of Tigernach and the Annals of Ulster are our best guide to the contents of the original Iona

Chronicle. They can be found in: Annals of Tigernach, edited and partially translated by W. Stokes, *Revue Celtique*, xvi–xviii, 1895–7 (omnibus facsimile reprint: Felinfach, Wales 1993); *Annála Uladh: Annals of Ulster* edited and translated by W.M. Hennessy and B. MacCarthy (Dublin 1887–1901, reprinted 1999) and *Annals of Ulster*, i, edited and translated by S. Mac Airt and G. Mac Niocaill (Dublin 1983). Dr Daniel Mc Carthy's synchronisms for the annals, published on the internet in April 2005, is available at: http://www.cs.tcd.ie/Dan.McCarthy/chronology/synchronisms/annals-chron.htm.

The same author's paper arguing for a revision of the dates of the three main events in Columba's life is available at: http://www.celt.dias.ie/publications/tionol/dmcc01.

Modern editions of other sources used below will be referenced in the appropriate places.

Columba's Birth and Early Life

> On the seventh day of the mid-winter month [December] Colum Cille was born and on the ninth day of the mid-summer month [June] he died. And fitting to his life was the season he came into it, for wintry was his life in respect of cold and darkness, pain and penance, and in respect of his inflicting hardship and discomfort on his own body. And, further, fitting to the life he entered from this world was the season when he died, for it is the season that is purest and warmest and brightest, and most shining of all the year.
>
> Manus O'Donnell,
> *Betha Colaim Chille* (1532)

Just to the northeast of the Derryveagh and Glendowan mountain ranges, which dominate the centre of County Donegal, is the townland of Lacknacoo. Its anglicised name is derived from the Irish *Leac na Cumha*, the meaning of which will be returned to below. The wider surrounding area, known commonly as Gartan, lies on the more fertile lower foothills of the mountains on the edge of the magnificent but wildly desolate Glenveagh National Park. The area overlooks a cluster of three picturesque lakes: Lough Nacally, Lough Akibbon and, the largest of the three, Gartan Lough. At the centre of this peaceful and beautiful rural district, inside a small fenced area near the end of a grassy lane, is a low earthen mound on top of which is a U-shaped setting of stones. Immediately beside these is a large stone slab (*leac*), dotted with small 'cupmarks'. The position of the slab might indicate that, perhaps originally, it covered the other stones. It is not at all clear what sort of ancient monument this actually is but it gives the impression of something prehistoric, maybe dating to the Bronze Age.

Tradition (probably dating to no more than the past few centuries) has it, however, that the slab formed the floor of a tent in which the future Saint Colum Cille was brought into this world. As we will see – apart from its other associations – the stone can be taken as a symbol of the mixture of fact and legend that wraps itself around the character of the saint, making the tracking down of the actual details of his real life a relatively complicated task.

The name *Leac na Cumha* is difficult to translate precisely. *Cumha* is a word used widely in Donegal Irish to convey ideas of sorrow, homesickness, loneliness or nostalgia. *Leac na Cumha* is famous in the folk beliefs of County Donegal. In the nineteenth century it was the practice of poor local emigrants who thought they were leaving their homeland forever to come and stay there the night before their departure from Ireland. Most of those people would have been leaving on ships from the port of Derry about thirty miles away where, according to legend, in the middle of the sixth century Colum Cille himself was believed to have left his homeland as an exile. Those who came to the slabstone believed that as Colum Cille himself was an emigrant, sleeping there on the very spot where he was born would – as a contemporary Catholic bishop put it – 'help them to bear with lighter hearts the heavy burden of the exile's sorrow'. The customs practiced at that site have continued to evolve. Since the anniversary year of 1997 a tradition has commenced of 'pilgrims' scattering low value copper coins on the slab; in turn these have gradually begun to discolour the 'holy stone'.

Manus O'Donnell gives the story of the flagstone on which the saint's birth is said to have occurred, as he had heard it in the early sixteenth century. On the night before Colum Cille was born his mother Eithne saw a beautiful youth who told her that there was a flagstone in Lough Akibbon and that it should be brought to a place called *Rath Cnó* – 'The Fort of the Nuts' and that the saint would be born there. The flagstone was found floating on the surface of the lake and Eithne's family carried it to the place specified by the 'angel'. At the moment that the baby was delivered the stone spontaneously opened a cross-shaped niche for him. Eithne was also believed to have brought forth a round, blood-coloured stone, *an cloch ruadh* – 'the red stone'. According to O'Donnell, Colum Cille left that stone in Gartan 'to work marvels and wonders, and it would not allow a covering of gold or silver for itself despite that such was often attempted but it did "suffer" a case of silver or of gold'. Cormac Bourke suggested that the original reference to this object could have been to *an clog ruadh* 'the red [perhaps bronze?] bell', rather than to a stone.[1] An early medieval bronze Gartan Bell does exist and is now preserved in the National Museum of Ireland.

About half a mile to the north of Lacknacoo in the neighbouring townland – Churchtown – is another site also associated with the birth and early life of the saint. The historian Fr Pádraig Ó Gallachair, who spent a lot of his life studying the monuments and traditions of County Donegal, felt that the story of the saint's birth and the flagstone at *Ráth Cnó* fitted the Churchtown site better than Lacknacoo.[2] For instance the slab known as *Leac na Cumha* has no inscribed cross (at least on its visible surface), as seems to be required by

[1] C. Bourke, 'Insignia Columbae II', in C. Bourke, *Studies in the Cult of Saint Columba* (Dublin 1997), 162–83, pp 170–1.

[2] Rev. P. Ó Gallachair, 'Where was St. Colmcille born at Gartan', *Donegal Annual* (1963), 219–22.

Manus O'Donnell's description. At Churchtown on the other hand there is the ruins of a tiny sixteenth-century chapel, and nearby are the badly preserved remains of two plain stone crosses, the foundations of a small rectangular structure known as the 'Abbey', and a 'holy well'.[3] A *turas* or pilgrimage in honour of Colum Cille has been performed at this place from time immemorial on his feast day – 9 June, and even today the little altar inside the ruined church is usually heaped with the trifle offerings of those who come to seek the assistance or protection of the saint. All sorts of things (from small religious objects, to children's toys and coins, even a ticket for a Glasgow Rangers football match) have been left – one might even say 'sacrificed' – there in recent years.

Another tradition, still widely respected in the surrounding area, is that the unusual white 'Gartan Clay' is a powerful protective and curative charm. A similar tradition regarding clay from Tory Island is also part of Columban lore. Ancient protocols require that members of the Ó Dúgáin family have to extract the special clay on Tory; at Gartan the same function must be performed by the O'Friels. Another tradition about Gartan Clay is that it must never be requested; instead it should be given freely as an unasked for gift. Modern legends abound as to the variety of its contemporary uses and occasional embarrassing discovery by foreign police and customs officials who did not have the advantage of schooling in the esoteric nature of Irish folk customs. Some international footballers of Donegal extraction are even believed to carry Gartan Clay 'into battle', anxious to secure whatever extra assistance the saint can make available to them by virtue of its special properties.

Manus O'Donnell said that the semi-secret place where Gartan Clay is found is where Eithne first felt 'the sickness of childbirth' and where she spilled some of her blood.

> Flour isn't whiter or finer than that clay and whoever eats it or carrys it with him is never burned or drowned. Nor shall he die without a priest. And every woman in the pangs of childbirth who eats it shall be helped. And whoever puts it on his tongue on the first day that he is seized by a fever will have no bitter taste in his mouth as long as the fever lasts. And it is its nature to heal every disease. But it must be one of the natives of Gartan [the O'Friels] that digs the clay for distribution, for it is said that once a stranger went to dig it but [the clay] fled from him and went into the heart of a tree or a great trunk nearby, and it was not found again in its own place until holy water was sprinkled there and the place was blessed.

The truth, of course, is that we do not know where exactly Columba was born or grew up. The earliest surviving evidence – that from his Life by Adomnán, which was written about a century after his death – tells us simply that:

[3] B. Lacy, *Archaeological Survey of County Donegal* (Lifford 1983), 252.

> the holy Columba was born of noble parents having as his father Fedelmid, Fergus's son, and his mother, Eithne by name, whose father may be called in Latin 'son of a ship', and in the Irish tongue *Mac-naue.*

Unfortunately there is no historical source earlier than the twelfth century connecting Colum Cille with the Gartan area, with the possible exception of the explanation of the name of nearby Kilmacrenan – *Cill Mhic Réanáin.* One of the saint's sisters is said, in a source dating to about the beginning of the eighth century, to have been the mother of the sons of Enán – *Mhic Réanáin* [nEnáin] – after whom the place was allegedly named.[4] If that tradition was true, then it would be the oldest actual connection of the saint with the general Gartan area. However, there is a sort of geographical logic that points to that part of Donegal as a likely location for the saint's birth.

Our historical records for this early period are so meagre and confused that the sources are not even agreed on the year of the saint's birth. The various sets of annals – which, at face value, are extremely unreliable as guides to events at this early period – record dates as diverse as: 518, 519, 521 and 523. Adomnán implies that the saint was seventy-six years of age when he died but does not tell us in what year that event occurred. There used to be a consensus among those who had studied the fragmentary evidence that Columba was probably born in 521, left Ireland for Iona in 563 and died in 597. However, as mentioned above, in a major revisionary study of the chronology of the Irish annals Dr Daniel Mc Carthy has claimed recently that these events are more likely to have happened in 520, 562 and 593, respectively.[5] Late tradition also claims that the saint's birthday fell on 7 December and that the day was Thursday. 7 December 520 was actually a Saturday, although that date did fall on a Thursday in 519. The fact that the change of year was marked at the time on 25 March (rather than 1 January) might possibly be a reason for such confusion. In folklore there are many associations linking Colum Cille with Thursdays, especially in the Hebridean traditions but also in the customs and beliefs of Donegal and the northwest of Ireland generally.

> On a Thursday was born Colum Cille,
> In Gartan, angelic and dear,
> As generous Patrick predicted to Brigid,
> When the time of his death came near.
>
> On a Thursday fair Colum was christened,
> In Templedouglas of fame.
> Just 'Crimthann' is all that they called him,
> Before 'Colum' was used as his name.

[4] A.O. & M.O. Anderson, *Adomnán's Life of Columba* (Edinburgh 1961), 548–9; the letters 'n' and 'r' are often interchangeable in Irish.
[5] http://www.celt.dias.ie/publications/tionol/dmcc01.

On a Thursday without any sorrow,
I tell you, he took his very first walk.
On a Thursday they baptized that baby,
Always good-natured in deed and in talk.

Each Thursday, no evil exchanges
With God's angels, talking in heaven.
They altered his name to 'Colum Cille',
And ignored the old one, 'Crimthann'.

And again:

I am Colum Cille,
Without mirth or boastfulness.
I'm in heaven every Thursday,
But in my body, nevertheless.[6]

Those beliefs may be related to the widespread understanding that the saint could offer special protection from thunder and lightning. In the Germanic and Scandinavian languages – although not in Irish or Scottish Gàidhlig – Thursday is the day of the god Thor, the ruler of thunder. We know that the earliest Gaelic Columban traditions in the Hebrides were overlain by a layer of Norse customs brought there subsequently by the Viking settlers of those islands who, in time, would convert to Christianity. Such a cultural mix could have provided the background to the later beliefs expressed in the following Scottish charm.

Thursday of Columba benign,
Day to send sheep on prosperity,
Day to send cow on calf,
Day to put web in the warp.
Day to put coracle on the brine,
Day to place the staff to the flag,
Day to bear, day to die,
Day to hunt the heights.
Day to put horses in harness,
Day to send herds to pasture,
Day to make prayer efficacious,
Day of my beloved, the Thursday.[7]

[6] Lacey, *Manus O'Donnell*, 93–4.

[7] Translated by Alexander Carmichael, *Carmina Gadelica: Hymns and Incantations* (1994 edition), 80. The *Carmina Gadelica* is an assemblage of folk material, much of it Columban in nature, collected by Alexander Carmichael in the nineteenth century in the Highlands and Islands of Scotland. It was edited by Carmichael himself (first two vols) and others, and published in six volumes between 1900 and 1971. A one-volume edition, representing the complete collection of translations but without the original Gàidhlig texts, was edited by C.J. Moore (Edinburgh 1992, reprinted 1994).

Columba's father Fedelmid (modern: Felim or Phelim) was said to be a grandson of the legendary Conall who was believed to have given rise to the celebrated Donegal Cenél Conaill dynasty, as also to *Tír Chonaill* – the name in Irish for the greater part of Donegal. We cannot be certain that such an individual actually existed as his 'life' would have occurred before the onset of 'history'; in fact, many other early Irish population groups claim to be descended from a late prehistoric Ulster figure called Conall. The Cenél Conaill seem to have originated in the very good agricultural land of east Donegal – the lower valley of the River Finn which was known in ancient times as *Mag nItha*.[8] However, before Columba died that kingdom – under their powerful and ambitious kings Ainmire mac Sétna and the latter's son Áed mac Ainmirech, both of whom were close relatives of Columba – had probably been expanded to at least double its original extent. Before Áed died in 596, the Cenél Conaill kingdom probably stretched already from Derry in the north to the area a few miles south of where Donegal town is nowadays located. The actual southern boundary of the kingdom may have been marked by the Columban or at least Cenél Conaill church of *Druim Tuama* or Drumhome, which will be mentioned again below.

The Cenél Conaill remained extremely influential in the northwest of Ireland for many centuries. The later medieval lords of Donegal, the O'Donnells, claimed – probably falsely – to be descended from them. The original Conall and what were said to have been his many brothers were reputed later in the Middle Ages – again probably falsely – to have been sons of the legendary king Niall Noígiallach or Niall 'of the Nine Hostages', from whom were allegedly descended most of the politically important families of early medieval Ireland. These families were later known collectively as the Ui Néill (literally: 'the descendants of Niall'), although that dynasty was, at the very least, partly artificially-constructed retrospectively in the eighth century. From the sixth century onwards, however, the group of families who would become known as the Uí Néill had ruled over most of the northern half of Ireland. As well as their own individual local kingdoms, they shared among themselves the originally sacral high-kingship of Tara. The primacy of that kingship over all the other kingdoms of Ireland was repeatedly asserted throughout the second half of the first millennium, although that superiority was not always recognised or unequivocally accepted by the other kingdoms and dynasties throughout the rest of the country.[9]

Columba's relations, the Cenél Conaill, were thus a very powerful political group. That reality gave rise to the later exaggerated legends that Colum Cille himself would have been eligible for the kingship of Tara, although he was

[8] B. Lacey, *Cenél Conaill and the Donegal Kingdom: AD 500–800* (Dublin 2006), 131–43.
[9] See E. Bhreathnach (ed.), *The Kingship and Landscape of Tara* (Dublin 2005).

definitely born into a vigorous and expansive aristocracy. In later medieval times the O'Friel family – the family who have the prerogative for gathering the wonder-working Gartan Clay – claimed the privilege of being his closest blood relatives. According to their genealogies – whatever about historical reality – they claimed to be descended from Iogen or Éogan, the saint's brother.

Columba's mother was said to have been called Eithne. Eithne was also the name of a widely honoured pre-Christian territory goddess,[10] so we have to be especially cautious about accepting the traditions about her. Some of the stories claim that the saint's mother belonged to the Leinster people known as the Uí Bairrche who lived in what is now County Wexford. In the southeast of that county is an overgrown graveyard called Ardcolum ('Colum's Height'), formerly an ancient ecclesiastical site. Also close by is a holy well dedicated to Saint Colum Cille. This unexpected honouring of a saint from the opposite extreme of the country (they had of course many local saints of their own in that part of Ireland) may be a reflection of the medieval belief about the birthplace and origins of his mother. The so-called Middle Irish Life of Colum Cille, written in the second half of the twelfth century, says that Eithne belonged to a people known as the *Corpraige* of Leinster. An alternative genealogical tradition links her to a population group that lived beside Lough Erne in what is now County Fermanagh.

An altogether more likely origin for his mother, if we are to accept the cumulative traditions concerning the place of the saint's birth and early childhood, is that she belonged to the *Corpraige* of the Fanad peninsula,[11] which lies just to the north of the Gartan area. We know very little about these people but they appear to have been a relatively unimportant ancient tribal unit that came to be dominated, by the mid-seventh century at the latest, through the expansion of Columba's own people, the Cenél Conaill. Apart from their possible association with Eithne, we have no other evidence for the existence of the *Corpraige* of Fanad. However, in the early sixth century Fanad was probably the designation of a polity somewhat larger than the present peninsula of that name and may have included the Gartan area to its immediate south. The lands of the *Corpraige* then might have been – more or less – adjacent to the territory of the Cenél Conaill, the people to whom Columba's father belonged. It is quite possible and certainly logical that he could have chosen a wife from such a neighbouring kingdom.[12]

In modern times the idea of what constitutes Fanad has tended to 'move' further north – towards the top of the peninsula itself, but that may not have

[10] D. Ó hÓgáin, *The Lore of Ireland: an Encyclopaedia of Myth, Legend and Romance* (Cork 2006), 192–3.
[11] P. Ó Riain, *Corpus Genealogiarum Sanctorum Hiberniae* (Dublin 1985), 61, 78, 173 and 184.
[12] Lacey, *Cenél Conaill*, 189–90.

been the case in the early sixth century. Fanad is a long peninsula surrounded on three sides by deep sea loughs and the open ocean. It is very likely that in the sixth century almost any one of its male inhabitants could have been described as the 'son of a ship – *Mac-naue*', as Eithne's father (Columba's maternal grandfather) was called according to Adomnán. Unlike Fedelmid, Eithne was later treated as a saint herself. There is a nineteenth-century tradition that she was buried in Scotland – on the island of *Eileach an Naoimh* in the Garvellachs south of Mull. While there is not much reason to accept the historical truth of that tradition, what is believed to have been the actual place of her burial is marked by a small, circular enclosure about three meters in diameter, with a number of upright slabs, one of which has an incised cross on it.

Conall Gulban
I
Mac-nave Fergus
I I
Ernán ——?——Eithne================Fedelmid ——————————————Brendan
I I
Mac-decuil=Cuimne–Columba (593)—Éogan—Sinech—Mincoleth==Enan Cobthach-Báithín (596)
I I I
Mernoc–Cascene–Meldal–Bran I Aidan—Conrí Colmán & *other sons of Enan*
I *Men of mocu-Céin*
I______________
Tochumme
grandson of Sinech

Table 1: Colum Cille's relatives, according to genealogical tradition.

We seem to know something about the other close members of Columba's family from a list that appears to have been drawn up about the beginning of the eighth century.[13] That list was preserved – apparently uniquely – among the records of Durham cathedral in England where there was a devotion of some sort to Colum Cille which continued right up to the later middle ages.[14] The list tells us that he had a younger brother called Iogen (Éogan?) and three sisters: Cuimne the wife of Mac-decuil whose four sons were called Mernoc, Cascene, Meldal, and Bran who was buried in Derry; Mincoleth mother of the sons of Enán after whom the monastery of Kilmacrenan near Gartan was named (one of whom was called Colmán – a hypocoristic or 'endearing' form which means something like 'little' or 'dearest' Colum); and Sinech, mother of the men of mocu-Céin (probably the people known as the Ciannacht from the valley of the River Roe in the present County Derry) whose names were Aidan (a monk) and Conrí (probably another monk) who was buried at the Columban monastery of Durrow in the midlands, now in County Offaly. Sinech was also the grandmother of To-chumme, a priest who died in old age on Iona. To-chumme also seems to be an endearing or hypocoristic form of the root name Colum. Ernán who went with Columba to Iona was one of his uncles, probably his mother's brother. Another uncle, Brendan, was his father's brother and his two sons, Baithín (also called Conín) and Cobthach – first cousins of Columba, were among those who left Ireland with the saint for Iona.

The various Lives of the saint, as would be expected in hagiographical texts, have prophetic stories in which the birth of this holy man is 'forecast' (retrospectively). Many of the other well-known Irish saints, including Patrick and Brigid, are said to have predicted the success of his life. Adomnán tells a number of those stories. In one of them, before the boy was born his mother is said to have had a dream in which she was visited by an angel who gave her a marvellously embroidered robe. The robe moved away from Eithne but grew greater in size than the plains, mountains and woods. Then the angel told Eithne not to grieve the loss of the robe as she would bear a son 'of such grace that he, as though one of the prophets of God, shall be counted in their number; and he has been predestined by God to be a leader of innumerable souls to the heavenly country'.

[13] R. Sharpe, *Adomnán of Iona* (London 1995, reprinted 2005), 354.

[14] The list is preserved in the late twelfth-century manuscript, now British Museum Additional 35110, and printed in various modern editions of Adomnán's *Vita Columbae*: see esp. Andersons, *Columba*, 546–9; Sharpe, *Adomnán*, 354, although the identification of Colum Cille's sisters there differs from that presented here; Marsden, *Illustrated Columcille*, 182, where, in addition to the translation of the list, there is an excellent photograph of the original manuscript text.

As in many similar stories told about other Irish saints such as Brigid, the description of the expansion of the robe is used retrospectively to suggest the foreknowledge of the growth of the influence of the person in question. Two almost identical stories about the expansion of Colum Cille's own cloak during his lifetime occur in the folklore of Tory Island off County Donegal and Inishmore in the Aran Islands off Galway Bay. *Gort a' Chochaill* (but sometimes inaccurately, *capaill* or 'horse') or 'the field of the cloak' is still pointed out on Inishmore.

Even more fantastically, Manus O'Donnell claimed that:

> not alone was it the saints of Ireland and the patriarchs, who had the spirit of prophecy from God, that foretold the coming of Colum Cille but the druids and those that hadn't the faith foretold his birth a long time before it happened.

O'Donnell instances as one example the story of the legendary ancient hero Finn mac Cumhail, who set his famous dog Bran loose after a deer at a stream at the head of *Senglenn* ('the old glen') in southwest Donegal that was known in O'Donnell's time and to this day as Gleann Cholm Cille. The hound refused to pursue the deer across the stream; something it was never known to have done before. Then Finn who was famous for his 'gift of knowledge' revealed the explanation. He said that Colum Cille would be born and that he would have many graces and much influence. He would come and bless the glen from the same stream so that it would be a sanctuary for everyone that would go there for evermore. It was in honour of the holy man that the dog had mercy on the deer and, therefore, did not pursue it across the stream. 'And from that time *Belach Damhain* – "the path of the stag" – is the name of the place where Bran spared the deer.'

About four miles southeast of Gartan is the remains of the ancient church of Templedouglas – *Tulach Dubhglaise*. Tradition says that it was there that Colum Cille was baptised. Just over a mile to the north is the *Cédimthecht* (literally: 'the first going') *Choluim Cille*, the place as reported by Manus O'Donnell where the future saint is said to have taken his first few walking steps as a baby. A section of rock outcrop has two carved 'footprints' which are said to mark the location of the latter event. There were also other sites and landscape features in the immediate vicinity of Templedouglas, associated with such Columban stories. It is, of course, very unlikely that knowledge could have been preserved of where such ordinary events would have taken place in the early life of what was – despite his undoubted aristocracy and later fame – still a relatively ordinary boy at the beginning of the sixth century. Those beliefs testify more to a much later desire by some of his devotees to provide real locations for the drama of the saint's life, and to associate what were probably already ancient sites in the landscape with an important local hero. Colum Cille appears frequently in Irish and Scottish folklore, but particularly in that from County Donegal.[15] One of the principal characteristics of those stories is to associate him with very specific geographical locations and features that are still to be seen in the modern landscape.

However, notwithstanding the caution expressed here, it is very likely that the boy was born, was baptised, did learn to walk, and did begin to study in a general sense in northwest Donegal – almost certainly in the beautiful countryside around Gartan and Kilmacrenan.

Manus O'Donnell tells us – although we have no way of knowing if it is true – that the boy was at first called Crimthann, an Irish name that means something like 'fox' or 'deceitful one'. However, 'the angels of heaven' knowing that this was an inappropriate name for a would-be saint inspired the other boys that played with him to call him Colum Cille, that is 'dove of the church'. This is the name by which he came to be known widely in the Gaelic traditions of Ireland and Scotland. However, it is not at all clear that this formulation was ever used during his own lifetime. Adomnán – writing close to the year 700 – always uses the plain Latin form Columba (literally 'dove') as does, for the most part, Bede writing in 731. The Irish language poem possibly written originally about 600 (but now surviving only in a later version – see below) known as the *Amrae Coluimb Chille*, 'the Eulogy of Colum Cille', refers to him several times as Columb, but one line, *ro- Columb ó Chille – cúalamar* – 'which we have heard from Colum Cille' – seems to use a tmesis or split form of the cultic name as a literary device.[16] However, two poems written in Irish apparently before 677 and maybe as early as the 640s interchangeably use the names Columb and Columb Cille.[17] It seems that his actual 'Christian' name was some variation of Colum in Irish, probably originally in the form 'Columb' (that is, with a final 'b') and Columba in Latin. This was later anglicised as Colm in Ireland and Calum in Scotland.[18]

A very popular practice associated with personal names in Ireland during the very earliest phases of historic times was the giving of hypocoristic – that is, diminutive or endearing – forms of the root name. Depending on what prefixes and endings were attached to the original root or 'radical' name, as well as some other linguistic variations that might have included for example dialect or other local differences, a single name could be transformed into a whole host of variations. Prof. Pádraig Ó Riain has shown, for example, that

[15] See for instance Seán Ó hEochaidh, 'Colm Cille sa tSeanchas', *Irisleabhar Muige Nuadhat* (1963), 33–50 and Carmichael, *Carmina.*

[16] Clancy & Márkus, *Iona,* 108–9.

[17] *Ibid.,* 136–51.

[18] See N. Ó Muraíle, 'The Columban Onomastic Legacy' in Bourke, *Studies in the Cult,* 193–218, pp 193–4.

the simple name Colum could be changed in this way (among others) into: Caimme, Caimmíne, Cainne, Cainnech (often anglicised in Scotland as Kenneth), Cainneóc, Cammán, Cammóc, Coimme, Coinne, Colmán, Commae, Commán, Conna, Conóc, Cuimmíne, Cumma, Cummóc, Dochonna, Mocholmóc, Mochonna, Mochonóc and Mochumma.[19]

At a period when communication across distances would have been extremely difficult, it is easy to see how the same person, but referred to in different places by different variations of their name, could be 'split' as it were into a number of distinctly different characters. In this way the original connections and associations of an individual could be forgotten and a new 'character' invented. In at least one or two instances such a 'fate' may have befallen Colum Cille. For example, Prof. Ó Riain has suggested that two saints who are usually thought of as absolutely separate individuals – Colmán of Dromore in County Down and Cainnech – may in fact be aliases of Colum Cille.[20] The name Cainnech is an element in that of Kilkenny (*Cill Cainnigh* or 'Cainnech's church'), as well as of several other places in Ireland and Scotland.

In addition Columbanus, which is the Latin form of the diminutive Irish name Colmán ('little Colum'), was often confused in medieval Latin sources with the name of Columba. Columbanus was definitely the name of another genuinely Irish saint – the founder of the continental monasteries at Luxeuil in France and Bobbio in Italy – who died in 615. Along the same lines, a female but non-Irish Saint Columba – associated with Sens in what is now northern France – was also occasionally confused with the saint of Iona.[21]

Although almost certainly born in the Gartan area in the territory of his mother's family, the boy Columba probably grew to manhood in the kingdom of his father's people, the Cenél Conaill. This was located during the first half of Columba's own lifetime in the agriculturally rich valley of the lower River Finn, the area known then as *Mag nItha*. Nowadays that area lies along the Irish border, roughly between the towns of Strabane, Raphoe and Ballybofey. It is probably relevant that there is in that area an instance of one of the apparently earliest stratum of Christian church foundations in Ireland, *Domnach Mór Maige nItha* (Donaghmore, Co. Donegal). Churches incorporating in their names the element *Domnach* (borrowed into Irish from the original Latin word *Dominicum* – meaning 'the Lord's house') are believed to have been among the first generation of ecclesiastical establishments in the country. In fact, because of that, those churches are frequently said to have

[19] P. Ó Riain, 'Cainnech *alias* Colum Cille, Patron of Ossory', in P. de Brún, S. Ó Coileáin & P. Ó Riain, *Folia Gadelica* (Cork 1983), 20–35.
[20] *Ibid.*
[21] For an analysis of the confusion with Columbanus and Columba of Sens, see J.M. Picard, 'Adomnán's *Vita Columbae* and the cult of Colum Cille in continental Europe', *Proceedings of the Royal Irish Academy*, Vol. 98, Section C, Number 1 (1998), 2.

been founded by Saint Patrick, as was the case of the church at *Domnach Mór Maige nItha.*[22]

Another intriguing possible connection between the boy Columba and Saint Patrick is hinted at in a story in the Middle Irish Life.[23] There we are told that the boy was brought one Christmas time to visit a holy man named Brugach mac Dega at a place called *Ráith Maige Enaigh*, which may have been, as we will see below, only a few miles from his home. Brugach seems to have been remembered as belonging to one of the very earliest cohorts of Christians in that part of the world and, although admittedly the reference is quite late, one not entirely impossible tradition claims that he had been baptised by Saint Patrick.[24]

Stories about Colum Cille's childhood are preserved in the later Lives but our earliest historical evidence, much as we would expect, has actually very little to say about those years. Adomnán tells us, in what might be no more than hagiography, that Columba was 'devoted even from boyhood to the Christian novitiate and the study of philosophy'. In another story Adomnán recounts how on one occasion the boy's foster-father, the priest Cruithnechán, saw a ball of fire above the sleeping child. Cruithnechán understood this as a sign of the special favour of the Holy Spirit for the boy. Fosterage or the sending away of children to be reared, educated and socialised by another family was a common practice among the aristocracy in early Ireland. Among other things, this must have helped to reduce the many inter-kingdom and inter-family conflicts and disputes. However, fosterage with a Christian priest must have been a fairly unusual practice and was possibly recognised as a form of novitiate for the clerical life. Columba himself is said to have been the foster-father of Baithín, his younger first cousin and the man who would succeed him as second abbot of Iona.

An amusing tongue-in-cheek story in the Middle Irish Life purports to explain how the commencement of Colum Cille's formal education came about. When Cruithnechán thought that the time was appropriate he went to see a local seer (*faith*) for confirmation. The seer scanned the heavens and told Cruithnechán to write out the alphabet for the boy. This was written on a loaf of bread which Colum Cille promptly ate, thus beginning his life of learning. Although the reference is late, the mention of a 'seer' might suggest that Irish society was still essentially pagan at the time of Columba's childhood, just as we would expect it to have been.

The later traditions claim that the place where he was fostered was at Kilmacrenan, originally known as *Doire Eithne* – 'oakwood of Eithne' (his

[22] L. Bieler, *The Patrician Texts in the Book of Armagh* (Dublin 1979), 160–1.
[23] M. Herbert, *Iona, Kells and Derry* (Oxford 1988), 253.
[24] Lacey, *Cenél Conaill*, 131.

mother's name). The earliest church there is said to have been named in honour of the sons of Columba's sister Mincoleth and her husband Enán. There is not much visible in the landscape there today to remind us of what it might have looked like in the early sixth century. Sometime in the first few decades of the sixteenth century, Manus O'Donnell, who composed the *Betha Colaim Chille* and from 1537 was chieftain of the O'Donnells, built a friary there for the Franciscans. Some of the ruins of the out-buildings and friary church still survive.[25]

Just as with his childhood, tradition is rich with stories about Colum Cille's days as a student and young cleric. Again our actual evidence is very limited. Adomnán, on whom we can probably rely somewhat for this sort of information, tells us that he spent at least some time while still a deacon in Leinster studying with an 'aged master (*magistrum*)' called Gemmán. In some later sources Gemmán was identified as a Christian poet, a title that might suggest that he was remembered as some sort of Christianised druid. We also know from Adomnán that Columba studied sacred scripture in Ireland with a bishop called Findbarr who is often identified with one of the two saint Finnians, respectively associated with the monasteries of Movilla in County Down and Clonard in County Meath. There is no specific evidence to support either of these identifications and some scholars have argued, anyway, that the two 'saints' may actually represent just one historical person.[26]

A lot of confusion has arisen about the identity of that Findbarr who Adomnán also refers to by the alternative versions of his name, Vinniavus and Finnio. These other names have a British Celtic (what we would now think of as 'Welsh') appearance to them, suggesting that either Findbarr was himself British or that his name was for some reason remembered in a British form. More recently it has been suggested that the same Findbarr/Finnian should also be equated with the famous British saint, Ninian.[27] There were, of course, many connections between the Christian church in sub-Roman Britain and that in Ireland in this early period. Patrick, 'the apostle of Ireland', was British and not Irish as many of the people who celebrate his memory all over the world on 17 March usually assume. The oldest Irish 'penitential' or list of sins coupled with their appropriate penances is the so-called penitential of Vinnian dating to between about 540 and 590.[28] Some authors have suggested that this Vinnian might be the Findbarr who was the teacher of Columba. Pádraig

[25] B. Lacy, *Archaeological Survey*, 338–9.
[26] D. Ó Corráin, 'The Historical and Cultural Background to the Book of Kells', in F. O'Mahony (ed.), *The Book of Kells. Proceedings of a Conference at Trinity College Dublin*, 6–9 September 1992 (Aldershot 1994), 5.
[27] See J. Fraser, *From Caledonia to Pictland: Scotland to 795* (Edinburgh 2009), 69–71.
[28] L. Bieler, *The Irish Penitentials* (Dublin 1975), 74–95.

Ó Riain has shown how 'his cult spread, very often, it seems, in conjunction with that of Columba of Iona.'[29]

We have to surmise that Columba was ordained a priest as, strictly speaking, this is not recorded in any contemporary or near contemporary historical source although Adomnán writes about him celebrating Mass on a number of occasions. A late tradition claims that he was ordained by Etchen said to have been a brother of the Cenél Conaill king Áed mac Ainmirech.[30] This is extremely unlikely as Áed definitely (and hence his alleged brother Etchen) belonged to the generation following that of Columba.

In fact, we have very little information about any of his activities before the year 562 when he left Ireland for Scotland. By then he was a man of about forty-two years of age, presumably having led something of an eventful life before that. Adomnán refers to him as 'the father and founder of monasteries'. Whether he was the founder of any monasteries in Ireland before he left for Scotland, however, is a major question. Bede says that 'before he came to Britain, he had founded a noble monastery in Ireland known in the Irish language as *Dearmach*, the "Plain of Oaks", because of the oak forest in which it stands.' This is Durrow in the Irish midlands – now in County Offaly. But Bede's version is contradicted by the presumably more reliable words of Adomnán who implies that Durrow was not founded until the 580s. We will return to the founding of the monastery of Durrow below.

The later legends are all quite definite that Colum Cille founded the monastery of Derry – his first and thus most beloved monastery – well before he left Ireland for Iona. The earliest surviving version of this legend is found in the tenth or early eleventh century preface to the Latin prayer/poem known as *Noli Pater Indulgere* – 'Father do not allow', which claims to explain when, where and why the poem was composed by Colum Cille:

> Once at the time of king [Áed mac Ainmirech], Colum Cille went to Derry to have a conference with him and there was offered to him the place with its appurtenance. At that time Colum Cille refused the place because Mo Bhí [abbot of Glasnevin, near Dublin] had prohibited him from accepting it until he should hear of [Mo Bhí's] death. But when Colum Cille came to the door of the place, there met him three of Mo Bhí's people who had with them Mo Bhí's girdle [as proof] and who told him that Mo Bhí had died.
>
> Colum Cille went back to the king and said 'The offer you made me early this morning, give it to me now.' 'It shall be given', said the king. Then the

[29] P. Ó Riain, *Beatha Bharra: St Finbarr of Cork – The Complete Life* (London 1994), x. Also P. Ó Riain, 'Towards a Methodology in Early Irish Hagiography', *Peritia* I (1982), 146–59, pp 148–51.

[30] W. Reeves, *The Life of St. Columba, Founder of Hy; Written by Adamnan, Ninth Abbot of that Monastery* (Dublin 1857), 349 and 371.

> place was burnt with all that was in it. 'That is wasteful', said the king, 'for if it had not been burnt, there would be no want of garments or food there till Doomsday.' [However, Colum Cille explained that everything would be alright.] Now the fire from its size threatened to burn the whole oakwood [*Daire*], and to protect it the hymn [*Noli Pater Indulgere*] was composed ... and it is sung against every fire and thunder from that time to this; and whosoever recites it at lying down and at rising up, it protects him against lightning flash, and it protects the nine persons of his household whom he chooses.[31]

The legend in its most developed form, as recounted by Manus O'Donnell, tells us that Colum Cille was studying at Saint Mo Bhí's monastery at Glasnevin, now in Dublin. The plague known as the *Buidech connaill* – 'Jaundice of the colour of stubble', broke out and the students there at the time were dispersed around the country for safety. Colum Cille went north to his homeland in *Tír Chonaill* (Donegal) where king Áed granted him one of his own fortresses at *Daire Calgaich* (Derry) as the site for a monastery. Colum Cille first set fire to the place, in what might be read as some sort of rite of exorcism, to cleanse it of 'the works of worldly men that he might consecrate it to God and to himself'. When the fire grew too large the holy man pronounced the short prayer/poem known as *Noli Pater Indulgere*, 'Father do not allow'.[32]

> Father, keep under the tempest and thunder,
> Lest we should be shattered by Thy lightning's shafts scattered.
> Thy terrors while hearing, we listen still fearing,
> The resonant song of the bright angel throng,
> As they wander and praise Thee, shouts of honour still raise Thee.
> To the King ruling right, Jesus, lover and light.

A chronicler working in Derry in the twelfth century, and on very insubstantial grounds, went so far as to give the date 545 as the year in which the foundation occurred, the year following the death of Mo Bhí. Colum Cille's church was said to have been called the *Dub Regles* or 'Black Abbey'. A church of that name certainly did exist in Derry in medieval times because, when it was burnt in a major fire in 1166, the annalist adds that this was something 'which had not been heard of from ancient times'. Notwithstanding the legend, we cannot say how old the *Dub Regles* was at that time.

However, despite a formidable ancient and modern tradition, historical evidence does not support either such an early date for the foundation of the

---

[31] J.H. Bernard & R. Atkinson, *The Irish Liber Hymnorum*, Vol. II (London 1898), 28.
[32] A recent scholarly translation of the poem can be found in Clancy and Márkus, *Iona*. I have preferred, however, to use here an older rhyming version by the 'Nun of Kenmare', Sr Mary Frances Cusack.

monastery of Derry nor the attribution to Columba.[33] The legendary version can be challenged on various grounds. No historical source supports the idea that Columba was a student at the monastery of Glasnevin or that he was taught by Mo Bhí its founder. Mo Bhí is also a hypocoristic form of Baithín – the name of Columba's first cousin, foster-son and successor in the abbacy of Iona. It seems likely that the stories connecting Colum Cille with Mo Bhí of Glasnevin are actually a confused memory of his genuine associations with Baithín. In fact other – admittedly equally late – tradition suggests that Colum Cille and Mo Bhí were both contemporary students of Saint Finnian of Clonard. Áed mac Ainmirech was probably not born as early as 545 and certainly was not king, even of his own dynasty the Cenél Conaill, before the 560s when his predecessor and father Ainmire is said (not without some probability) to have attained the higher office of king of Tara. More persuasively, there is separate evidence that the monastery of Derry was founded some time later and by someone other than Columba. That matter will be returned to below.

Adomnán twice relates the date of Columba's departure from Ireland to two years after the battle of *Cúl Dreimne*. We know that that battle was fought in 560 at the foot of Benbulbin Mountain, coincidentally in the vicinity of the later Columban monastery at Drumcliff near Sligo. The battle of *Cúl Dreimne* was clearly a significant encounter, the true circumstances of which have become obscured and enshrouded in later falsified, propagandistic myths.[34] The legendary version claims that the northern Uí Néill defeated their southern Uí Néill rivals led by the king of Tara, Díarmait mac Cerbaill. The cause of the battle is not recorded in contemporary texts but later annalists claimed that the northerners gained the victory 'through the prayer of Colum Cille'. The Annals of Tigernach adds that Díarmait had the benefit of an additional, exotic weapon – a druidic protective 'fence' of some kind. Whatever the facts, the battle seems to have been remembered in some quarters as a conflict between the forces of Christianity on one side and those of pagan druidism on the other.

The battle gave rise to many legends. The best known of them tells how Colum Cille himself was in a way responsible for it.[35] He was said to have been

---

[33] See full discussion in B. Lacey, 'Colum Cille, founder of the monastery of Derry? – "Mihi manet Incertus"', *Journal of the Royal Society of Antiquaries of Ireland*, 128 (1998), 35–47; Lacey, *Cenél Conaill*, 128–31.

[34] See full discussion in B. Lacey, 'The Battle of Cúl Dreimne – a re-assessment', *Journal of the Royal Society of Antiquaries of Ireland*, 133 (2003), 78–85; Lacey *Cenél Conaill*, 178–85; B. Lacey, 'The real cause of the battle of *Cúl Dreimne* in Co. Sligo, the so-called "Battle of the Book"', in M. Timoney (ed.) *Dedicated To Sligo: Thirty-four Essays on Sligo Antiquarian and Related Topics*, forthcoming.

[35] As with most of the stories about Colum Cille, the best version can be found in Manus O'Donnell's *Betha Colaim Chille.*

visiting the monastery of one of the Saint Finnians when he discovered a manuscript of the Psalms. Fearing that Finnian would refuse him permission to make a copy of it, he began to do so secretly. Some of Finnian's followers saw what was happening and reported this to their master. Finnian, however, decided not to intervene until the copy was finished. At the appropriate time he sent for Colum Cille and argued that the new transcript was now his property because he had given no permission for the copying. Colum Cille was furious and referred the matter to Díarmait mac Cerbaill, the high-king at Tara. But Díarmait found in favour of Finnian, uttering the famous judgement:

> *Le gach boin a boinín, le gach leabhar a leabhrán* — To every cow its calf [literally: 'little cow'], to every book its copy [literally: little book].

It is often claimed that this is one of the oldest references in history to the concept of copyright although the story almost certainly dates to much later than the reign of Díarmait mac Cerbaill. A very abbreviated reference to the copy story (although minus the famous judgement) as background to an account of the battle can be found in the text *De causa peregrinationis Sancti Columbe*, 'The reason for Columba's pilgrimage [to Iona]', in one of the major medieval collections of Irish saints' Lives now in the Bodleian Library in Oxford (formerly known as the Codex Insulensis), which dates broadly to the fourteenth century.[36] The copy story also occurs briefly – this time including the famous judgement but not as a specific cause of the battle – in the Irish language text *Cath Cúla Dreimhne* in the *Leabhar Cloinne Suibhne*.[37] That section of this Donegal manuscript, written for the Mac Suibhne's of Fanad, appears to have been composed around 1513 or 1514.[38] The fullest version of the story is found for the first time in Manus O'Donnell's *Betha Colaim Chille* composed in 1532. This has led to the suggestion that, far from being genuine sixth-century tradition, the anecdote (at least in its developed form) may be an early sixteenth-century reflection of the kind of problems that had arisen as a consequence of that most recent innovation of the time – the printed book. However, almost certainly there must have been some older kernel for the story.

[36] The text is printed in H.J. Lawlor, 'The Cathach of St Columba', *Proceedings of the Royal Irish Academy* C33, (1916–17), 408–12, esp. p. 409. See also R. Sharpe, *Medieval Irish Saints' Lives: An Introduction to* Vitae Sanctorum Hiberniae (Oxford 1991), esp. p. 279 n. 16, who states that a now lost leaf of the *Codex Salimanticensis* probably contained the same account. I am grateful to Prof. Raymond Gillespie for drawing my attention to the relevance in this regard of the *Codex Salimanticensis*.
[37] Royal Irish Academy MS 24P25. I am grateful to Dr Nollaig Ó Múraíle for drawing my attention to this text.
[38] Paul Walsh (ed.), *Leabhar Chlainne Suibhne* (Dublin 1920), xliv and lii.

At any rate in the story, Colum Cille – now doubly infuriated – promised to avenge what seemed to him an unjust decision by the king of Tara. At that time a son of the king of Connacht, Eochaid Tirmcharna, was a hostage at Tara. While playing hurling the young prince accidentally killed a son of one of king Díarmait's men. The boy fled for protection to Colum Cille but Díarmait, contrary to all custom, refused to recognise the holy man's 'sanctuary'. The youth was captured and executed but Díarmait, fearing Colum Cille's revenge, had the holy man watched so that he could not leave Tara. However, the cleric did escape and made his way back to the land of his own people in the northwest, *Tír Chonaill.* Although only at the start of his career, Colum Cille's kin were not prepared to accept such insults to their illustrious relative; so they prepared for battle. The so-called northern Uí Néill kingdoms of Donegal, including Colum Cille's own people the Cenél Conaill and the neighbouring dynasty – the allegedly closely-related Cenél nEógain, along with the forces of the king of Connacht made an alliance against the king of Tara, Díarmait. The result was the battle of *Cúl Dreimne.*

These late stories are of course fictional and the character of Colum Cille that comes out of them is very much at variance with that shown in the more sober and earlier sources such as Adomnán's *Vita Columbae.* In fact in reality, it has been shown recently that Columba and king Díarmait may have been first cousins[39] and that the king may have been actually leading the Donegal kingdoms in the battle rather than attacking them.[40]

There has been considerable debate among historians as to whether or not Columba had any real role in the battle or in whatever the circumstances were that had led to it. Some later legendary material suggests that guilt for his alleged role in the death of those who fell in the battle was the cause of his going into exile in Scotland. Adomnán records the fact that a synod held at *Tailtiu* (Teltown, near Kells in County Meath) excommunicated Columba 'improperly as afterwards became known'. If Columba did have some involvement in the events surrounding the battle, it is possible that he would have been disciplined by a gathering of his peers. If so, the synod in question may have taken place in the summer of 561 – the year after the battle, on the occasion of the *Oenach Tailteann,* the famous assembly held in honour of Tailtiu, the mother of the great Celtic god Lugh.

Adomnán tells us that when Columba came to the assembly, Saint Brendan, the founder of the midland monastery of Birr (now in County Offaly), rose and greeted the holy man. He remonstrated with his clerical

[39] A. Mac Shamhráin, 'Nebulae discutiuntur? The emergence of Clann Cholmáin, sixth-eighth centuries', in A. Smyth (ed.), *Seanchas: Studies in Early and Medieval Irish Archaeology, History and Literature in Honour of Francis J. Byrne* (Dublin 2000), 95.
[40] Lacey, *Cúl Dreimne.*

colleagues saying that he had seen a vision, which clearly indicated that Columba was greatly favoured by God and was predestined to be a great church leader. The assembly then retracted its decision of excommunication and honoured Columba instead. However, Adomnán does not explain further the reason for the original edict.

'Pilgrim for Christ': Founding the Monastery on Iona

> In the second year after the battle of Cúl Dreimne, the forty-second year of his age, Columba sailed away from Ireland to Britain wishing to be a pilgrim for Christ.
>
> Adomnán,
> *Vita Columbae* (*c.*700)

Whether these two events were related or not, two years after the famous battle, in 562, Columba allegedly with twelve companions set out from Ireland for Britain 'wishing to be a pilgrim for Christ'. That form of voluntary exile was to become known in the Irish church as 'white martyrdom'. Some of those who practiced it went on to found various other island monasteries. In the words of the Scottish archaeologist Ian Fisher, it was 'the maritime equivalent of the flight by the first monks and hermits to the Egyptian desert'.[1] The similarity between the suggested number of monks that travelled with Columba and that of the original twelve apostles has occasionally aroused scepticism. But, as Richard Sharpe has pointed out, Columba may have been consciously and deliberately imitating the model of Jesus and his close followers.[2]

A secondary hand to that of the main copyist in the Annals of Ulster describes this event as the '*navigatio Coluim Chille ad Insolam Iae anno etatis sue xlii* – the voyage of Colum Cille to the island of I[ona] in the 42nd year of his age'. However, the use of the cultic name for the saint is sufficient evidence to show that this was not a contemporary record of the event but must have been added sometime later. The problem is that we do not know how much later.

The Ireland that Columba was leaving was undergoing some profound changes. For a start – although only from our perspective – it was passing through the phase that would see it emerge from pre-history (the period when

[1] I. Fisher, *Early Medieval Sculpture in the West Highlands and Island* (Edinburgh 2001), 1.
[2] Sharpe, *Adomnán*, 19.

there were no contemporary written records) into the beginnings of the historic era. To most of his contemporaries this transformation would have been invisible and irrelevant. However, as we have seen, Columba and those associated with him may have been in some ways especially conscious of the need for such a change to be achieved, even if they did not conceive of it in precisely the same terms as we do now. Indeed, consciously or not, Columba and his followers seem to have taken a leading role in that momentous transformation.

The introduction of writing to Ireland had been part of the package of cultural and technical changes that had accompanied the arrival of Christianity. Christianity, as has been pointed out many times, has at its heart a book – the Bible; in fact Christianity (although not necessarily for every one of its adherents) is inconceivable unless accompanied by the knowledge and skills of literacy.

The Christian religion had probably been seeping into Ireland from the continent as well as from Roman Britain slowly and in various ways since perhaps the late fourth or early fifth centuries. Trade, captured slaves like the teenage Saint Patrick, and the activities of missionaries – again like Saint Patrick later in his life, would have provided the means of its introduction.

By the time that Columba was ready to leave Ireland it is very unlikely that the whole population had been converted to Christianity. Díarmait mac Cerbaill, the king of Tara mentioned above who may have been one of Columba's cousins, is recorded as celebrating what historians have seen as the important and overtly pagan *feis* or 'Feast of Tara' in 559. The Annals of Tigernach says that this was the last time that this was ever done, hinting at the probable non-Christian nature of the event and, simultaneously, at the fact that this was the end of some kind of era. Notwithstanding this, the new religion was sufficiently strong enough that by the mid-sixth century it had among its members high aristocrats such as Columba himself as well as many of his relations.

Major political changes were also taking place in the Ireland of his day, with new dynasties and new kingdoms coming to the fore as older – technically prehistoric – political units which we can now only perceive very dimly were being shattered and re-formed.[3] It seems almost certain that a 'revolution' or major political upheaval of some sort had occurred relatively recently, at least within the previous century, when a group of people from the west of Ireland – probably from north Connacht, crossed the Shannon and conquered the eastern midlands. Those people were remembered as Niall of the Nine Hostages and his descendants. Their conquests included the

[3] For a recent comprehensive account of what we know about those events, see T. Charles-Edwards, *Early Christian Ireland* (Cambridge 2000). For the situation in the saint's own homeland in Donegal, see Lacey, *Cenél Conaill.*

sacred complex of sites and monuments on the Hill of Tara, as well as its kingship. That office seems to have had some kind of 'national' or at least widespread ritual significance. Those ambitious newcomers would become known in later times as the Uí Néill. Later other powerful and ambitious dynasties like Columba's own people – the Cenél Conaill – would also capture the kingship of Tara and ultimately and consequently be recruited retrospectively into the ranks of the Uí Néill elite.[4]

Traditionally it is said that in early medieval Ireland there were about one hundred and fifty individual small kingdoms; in fact, there may have been many more! These were grouped together by means of power politics and violent conflicts into various regional and provincial hierarchies. It is difficult to be precise about these matters; our records are very vague for that period and it is unlikely, anyway, that there was any form of agreed 'system'. To a large extent *realpolitik* based on the exercise of force and domination, rather than immemorial custom, must have ruled the day. The situation was extremely fluid and, although the attainment of the kingship of Tara seemed to signal some sort of 'national' eminence and influence for the incumbent and his dynasty, there was certainly no centralised kingship of Ireland as used to be argued.[5] Instead there seems to have been a handful of provincial overkingdoms, the rulers of each of which vied with each other for greater power and influence.

A list that survives in a text apparently compiled about one hundred and fifty years later than Columba's departure from Ireland gives the names of the twelve individuals who are said to have accompanied him on his voyage of exile.[6] There was Baithín and Cobthach who were first cousins of Columba on his father's side. They were sons of one of Columba's uncles, Brendan. According to Adomnán, Baithín had been the *alumnus* of Columba – his 'pupil' or 'foster-son' as some authors translate the word. Again according to Adomnán, Báithin was also called Conín. Thomas Charles Edwards has suggested that the name Baithín – which seems to mean something like 'the foolish one' – may have been given to him as a pet-name by his master,[7] presumably when he was a child or young man in the care of the older cleric.

Baithín would eventually succeed Columba as second abbot of Iona on the latter's death. Before that, he had served as prior of the dependent monastery at *Mag Luinge* on Tiree, and Adomnán describes him operating also along with the saint at the still unidentified monastery of *Hinba* somewhere in the Hebrides. Ernán, another uncle of the saint (possibly a

[4] Lacey, *Cenél Conaill.*

[5] For the most comprehensive and authoritative discussion of the kingship of Tara, see Bhreathnach, *The Kingship … of Tara.*

[6] For this list, see note 16 above.

[7] Charles-Edwards, *Early Christian Ireland,* 5.

brother of his mother), is recorded as being prior at *Hinba* – but for no more than a few days as he took ill and later died on Iona. He is said to have been on the original voyage also.

Another of those who went with Columba is said to have been Scandal son of Bressal, son of Énna, son of Niall. The Niall of the reference has always been understood to be Niall of the Nine Hostages. Scandal clearly belonged to a people known as the Cenél nÉnnai. There were different peoples of that name in various parts of Ireland at the time, including a group who were settled in east Donegal in the area stretching between Derry and Raphoe. These would have been the neighbouring people to Columba's own home kingdom of Cenél Conaill and, for obvious reasons, therefore it was assumed by many authors down the centuries that Scandal belonged to these.

However, it has been shown recently that the Donegal Cenél nÉnnai are unlikely to have had any real connection with Niall or the Uí Néill, although later genealogists retrospectively attempted to prove that this had been so.[8] Therefore, it is more likely that Scandal belonged to a different Cenél nÉnnai, perhaps the people of that name based in the eastern midlands, although another group from near the southern border of Donegal and Fermanagh could also be a possibility. Like Ernán, Scandal was probably one of the older men who accompanied Columba as, apparently, he belonged to the same generation as the latter's father.

Another Donegal man who travelled with Columba was Cairnan son of Brandub, son of Meilge. Allegedly, Cairnan's great-grandfather was Énna Bógaine the eponymous ancestor of the Cenél mBógaine who lived in southwest Donegal. This is the area in which *Gleann Cholm Cille* is situated, although whether that valley actually had any contemporary association with Columba is very much open to question as we will see below. Until recently the Cenél mBógaine had been understood to have been part of or, at least related to, Columba's own people the Cenél Conaill. However, recent research has thrown a lot of doubt on that claim.[9]

Also among those who sailed away with the saint was the monk Diormit (or Díarmait), who is described as Columba's *ministrator* ('attendant'). Diormit would figure in many of the subsequent stories told about events on Iona. The other monks that travelled with Columba are named as: the brothers Rus and Féchno (whose father was called Ródan), Grillan, Echoid, Tochannu moccu fir-Chetea and Lugaid moccu Theimne. It has not been possible to establish with any degree of certainty to which kingdoms or dynastic groups the rest of these individuals belonged. Tochannu moccu fir Chetea seems, however, to have had a 'tribal' name somewhat similar to the

[8] Lacey, *Cenél Conaill*, 120–31.

[9] *Ibid.*, 76–84.

place name *Druim Cett* where Columba would attend the famous Convention or 'meeting of the kings' at a later date, as we will see below. In addition, his first name Tochannu looks a little bit like a hypocoristic version of the name Cainnech or Canice. Columba, of course, is associated frequently in the early sources, including Adomnán's *Vita Columbae*, with an individual called Cainnech who is also remembered as a separate saint. However, Pádraig Ó Riain has suggested that Cainnech itself is a hypocoristic version of the name Colum and that, therefore, Cainnech and Columba may have been the same person. Interestingly, Saint Cainnech is said to have been born and grew up in the area near to the location of the traditional site of the *Druim Cett* convention, and his chief church in the district – at Drumachose – is less than two miles to the northeast. There can be no certainty about any of these identifications but a further association with this district is, again as we have seen above, that Columba's sister Sinech is said to have been the wife of a man who was probably from that general area also.

Another of Columba's original travelling companions who remains unidentified is Lugaid moccu Theimne. It is possible that he belonged to the east Ulster people known as the Conailli Muirtheimne. There are now several reasons for thinking that Columba's own people, the Cenél Conaill, may have had some sort of genealogical links with the latter.[10]

Bede says that Columba left Ireland 'to preach the word of God to the provinces of the Northern Picts', but Irish sources are divided as to whether he went as a form of penance or simply to find a 'desert' place for prayerful contemplation. Most modern historians, as indeed the earliest evidence, would emphasise the latter interpretation. Twice Adomnán links the story of the departure with a reference to the battle of *Cúl Dreimne*, but it is not clear if he is hinting that there is some connection between the two events or if he is just using the battle, which must have been a major and well-remembered conflict, as a sort of benchmark dating device.

Although there is no relevant historical evidence, tradition has it that Colum Cille and his companions left from Derry, sailing down Lough Foyle and across the northern channel to the Scottish coast. The legends make out of this departure one of the great dramas of the saint's life, indeed of the history of Ireland. Later poets put words into the mouth of the saint at the point of his leaving:

> The great cry of the people of Derry
> Has shattered my heart into quarters.
>
> Derry of oaks we are leaving,
> Tearful with gloom and with sorrow,

[10] Lacey, *Cenél Conaill*, 157, 177 and 187.

> Leaving here broken-hearted,
> To go to the land of the strangers.[11]

The medieval writers heaped image upon image, not only making all the local people – but all of nature – lament Colum Cille's departure:

> Because of this, the seagulls and the birds of Lough Foyle pursuing the boat on both sides were screaming and screeching for grief that Colum Cille was leaving Ireland.

The fact that 'screaming and screeching' seagulls follow almost every boat that leaves Lough Foyle – as well as every other harbour in the world – hardly detracts from the appropriateness of the poetic image thus evoked.

Again, we have very little actual information about the voyage. Despite the existence of a number of sites along the western shore of Lough Foyle and the northern coast of the Inishowen peninsula – which are pointed out as having had some connection with the story, we do not know accurately where Columba and his companions left from or, indeed, where they actually went to. Fourteen hundred years later in 1963, a group of thirteen Church of Ireland clergy and laymen 're-enacted' the voyage from Derry to Iona.[12] Their thirty-foot long canvas boat was specially constructed for the voyage by Jim Boyd, a professional currach-builder from Carrickfin in County Donegal.

That boat left Derry in the early afternoon of 4 June and arrived at Martyr's Bay Iona just after eleven o'clock in the morning eight days later; they were met among others by the then Archbishop of Canterbury, Dr Michael Ramsey. Each evening the crew had landed on an island or on the adjacent mainland and camped till the following morning. According to the written account of the journey, in some of the more remote Scottish places where they landed – in those largely pre-television days – they seem to have been greeted almost as if they were a reincarnation of the sixth-century saint and his associates.

The 1963 currach was equipped with a one-hundred-and-twenty foot square lug sail but, even when wind conditions were suitable for its use, it was still necessary to keep the oars operating continually in order to maintain the correct course. The boat is now preserved by the Museum Service in Derry. Since 1963 a number of similar re-enactment voyages have been organised.[13]

It is not at all clear that Columba and his companions went directly to Iona once they left Ireland. Alfred Smyth has argued that a close reading of Adomnán's *Vita Columbae* allows us to see that the monks' earliest 'base in

[11] Lacey, *Manus O'Donnell*, 106.

[12] For an account of the 're-enactment', see J. Barry, *Joyful Pilgrimage* (London 1963).

[13] The most recent, taking 5 days, was in July 2012, for the BBCNI-commissioned television documentary *Turas go hOileán Í*. The programme was presented by the author of this book.

Scotland' may have been on the still unidentified island of *Hinba*.[14] There certainly was a Columban monastery on *Hinba* during the saint's own lifetime – it is mentioned several times by Adomnán. At one such mention he seems to suggest that *Hinba* existed already by the time of the inauguration of the Scottish king, Áedán mac Gabráin, probably in 573 or 574. Since the nineteenth century at least, a great deal of energy has been expended by historians and archaeologists in attempting to identify which of the Hebridean islands may have been the location of the unidentified *Hinba*. A variety of islands – as far north as Uist – have been suggested, but in recent years Jura, Canna and Colonsay seem to have attracted most support. Wherever it was, Richard Sharpe has strongly countered Prof. Smyth's claim that this was where Columba founded his original Scottish monastery, arguing instead that, as always understood, Iona was the place that had that honour.[15]

At the time of his arrival there, what we now call Scotland was divided among three linguistic or ethnic population groups and at least seven (and probably a lot more) distinct polities.[16] Before another half century had passed an additional ethnic group, the Anglo–Saxons from Northumbria, would also become significant players in the complex politics of the northern parts of early medieval Britain.

Historical evidence for this period in Scotland is very meagre but study – particularly of place names – has allowed a picture of the ethnic mix at the time to be discerned with reasonable certainty. South of the Forth–Clyde line were several peoples who spoke a form of the British Celtic (or P Celtic) language. That language is sometimes called Cumbric by modern commentators and was clearly related closely to the ancestor of present-day Welsh. Those people seem to have been divided into at least three kingdoms. There was a kingdom in the Strathclyde area with its caput at Dumbarton (also known as *Ail Cluaithe*, 'the rock of the Clyde') on the north side of the River Clyde downstream from modern Glasgow. The kingdom of the Gododdin (formerly the Votadini) was located in the Lothian area on the east side of Scotland with its caput at *Din Eidyn*, modern Edinburgh. Finally there

---

[14] A.P. Smyth, *Warlords and Holy Men: Scotland AD 80–1000* (Edinburgh 1984), 100.

[15] Sharpe, *Adomnán*, 18–19.

[16] Several descriptions of the ethnic and linguistic make-up of Scotland in this period are available. For a specialist treatment see, for instance, I. Ralston & I. Armit, 'The Early Historic Period: An Archaeological Perspective', in K. Edwards & I. Ralston (eds) *Scotland Environment and Archaeology, 8000 BC–AD 1000* (Chichester 1997), 217–40. For Dál Riata see R. Sharpe, 'The thriving of Dalriada', in S. Taylor (ed.) *Kings, Clerics and Chronicles in Scotland, 500–1297* (Dublin 2000), 47–61. Historic Scotland's excellently readable series, *The Making of Scotland* (Edinburgh 1999), also has a number of volumes which cover these matters, esp.: C. Lowe, *Angels, Fools and Tyrants: Britons and Anglo–Saxons in Southern Scotland*; M. Carver, *Surviving in Symbols: A Visit to the Pictish Nation*; E. Campbell, *Saints and Sea-kings: The first Kingdom of the Scots*. The most recent comprehensive account can be found in Fraser, *From Caledonia*.

was the kingdom of Rheged in the southwest borders area, around the shores of the Solway Firth and extending into the northwestern part of modern England, an area still appropriately called Cumbria.

North of the Forth–Clyde line – particularly on the eastern side – were the Picts; divided, at least, into northern and southern groups probably by the line of the mountainous area of the Mounth. There must have been other sub-divisions and petty kingdoms as well, such as that ruled by the *subregulus* ('subordinate king') in the Orkneys, mentioned by Adomnán. The earliest Pictish list of kings, which dates to about 900, suggests that there may have been as many as seven separate provincial Pictish kingdoms. We seem to have the names of some of those separate mainland units, a few of which are still preserved in the titles of modern districts: *Fib* –Fife; *Athfotla* (which literally means 'new Ireland') – Atholl; *Fortriu* – Fortrenn; *Cat* – Caithness and Sutherland; and *Ce.*[17]

Many bizarre things have been written over the years about the Picts: their alleged small physical stature, their allegedly extraordinary painted or tattooed bodies, and their peculiar matrilineal succession customs. In fact, apart from minor cultural differences, the Picts were probably very similar in appearance and lifestyle to their contemporaries elsewhere in these islands. They were not a mysterious or fabulous people but simply the post-Roman and early medieval descendants of the native Iron Age population of that part of Britain. Because they did not leave much in the way of writing behind them, they are best known nowadays for their extraordinary and evocative works of art – particularly their impressive stone carvings as well as some beautiful metalwork.

The Picts first appear in history as the *Picti* – 'the Painted People' (a nickname), in AD 297 when they are mentioned by the Roman writer Eumenius.[18] Surviving Pictish writing and symbols – mainly in the form of proper names – are very scarce and difficult to understand, but almost certainly they had a P Celtic language similar to, but nevertheless different from, their countrymen to the south of the Forth–Clyde line. All these languages, which are related to modern Welsh, were very different from the so-called Q Celtic language used by the monks who came from Gaelic-speaking Ireland; in fact, we know from Adomnán that Columba could only preach to the Picts through an interpreter.

Interestingly but also very puzzlingly, when the Picts were referred to in some of the medieval sources from Ireland they were given the same name, Cruithin, as a group of people who occupied much of central Ulster at the

[17] S. Foster, 'Before Alba: Pictish and Dál Riata power centres from the fifth to late ninth centuries AD', in S. Foster, A. Macinnes & R. Macinnes, *Scottish Power Centres from the Early Middle Ages to the Twentieth Century* (Glasgow 1998), 1–31, p. 5. See also Fraser, *From Caledonia.*
[18] Carver, *Surviving in Symbols*, 8.

time as well as other parts of Ireland.[19] In fact it now seems likely that Columba's own people, the Cenél Conaill, may have had a Cruithin origin[20] and, as we have seen above, one of his foster-fathers was known as Cruithnechán (literally: 'little Cruithin'). The name Cruithin seems to be a Q (or Gaelic) Celtic variation of the P Celtic word that was the ancestor of the modern name 'Britain'. Despite this sameness of names in Irish, ancient authors such as Adomnán, when writing in Latin, made a definite distinction between the Picts of Scotland and the Cruithin of Ireland. Like the Picts of Scotland, the Cruithin of Ireland have been the subject of considerable misinterpretation. However, as far as can be determined now, they seem to have been linguistically and culturally indistinct from the rest of the population of the country at the time.[21]

The third linguistic group living in Scotland at the time of Columba's arrival there were the Gaelic-speaking people who would become known collectively as the Dál Riata.[22] Their origin legends claimed that their ancestors had migrated from the north of Ireland around the fourth or fifth centuries when they, allegedly, drove the previously indigenous Picts out of Argyll and the surrounding districts and islands. The legends say that about AD 500 their king Fergus Mór – who had led them to Scotland – died. Unfortunately, the historical records are not sufficient to demonstrate the truth or otherwise of that claim and it has been suggested occasionally that the migration may have actually occurred somehow in the opposite direction.[23] Whatever happened, the Dál Riata in Scotland seem to have been closely related to their 'cousins' of that name in Ireland, who were located in the north of what is now County Antrim.

Just as with the segmented kingdoms in Ireland, Scottish Dál Riata was subdivided into a number of smaller units, allegedly founded by a series of eponymous ancestral brothers who were said to be sons or other close relatives of Fergus Mór. Those kingdoms, like their counterparts in Ireland were known by the names of the dynastic segments that ruled them. In a generalised way they can be assigned to territories as follows: Cenél nGabhráin mainly in Kintyre; Cenél Loairn in the district of Lorne, Colonsay, Mull, Tiree, Coll and Ardnamurchan; and Cenél nÓengusa on Islay.[24] Cenél Comgaill, which appears to have been fairly closely related to Cenél nGabhráin, emerged as a separate unit in what is now the district of Cowal.[25]

---

[19] See discussion in F.J. Byrne *Irish kings and High-kings* (London 1973, reprinted Dublin 2001), esp. p. 108.

[20] Lacey, *Cenél Conaill*, esp. 155–7.

[21] But see now Fraser, *From Caledonia*, esp. 48–9 and 148–9 for a more complex analysis.

[22] See for instance R. Sharpe, 'The thriving of Dalriada'.

[23] See Fraser, *From Caledonia*, 144–9.

[24] Campbell, *Saints and Sea-kings*, 17.

[25] Fraser, *From Caledonia*, 165.

We cannot be certain that these Gaelic territories extended as far north as Iona in 562, as they certainly would do somewhat later. This uncertainty results in the confusion as to how Colum Cille and his monks acquired control of that island. A retrospective entry in the Irish annals says that Iona was given to them by Conall son of Comgall, the king of Dál Riata. However, Bede, whose sources were limited for this early period, says that it was granted to the monks by the Picts after they had been converted to Christianity.

Adomnán makes no reference to the island being granted to Columba by anyone. He does tell us that the saint made a visit to king Conall shortly after his arrival in Britain, perhaps even before going to Iona and for the purpose of seeking land or permission to establish a base there. That visit was made to the king at what Adomnán called his *caput regionis*, or chief place. It is generally assumed that this was the major hilltop fortress at Dunadd on the Scottish mainland, which seems to have been one of the chief royal residences of the kings of Scottish Dál Riata.[26]

Excavations carried out at Dunadd in the 1980s[27] as well as earlier in the twentieth century revealed that the site had two phases of use during the Iron Age: from around 400 to 200 BC and again from about 100 BC to around AD 100. However, the bulk of the finds and the radiocarbon dates from the site indicate that it was used mainly from about the fourth century AD down to the tenth century. The most intense period of occupation was from the sixth to the eighth centuries. The elaborate hilltop fortifications there were remodelled on several occasions over that period, presumably in order to extend the site and improve its defences.

The excavations turned up substantial evidence in the form of mould and crucible fragments for a seventh-century metalworking workshop which produced objects comparable to those from other contemporary high status sites in these islands, such as Moynagh Lough crannog in County Meath. The evidence showed that gold, silver, copper alloys, lead, tin, iron and glass, were all being worked on the site. The moulds were used for making pins, buckles and discs, but mainly for producing penannular brooches. The excavators concluded that the site was of major importance in the integration of Germanic (Anglo–Saxon) and Celtic styles in the insular art of the period, such as is represented by the decoration in the Book of Durrow and other major contemporary works of art. The site also produced evidence for long-distance trading links – from as far away as the Mediterranean. In addition the various rock-carvings on the site, particularly the carved footprints, would seem to confirm its importance as a major royal establishment and possibly as the inauguration place of kings.

[26] Fraser, *From Caledonia*, 243, has suggested, instead, the ancient fort of Dunollie on Oban Bay as the likely location.
[27] A. Lane & E. Campbell, *Dunadd: An Early Dalriadic Capital* (Oxford 2000).

Whether it was at Dunadd or not, we do not know how long Columba's visit to king Conall actually lasted. Adomnán suggests that the Irish monks arrived in Britain in early June; some later tradition claims that they arrived on the ninth day of that month. Coincidentally or not, this was commemorated as the date of Columba's death.

The doubt as to whether it was the Dál Riata or the Picts who controlled the area in which Iona was located at the time, may be because it was situated in a largely uninhabited border zone. It may have been in some sort of no-man's land, located between the area really controlled by the Dál Riata and the former lands of the Picts. We know that monasteries of the same period in Ireland were often founded in precisely such types of territories. The only two monasteries named by Adomnán in Columba's home territory – Derry and *Druim Tuama* (Drumhome, County Donegal) – were almost certainly located in what were kingdom boundary zones at the time. Indeed, it seems clear that the Irish kings of the time often supported the founding of monasteries in exactly such locations precisely in order to define and secure their newly-established boundaries. It may be that Conall son of Comgall assisted the foundation of the monastery on the relatively marginal island of Iona with the express intention of thus extending his influence and power further north of the territory that, in reality, he actually controlled at the time.

Iona is a small island of about two thousand acres which lies less than a mile off its larger neighbour to the east, the Isle of Mull, which itself lies among the Inner Hebrides off the west coast of Scotland.[28] The island is about three miles in length – north to south, and about one and a half miles at its widest. Much of the island is rocky, exposing its Precambrian geology. A large area is over a hundred feet above sea level, while the hill of *Dún Í* at the northern end rises to over three hundred feet. Columba's monastery was located on a relatively level but gently sloping plain on the eastern side of the island, facing across the narrow sound back towards Mull and the Scottish mainland. The channel is so narrow that Adomnán suggests on a number of occasions that visitors going to the monastery from Mull could actually shout across in order to summon a ferry.

The western side of the island is more exposed to the open Atlantic, although it is there around the curving *Camus Cùil an tSaimh* – 'Bay at the Back of the Ocean' that the sandy level *machair* area is located. This is where, eventually, the monks as well as the later lay inhabitants cultivated their crops. Of course the rough Atlantic weather was a constant hazard as Adomnán frequently reminds us. He would have been painfully aware, as the Annals of

[28] The definitive relevant description of Iona can be found in Ian Fisher's 'The Royal Commission on the Ancient and Historical Monuments of Scotland (RCAHMS)', *Argyll Vol. 4 – Iona* (Edinburgh 1982).

Ulster tells us, that 'a great windstorm on the sixteenth of the Kalends of October [16 September 691] caused the drowning of some six of the community of Iona'. Adomnán was their abbot at that time.

The name Iona, although in use since the fourteenth century at least, appears to be one of the great spelling mistakes of history. It arises from a misreading by some unknown medieval scribe of Adomnán's Latin *Iova insula,* in which the original letter 'v' was misunderstood as an 'n'.[29] The most ancient version of the name of the island in Irish appears to have been *Í* or, as Bede gives it in a Latinized form, *Hii.* There is no definite explanation for the meaning of the name but some sources suggest that it derives from an old Irish word for a yew tree (in Latin, *Iova insula* – 'yewy island'?) although no evidence for ancient yew trees has been found there yet by archaeologists. Much later stories claim that the name was derived from the feminine pronoun in Irish used when the Columban monks first saw the island from their boat and cried out 'I see it [*'í',* literally 'her']'. Coincidentally, Adomnán is at pains in the prefatory material to his Life of the saint to point out that the Hebrew form of the Latin name Columba is Jonah, possibly pronounced similarly to Iona. Such a similarity could have contributed to the later confusion.

Bede says that Columba 'arrived in Britain in the ninth year of the reign of the powerful Pictish king Brude son of Maelchú; he converted that people to the faith of Christ by his preaching and example'. Several modern authors, however, have cast doubt on this. We know that the monks of Iona in subsequent times played a major role in the conversion of the Picts, but it is unlikely that much of this was achieved during the lifetime of the Donegal saint. It is also certain that other Christian clerics (some of them from Ireland) were present in Scotland around the same time and, indeed, that Christianity had already been established in at least the southern parts of the country before the Romans left. Adomnán confirms that Columba made a number of excursions into the territory of the Picts, and possibly more than one visit to king Brude at his fortress near Inverness. Brude may have been living at what was actually the much older fort of *Craig Phádrig.* Archaeological excavations there have shown that it was definitely occupied in the sixth century when Columba would have been in the vicinity.[30] An alternative location for the residence of the Pictish king may have been at Castle Hill in Inverness.[31]

Apparently, among the items discussed by the Pictish king and Columba was the safety of his monks as they voyaged around the western and northern isles. Adomnán depicts Columba specifically requesting Brude to persuade the un-named subject king of the Orkney Islands to guarantee the safety of the

[29] See Sharpe, *Adomnán,* 257–9 and Ó Muraíle, 'Onomastic Legacy', 198.
[30] Sharpe, *Adomnán,* 335.
[31] Foster, 'Before Alba', 16.

missionary Cormac ua Liatháin when he went there. Cormac later became the subject of a separate set of legends which highlighted his role as a sea voyager.[32]

As described by Adomnán – probably not too objectively – the visit or visits that Columba made to the Pictish royal court invariably became the occasion for a contest between the Christian miracle-working abilities of the saint and the pagan powers of the king's magician, Broichan. Columba was of course victorious in all these contests but Adomnán does not say that his wonder-working was rewarded with the conversion of the king or his people. Columba does not seem to have been able to speak the Pictish language; on a number of occasions we hear of him preaching through an interpreter.

On one journey in the territory of the Picts, Adomnán tells us that the saint had to cross the river Ness. There then follows what is surely the origin of the later stories about the Loch Ness monster. A 'water beast', attempted to attack one of Columba's companions who was swimming across the river. The saint ordered the beast to retreat and the man was saved. A group of 'pagan barbarians' watching, one of whose number had already been killed by the beast, was so impressed by 'this miracle that they themselves had seen, [that they] magnified the God of the Christians'. Scholars have debated whether this episode in the Life could be derived from a real event in which the 'monster' would have been a genuine sea animal such as a bearded seal or a walrus. Others have suggested that Adomnán may have drawn the inspiration for this story from one of the literary models for his own work, the *Dialogi* by Sulpicious Severus, in which a similar story is told about Saint Martin of Tours.[33] A separate miracle story told by Adomnán parallels that claimed later about Saint Patrick in Ireland. Columba did not drive the snakes off Iona but shortly before he died he was believed to have pronounced that 'all snake poisons will be powerless to harm either men or cattle on this island, so long as the inhabitants keep the commandments of Christ.'

As well as his contacts with the Dál Riata and Pictish kings, Adomnán tells one story that incidentally reveals Columba's friendship with the Christian king of the Britons of Strathclyde. This was 'Roderc son of Tóthal who reigned at Dumbarton', 'the fort of the Britons', also known as *Ail Cluaithe* or 'the Rock of the Clyde'. Rhydderch, as he probably would have been known to his own people, ruled over a kingdom which stretched from the Clyde southwards to below Ayr. However, his fortress at Dumbarton was on a dramatic rock outcrop on the northern bank of the river, downstream from modern Glasgow.

[32] See D. Tipp and J.M Wooding, 'Adomnán's voyaging saint: The cult of Cormac ua Liatháin' in J.M. Wooding (ed.), *Adomnán of Iona: Theologian, Lawmaker, Peacemaker*, 237–52.
[33] Jacqueline Borsje, 'The Monster in the River Ness in *Vita Sancti Columbae:* A study of a miracle', *Peritia,* Vol. 8 (1994), 27–34.

Adomnán gives very little chronological information about the events he describes in the Life, but it is possible to infer some dates from the details. Columba is said to be in Ardnamurchan when travellers arrived from Ireland with news of the deaths of the two Cenél nÉogain kings Báetán and Eochaid, which the annals place in the year 571. At that time the Cenél nÉogain, who would ultimately give their name to *Tír Éogain* – later County Tyrone, were confined to Inis Éogain – the Inishowen peninsula in Donegal just north of Derry.

When Conall son of Comgall – the king of Dál Riata – died in 573, his successor Áedán mac Gabrán came to Iona. Columba who had been on *Hinba* where he experienced a number of visions of an angel of the Lord instructing him to 'ordain' Aedán as king, crossed over to Iona and there according to Adomnán he performed the ordination ceremony. Although the exact nature of that ceremony (and even whether it truly took place) has been much debated by experts, some scholars consider that this is the earliest recorded instance in European history of the Christian inauguration of a king.[34]

The annals say that in 575 Colum Cille (*sic*) and his relative, the Cenél Conaill king Áed mac Ainmirech, attended the meeting that became known as the Convention of *Druim Cett*. Adomnán simply calls it 'the conference (*condictum*) of the kings' but confirms that it was held at *Druim Cett* in Ireland. The significance of that event has been obscured by its own set of fabulous legends but we know that it was principally a high-level conference between the Dál Riata king in Scotland – Áedán mac Gabrán – whose authority probably also ran in the related kingdom in north Antrim, and the king of the Cenél Conaill – Áed mac Ainmirech. Most probably the meeting was held to forge an alliance in opposition to Báetán mac Cerball, the powerful king who ruled most of Ulster east of the Bann and who may have been king of Tara also at the time.[35] If such an alliance was agreed between the two dynasties at *Druim Cett*, as seems probable, it seems to have held solidly until the battle of *Mag Roth* (Moira in County Down) in the year 639.

Legendary sources, the oldest written form of which appears to occur in the early eleventh-century introduction to the poem *Amrae Coluimb Chille*, say that three matters were discussed at the Convention of *Druim Cett*. Besides the issue of the alliance with Dál Riata, the subject of the holding as a hostage by Áed mac Ainmirech of Scandlan the son of the king of *Osraige* (effectively present-day County Kilkenny) and the proposed expulsion of the poets from Ireland were also dealt with. As a later poet said:

> For three reasons they held the assembly:
> So that Scandlan the prince could be freed;

[34] For a critical view see Sharpe, '*Adomnán*, 355–6; M. Enright, Royal succession and abbatial prerogative in Adomnán's Vita Columbae', *Peritia* 4 (1985), 83–103.
[35] Byrne, *Irish Kings*, esp. 110–11. Various dates for this meeting are suggested in the ancient sources and modern commentaries (see discussion below).

The obligations of Scottish Dál Riata;
And poets; for them, was there need?[36]

The legends maintain that it was argued that with the arrival of Christianity the poets should be expelled from the country, mainly on account of their almost universal greediness. That literary motif occurs in a number of other stories from ancient Ireland. If there is any basis to it in fact, it possibly reflects an uneasiness with the more pagan aspects of the profession of the poets as inheritors of some of the roles and privileges of the druids of pre-Christian times. The poets of the early historic period seem to have represented the survival into the Christian era of aspects of the pre-Christian pagan tradition at their most extreme. Colum Cille, who is remembered in tradition himself as a poet, is said in the legends to have intervened on their behalf at *Druim Cett*, saving them from their expected terminal fate. As a result of his successful defence of them, the leading poet Dallán Forgaill is said, again in legend, to have commenced the composition of the *Amrae* or praise poem in the saint's honour. However, Colum Cille asked him to desist until he himself would be dead; accordingly it was not finished at that time.

The most recent study of the introduction to the *Amrae Coluimb Chille* shows that 'it is entirely a literary construct' written in 1007–8 and cannot be taken as an accurate account of events in the late sixth century.[37] Scholars are agreed however that an alliance between the Scottish Dál Riata and the Cenél Conaill was a genuine result of the Convention. Whatever about any of the other issues that were discussed, it is extremely unlikely that this meeting took place in 575. Richard Sharpe has suggested that it was held about the year 590 and that its purpose was the forging of a local alliance rather than the holding of the great national assembly as is suggested in the legends. However, if that alliance was against the king Báetán son of Cerball, then the meeting must have been held before he died in 579. There is some other circumstantial evidence associated with the foundation of the monastery at Derry that would support such a date, around 578 or 579.[38]

It is clear from the incidental stories that Adomnán tells us about the events surrounding the Convention that the meeting was held in a location in what is now north County Derry. The Donegal ecclesiastical writer John Colgan said in 1645 that local tradition in his day was very precise that the Convention of *Druim Cett* of over a thousand years before had taken place at the Mullagh (literally, 'the summit') or Daisy Hill, a prominent rise in the landscape just outside the present town of Limavady. The site, on the south bank of the River Roe is now in the grounds of a hotel and golf course. Even

[36] Lacey, *Manus O'Donnell*, 173.

[37] Máire Herbert, 'The Preface to the Amra Coluim Cille', in D. Ó Corráin, L. Breatnach and K. McCone (eds.), *Sages, Saints and Storytellers* (Maynooth 1989), 67–75.

[38] Lacey, *Cenél Conaill*, 200–2 and see below.

in Colgan's time, a celebration was held there each year on All Saints Day to commemorate the great sixth-century gathering.[39] All Saints Day (1 November) coincides with the ancient festival of *Samain,* the beginning of the 'Celtic' new year. This would have been an appropriate occasion for the holding of assemblies and the making of alliances and agreements, but the evidence of Adomnán seems to be that the Convention of *Druim Cett* was held much earlier in the year. He describes a meeting between Columba and Comgall the founder of the monasteries of Bangor in County Down and Camus on the lower Bann near Coleraine. The meeting took place 'on a fine summer day ... after the conference of the kings in *Druim Cett,* when the blessed man [Columba] was returning to the plains of the [northern] sea-coast'. There is one way in which the different times suggested for the meeting might be reconciled. Possibly the meeting had been held at the beginning of November but Columba may then have remained in Ireland over the winter, only going back to Iona when the good travelling weather returned the following summer.

In the late sixth century the area around Limavady belonged to the people known as the Ciannacht of *Glenn Geimhin.*[40] These constituted a relatively unimportant petty kingdom. Their territory, which included much excellent farm-land, stretched along the River Roe from the fortress at Dungiven (*Dún Geimhin*) to below their other great fortification that still survives near to the Mullagh, known now as the Rough (Roe?) Fort. Precisely why the Convention would have been held there is something of a mystery but as we have seen one of Columba's sisters – Sinech – appears to have been the wife of a member of the Ciannacht. The traditional site of the meeting, which might be said to have been at the time in neutral territory, is a level-topped and possibly partly-artificial mound which has a wonderful commanding view of the surrounding countryside.

Possibly sometime around the same date, perhaps while visiting Ireland for the Convention of *Druim Cett,* Columba may have had some role in the foundation of the monastery of Derry. Almost all surviving ancient tradition is certain that Derry was the first of the saint's foundations and the one dearest to his heart, but such stories are the product of Derry propagandists of much later times than the sixth century. The Annals of the Four Masters, written in the early seventeenth century and without any additional historical support, says that Derry was founded by Colum Cille in the year 535. This is impossible; the would-be saint was at most about fifteen years of age at the time.

The usually more reliable Annals of Ulster says that 'Derry of Colum Cille was founded' in 545 but, importantly, the identity of the founder is not actually stated. The use of the cultic name 'Derry of Colum Cille', however,

[39] Reeves, *Adamnan,* 37.

[40] For a description of the Ciannacht of *Glenn Geimhin,* see B. Lacey, 'County Derry in the Early Historic Period', in G. O'Brien (ed.), *Derry and Londonderry: History and Society* (Dublin 1999), 115–48.

betrays the entry as a retrospective insert as it is not used again in those annals until the early twelfth century. We know that the contemporary source for what would become the Annals of Ulster was actually being augmented in Derry in the late twelfth and early thirteenth centuries.[41] The 545 entry is no more than a piece of twelfth-century propaganda inserted in the annals at that time by those seeking to boost the fortunes of Derry through linking the story of its foundation with the famous saint. In fact, there is no historical evidence of any kind that Columba founded the monastery of Derry.

Almost certainly another entry in the annals – which there is no reason to doubt – gives the more correct picture. In 619 Fiachra son of Ciarán, son of Ainmire, son of Sétna died. In some of the sets of annals he is also identified as 'the [other] founder of Derry'. Whatever this may mean, it is clear that an alternative interpretation to the official version has survived accidentally.[42] Although we do not know what age Fiachra was when he died, we may presume that his involvement in the foundation of Derry occurred about thirty or forty years earlier, that is at any time from the late 570s onwards. Fiachra was a younger relative of Columba and a nephew of the king Áed mac Ainmirech who is said in the legends to have given his fortress as the site for the new monastery. We know that Áed was victorious in a battle with the Cenél nÉogain of Inishowen in 578 at a place called *Druim Meic Ercae* which may have been very close to Derry.[43]

Conall Gulban
I
Fergus
I
Sétna——————Fedelmid
I I
Ainmire (568) Colum Cille (593)
——————I
Áed (596) Ciarán
I
Fiachra (619)

Table 2: Genealogy of Fiachra, the 'founder' of Derry.

[41] Gearóid Mac Niocaill, *The Medieval Irish Annals* (Dublin 1975), 29; D.P. Mc Carthy, *The Irish Annals: their genesis, evolution and history* (Dublin 2008), esp. 238–41.
[42] Lacey, 'Colum Cille, founder of … Derry'.
[43] Lacey, *Cenél Conaill*, 114.

There are reasons for thinking that very shortly after that battle Áed may have been involved as a lay benefactor in the foundation of the church at Derry.[44] Although there is no evidence to support the contention, it may be that following his participation in the Convention at *Druim Cett*, which as has been argued above also had to take place about 578 or 579, Columba may have come to Derry where he could have been involved in some secondary capacity along with Fiachra in the foundation of the monastery. The traditional site of the Convention is probably less than a day's walk from Derry and the same journey on the waters of Lough Foyle would take even less time. Adomnán mentions Derry on a few occasions as a port of embarkation for the journey between Ireland and Iona or Britain. One story in the *Vita Columbae* implies that Columba at least knew about the existence of a church with its graveyard in Derry before he died in the 590s.

But the saint's principal foundation in Ireland was clearly the monastery of Durrow (now in County Offaly) as indicated by Adomnán, and not Derry as is claimed in the legends. Durrow or *Dairmagh*, like Derry, has a name derived from the Irish word for an oak-tree or oak-grove, *Daire*. This similarity of names may well have contributed later to the confusion about the foundation stories of the northern monastery. Bede says that Durrow was founded before the saint left Ireland in 562. However, references to Durrow by Adomnán, who was closer to the event both in time and in terms of relationship to those involved, seems to show that the foundation occurred much later. The Annals of Ulster records the death of Áed mac Brénainn, king of *Tethbae* (roughly County Longford), in 587 and a note entered in the margin adds that 'it was he who granted Durrow to Colum Cille'. This date fits closely with a reference by Adomnán to Alither who was abbot of Clonmacnoise at the time that Durrow was founded. Alither became abbot about 583 and died in 597. However, Durrow was not located in *Tethbae* and if a king called Áed was involved in its foundation it is more likely that the actual person was Áed mac Ainmirech – Columba's relative, who was most probably king of Tara at the time.[45] Adomnán, who may have had his own particular connections with Durrow,[46] argues for Columba's close interest in the affairs of that monastery and his detailed knowledge of what was going on there.

---

44 *Ibid.*, 128–30.

45 See Herbert, *Iona*, 32.

46 A.P. Smyth, *Celtic Leinster* (Dublin 1982), 118–22, claims that Adomnán may have begun his monastic career at Durrow and may even have taught the future king of Northumbria, Aldfrith, there. However, other authors have not concurred; see for example Herbert, *Iona*, 48 and Sharpe, *Adomnán*, 45–6.

The only other possible Columban church in Ireland mentioned by Adomnán is Drumhome in south Donegal, although it is not definite that it belonged to the confederation of the saint's churches during his own lifetime.[47] Most of the other well-known Irish Columban churches seem to have been founded at much later dates by clerics who belonged to the *familia* or community of Colum Cille.

What is clear from Adomnán's account is that Columba made several separate visits to Ireland subsequent to the foundation of the monastery of Iona. The late medieval legendary sources, claiming that he had left his homeland as a penance, held that he had vowed never to return to Ireland again. However, as it was well known that he did return, the storytellers were forced to invent extraordinary explanations of this apparent breach of promise. Manus O'Donnell put it most succinctly:

> A wonder to tell but Colum Cille did go back to Ireland, he having promised when he was leaving that he would not set foot on Irish soil ever again nor look upon her men or women nor consume her food or drink. But Colum Cille fulfilled his promise completely for he had a sod of Scottish soil under his feet all the time he was in Ireland and there was a cere-cloth [a waxed blindfold] over his eyes and his cap was over that again and the hood of his cowl was over that also. In that way he saw not an Irish man or woman just as he had promised. And he brought with him sufficient provisions so as not to have had to consume any of the food or drink of Ireland as long as he was there.

[47] See B. Lacey, 'Tírechán's Sirdruimm, Adomnán's Dorsum Tómme', *Journal of the Royal Society of Antiquaries of Ireland*, 132 (2002), 148–50.

Everyday Life on Iona

Fedelmid's son, Colum Cille,
In his mouth every week, I feel,
Put as much of his food and his sustenance,
As would not serve a beggar one meal.

Three fifties of psalms he repeated,
Each night, and in terrible pain;
In the sea near his church, beside Scotland,
Before the sun had arisen again.

Manus O'Donnell,
Betha Colaim Chille (1532)

Our knowledge of what daily life was like in Columba's monastery on Iona can be gleaned from two distinctly different types of evidence. Adomnán's *Vita Columbae* provides more or less contemporary documentation about the Columban monastic way of life. In addition, various forms of archaeological investigation help to build a picture of the material culture at the time. As we will see below in the present state of our knowledge the evidence drawn from these two separate sources can occasionally appear to be contradictory; sometimes even irreconcilable.

Although it was not part of Adomnán's intention to give us a description of what the monastery was like or how it functioned, in the *Vita Columbae* the incidental details mentioned as part of the various stories about the saint do give us some impression of the daily life of the monks and of their surroundings. One of the main problems with that source, of course, is that it was written around 700, almost one and a half centuries after the foundation of the monastery. However, it seems a reasonable assumption – based on our understanding of developments in the early medieval period in general – that day-to-day life on the island had probably changed very little in the intervening period.

On the other hand, the main problem associated with the archaeology of Iona is that there has not been – and because of the existence of the restored abbey there it is unlikely that there ever will be – total or even significant excavation of the site of the original monastery. There have been 'excavations' of a kind on the island since at least the end of the nineteenth century; in the twentieth century these became increasingly more scientific. However, even these latter excavations have been piecemeal and sporadic and necessarily dependent on modern development requirements at the site rather than part of any overall integrated research plan.[1]

Evidence from modern archaeological work seems to prove that Iona had been inhabited in earlier prehistoric times as well as in the more recent centuries before the foundation of the monastery. Very few traces of the earliest monastery survive to the present above ground but it is certain that it was located on the gently sloping land on the eastern side of the island. The site is now dominated by the restored Benedictine Abbey which was founded about 1200 by Reginald of Islay – son of the more famous Somerled. The only structures that survive to the present from before the construction of that Abbey are themselves relatively late and certainly do not go back to the times of Columba. The two relevant buildings are the heavily restored little chapel known as Saint Columba's Shrine, now squashed up against the later Abbey walls, and St Orans' twelfth century church which stands somewhat apart from the present Abbey building. In addition, there are the high crosses which date almost certainly to the late eighth century and which will be discussed further below. The constant rebuilding and extension of the original monastery over the centuries, and more importantly of the later medieval Abbey, also damaged much of the below-ground archaeological deposits. Similar damage was also caused by what appears to have been the intensive horticultural activity of the later medieval Benedictine monks in the core of the original ancient monastic site, as well as the constant need to improve drainage throughout the medieval period.

We do know from Adomnán that the original monastery was at least partly surrounded by a *vallum* or 'boundary' of some sort, which seems to have included elements of both bank and ditch or ditches. Some evidence for this *vallum* still survives. However, the sequence of ditches as revealed by excavation is quite complex and not yet fully understood; particularly scarce is any evidence for a fully enclosing bank. Finbar McCormick, one of the archaeologists who has excavated at the site, has concluded from this that 'the *idea* of the *vallum* was more important than its monumentality.' Nevertheless,

[1] See F. McCormick, 'Excavations at Iona, 1988', *Ulster Journal of Archaeology*, Vol. 56 (1993), 78–107, where there are comprehensive references to previous archaeological investigations on the island. See also the same author's, Iona: the Archaeology of the Early Monastery, in Bourke, *Studies in the Cult*, 45–68. Much of what follows in the next section has been based on those two papers. Of particular importance also is J. Barber, Excavations on Iona, 1979, *Proceedings of the Society Of Antiquaries of Scotland* 111 (1981), 282–380. The most recent review of the excavation history on Iona is J. O'Sullivan, 'Iona: archaeological investigations, 1875–1996', in D. Broun & T. Clancy, *Spes Scotorum, hope of Scots: Saint Columba, Iona and Scotland* (Edinburgh 1999), 215–44.

studies of what appear to be the surviving remains of the *vallum* indicate that it enclosed a slightly rectangular-shaped space about eight acres in extent which appears to have been open on the eastern or shore side. Until recently the shape of that enclosure was considered problematic by archaeologists, as what appear to be contemporary early monastic sites in Ireland were almost invariably circular or subcircular in plan.

However, recent study of sections of the surviving bank on Iona seems to demonstrate that at least parts of that enclosure are actually older than the monastery and may date to the Iron Age. That abandoned enclosure – already quite ancient – was later re-used by Columba and his monks in the sixth century. The evidence of oak and ash trees recovered from the bottom of a part of the enclosing ditch would seem to indicate that some time – sufficient for the growth of such trees – had elapsed since the previous occupiers had left the site but before the monks had arrived. Although it is likely that people had been living there at some stage in the relatively recent past, the island was almost certainly largely deserted when the Irish monks came there – probably but not definitely in 562 or, perhaps, 563.

Adomnán mentions several of the monastic buildings of which the most important was the church. This would have been built in what Bede called the 'Irish manner', that is from timber. Some of the required wood would have had to be brought over from Mull or, possibly, from the Scottish mainland. It is probable also that as the monastery developed over the centuries other separate churches or chapels were built – possibly outside the *vallum* and in other parts of the island. The huts where the monks worked and lived are mentioned, including a particular place where Columba slept – allegedly on the bare rock with a separate stone as a pillow. What was claimed as that 'pillow stone' was said to have been used later as the saint's grave marker.

Columba had another private space, apparently built on a rise or a height of some sort overlooking the rest of the monastery. That was where he wrote and worked on his books. Excavations at the rock outcrop known as Tòrr an Aba, 'the abbot's mound', to the west of the Abbey, where such an outlook would have been possible, produced evidence that it had been revetted and had a structure of some sort on top. This has led to the interpretation of this feature as Columba's hut site, but there is no definite proof that this was so. At least some of the huts were made from wattle; we read in the *Vita Columbae* of wattles being procured for precisely that purpose. There was some evidence for the use of wattles on the top of Tòrr an Aba.

There may have been a special scriptorium and a library in the monastery. One study lists at least twenty-five texts that – based on quotations and references – must have been available on Iona before the beginning of the eighth century quite apart from those that were actually composed there.[2]

[2] Clancy and Márkus, *Iona*, 211–22.

The books were probably kept in satchels hanging from pegs in the wall, rather than lying on shelves.

Various sheds and barns are referred to, some of which may have been outside the main enclosure. Traces of a circular wooden structure, although not necessarily a 'roofed building', were found inside the enclosure fairly close to the present Abbey building. The location of the latter is always taken as a general guide to the whereabouts of the core of the Columban monastery. There is a supposition that the Abbey church – although much bigger – may have been located in the same general area as the ancient monastic church, although there is no definite archaeological evidence to prove that. The circular structure was composed of two concentric circles of posts, with an overall diameter of about 18 metres. It seems to have been built in the early medieval period. The nature of this structure is highly problematical as it would have presented a relatively enormous engineering problem to have covered it over with a roof. Nevertheless such a possibility cannot be discounted.

There seems to have been a smithy for iron-working and a disused millstone was used subsequently as the base for a cross. Adomnán tells us that crosses were set up at sites connected with special events in the saint's life such as the two erected to commemorate the death of his uncle Ernán: one outside the shed where the old man fell and the other close by where the saint himself was standing at that time. We do not know what material these crosses were made of but they were probably wooden. The surviving finely sculpted stone crosses on Iona, of course, date to much later times – from the middle of the eighth century onwards. Those crosses seem to have been the end of an evolutionary process that started with wooden crosses, included crosses made of stone pillars with wooden transoms as an intermediate stage, and ended with the fully stone cross. In that scenario, the distinctive ring of the so-called 'Celtic Cross' may have originated from the need to provide support struts for the heavy cross arms; indeed St John's Cross on Iona – of about AD 750 – may have been the very first such cross ever erected in these islands.[3]

There was also, of course, a monastic burial ground. Adomnán tells us that the first of the monks to die and be buried on Iona was a Briton – or perhaps a monk called Brito. There is no historical justification for the rather gruesome folkloric story told in the later fictional sources about the 'foundation sacrifice' of the monk Oran whose voluntary death was said to have been needed in order to consecrate the ground to God.[4] Oran does not figure in the list of monks who are said to have accompanied Columba originally from Ireland. Finbar McCormick has argued that the original monastic burial ground was probably on the site now known as *Reilig Odhráin*

[3] For the evolution of the stone cross on Iona, see esp. Fisher, *Early Medieval Sculpture*, 15.
[4] See 'Middle Irish Life of Colum Cille (section 52)' in Herbert, *Iona*, 261.

– 'Oran's Graveyard', which seems to have been separated from the core of the monastery by a deep ditch. More recently, Tomás Ó Carragáin has suggested that the alleged site of Columba's own grave under the small shrine chapel adjacent to the west wall of the late medieval Abbey church may have been 'in the principal monastic graveyard'.[5] From relatively early in its history and up to the end of the eleventh century many Scottish and some Irish and Norse kings were buried on Iona, but precisely where is not clear. Perhaps there was a separate cemetery for lay people.[6]

Excavations in the interior of Saint Ronan's church a few hundred yards to the south of the main monastic complex – itself probably dating to the late 12th or early 13th century – revealed evidence for fragmentary burials which were much earlier than that church. These seem to date to the early medieval period. This area was used later for the burial of women and children but whether that practice was a continuation of a much earlier custom could not be demonstrated. Another burial site, beside Martyr's Bay, yielded evidence for the burial of adult females who had not borne children – perhaps nuns of a later period. In fact, in the voluminous additional notes to his edition of Adomnán's *Vita Columbae* published in 1857, William Reeves listed no less than nine burial grounds in his day in various parts of this comparatively small island.

Detailed archaeological evidence for diet and agricultural practices in the early monastery is much better than that for its buildings. Various dumps of discarded food refuse, especially animal bone, have been found and pollen from a part of the *vallum* ditch has also been very useful in this regard. The pollen evidence seems to show that there was still fairly extensive covering of oak and ash woods on the island at that time, especially close to the monastery. However, relatively soon after the ditch was dug if not before, cereal, probably barley, began to be cultivated nearby. In fact, Adomnán tells us that Columba himself checked the grain store shortly before he died and was pleased that the monks had enough for the coming year despite the fact that it was only early June – well before the harvest of that year.

Evidence for the cultivation of cereals close to the monastery declines as time goes by, indicating perhaps that these crops were later planted elsewhere on the island; probably in the western *machair* area. In other words the earliest monks may have been sufficiently catered for by the crops grown close to the monastery itself but as time went by, and presumably as the number of monks increased, it was necessary to expand the amount of farmed land to other parts of the island. It seems from the finds of millstones that there was

[5] T. Ó Carragáin, 'The Architectural Setting of the Cult of Relics in Early Medieval Ireland', *Journal of the Royal Society of Antiquaries of Ireland* 133 (2003), 130–76, p. 168, footnote 59. See also most importantly I. Fisher, 'The monastery of Iona in the eighth century', in O'Mahony, *The Book of Kells*, 33–47, p. 41.

[6] A. MacDonald, 'Adomnán's Monastery of Iona', in Bourke *Studies in the Cult*, 24–44, p. 33.

definitely a watermill for processing the cereal on the island from early in the history of the monastery. Indeed, a millstream (*Sruth a Mhuilinn*) still passes close to the Abbey on its northern side, although we do not know how long it has had that name. Excavation at a kink in that stream revealed a large 'basin' (a pond?) that may have formed part of the workings of the mill. Unfortunately no dating evidence was found there.

The deposits of bones that have been found show that cattle were the dominant animal species, although Adomnán also mentioned sheep and goats and some bones of those animals were found as well. Pig bones were also found although whether these animals were actually raised on Iona remains an open question. As Finbar McCormick pointed out they could have been given to the monastery as tribute. We know that horses were used as farm animals. The famous story of the white horse that came to sympathise with Columba shortly before his death indicates an almost family-pet type relationship with some of the animals. Puzzlingly, horse bones with clear evidence of butchering marks were found indicating that, on at least some occasions, horse-flesh seems to have been eaten. This is most surprising given the well-established taboo against such a practice. However, there may well have been some special circumstances that gave rise to the occurrence of these bones.

There was also evidence for wild animals being hunted and eaten: bones of red deer, roe deer and seals were found. Adomnán specifically mentions a breeding colony of seals that seemed to have been recognised as actually belonging to the monastery and which were being farmed by the monks. McCormick suggests that the deer must have come from the adjacent but much larger island of Mull, where the monastery may have had some sort of off-site estate. The presence of badger, fox, wild-cat and otter bones in the collection has been interpreted as evidence that the skins of those animals were used by the monks. A fairly wide range of inshore and deep-sea fish as well as fowl and wild bird bones were also found, indicating that those food sources were also exploited – to some degree at any rate.

We know that by the middle of the eighth century at the latest, Iona was the centre of a school of excellent artists who could work in a variety of media. The surviving large crosses on the island, dating from around 750 onwards, as well as the near certainty that the Book of Kells was made there most probably before or around 800, is the best evidence of that kind of creativity. In addition there is archaeological evidence of metalworking – copper and tin (bronze) and of glassworking – such as has been found on other contemporary high status sites in Scotland and Ireland. Evidence for woodworking was also found, with samples of stave-built and lathe-turned objects. The lathe-turned bowls seem to have been made mainly from alder but evidence for the use of willow was also found. Some of these wooden bowls seem to have been modelled on ceramic exemplars imported from the continent, probably as part of the wine trade.

We know that there were carpenters among the monks and – unsurprisingly on an island – there is some evidence of boat-building, both timber-built vessels and skin-covered currachs. Excavation of part of the ditch produced remains of other kinds of woodworking in the monastery too, with evidence for the use of alder, ash, birch, fir, hazel, oak, pine, poplar and willow.

The ditch also produced evidence for leatherworking, especially shoe-making. Some of the shoes were decorated and others could be paralleled with those worn by the figure of Saint Matthew illustrated in the Book of Durrow. The range of hides used included: cattle, horse, red dear, seal, and goat or 'hairy sheep'. But no evidence was found for the specialized production of prepared calf-skin for vellum as has been found for instance at what now looks like another Columban (or at least Columban-period) monastic site at Portmahomack in northeastern Scotland which will be discussed further below. Some evidence of pottery-making was found, as well as evidence for exotic imported ceramics from as far away as the Mediterranean. The latter may have been imported as much for their contents as for the vessels themselves. It would have been necessary, of course, to have imported wine for use in the Eucharistic liturgies.

The Scottish archaeologist Aidan MacDonald has made Adomnán's *Vita Columbae* yield up a great deal of evidence about the monastery and its daily life by subjecting the text to detailed close reading and scrutiny.[7] He has commented that for Adomnán the whole island of Iona seems to have been regarded as a sacred space. Indeed Dr MacDonald's colleague Dr Jennifer O'Reilly has suggested that for Adomnán Iona was another 'holy land'.[8] Adomnán frequently seems to identify the Columban monastery with the entire extent of the island; not just the monastic buildings or the area enclosed by the *vallum*. MacDonald thinks that several of the stories told by Adomnán make it very unlikely that there was any secular population living on the island around that time. He suggests also that, as with other early Irish church sites, there seems to be on Iona a gradation of spaces in terms of their perceived, progressively increasing degree of holiness. Those divisions would have had several consequences such as the rules for restricting the admission of lay people to the various spaces demarcated in that way. We know that, following

[7] See for instance MacDonald, 'Adomnán's Monastery; and, Aspects of the Monastic Landscape in Adomnán's Life of Columba', in J. Carey, M. Herbert and P. Ó Riain (eds), *Studies in Irish Hagiography: Saints and Scholars* (Dublin 2001), 15–30, where references to several earlier articles are also cited. The following section owes much to all of those papers.

[8] J. O'Reilly, 'Reading the Scriptures in the Life of Columba', in Bourke, *Studies in the Cult*, 80–106, p. 86; see also Ó Carragáin, 'The Architectural setting', 144–6.

biblical examples, early medieval ecclesiastical sites were often subdivided into distinct zones that were categorised as: *locus sanctus*, *locus sanctior* and *locus sanctissimus*, that is 'holy', 'holier' and 'holiest' places.

For MacDonald the coastline of the whole island represented the outer boundary of this sacred space; the middle boundary was represented by the *vallum*; while a line of some kind enclosing the church and perhaps the space around it demarcated the innermost sanctuary. The space enclosed by the inner boundary may have been open only to clerics as well as, possibly, to select groups of the lay faithful who would have been admitted 'under strict supervision'. Indeed, MacDonald suggests that at that early stage of its history, as distinct from the practice much later, the Columban monks may have wished to discourage lay people from visiting the island. MacDonald stresses that Columba's and Adomnán's Iona, and its contemporary counterparts in Ireland and Scotland, were 'proper' monasteries, quite unlike the heavily secularised and possibly semi-urbanised ecclesiastical settlements which some of those places evolved into in later centuries.

> I suggest that 6th- to 7th-century Iona, and many other Irish monastic churches of the time, were originally regular cenobitic monasteries of a kind or kinds that would have been familiar enough in the late Roman world, East and West, or in contemporary Europe and (from the 7th century) Anglo–Saxon England. In other words, they were more or less enclosed and integrated religious communities living a common life under common discipline and authority – whether or not such communal organization was articulated explicitly in a written rule. While they acknowledged an interdependent relationship with the lay world around them, they lived secluded lives as detached as possible from that world for the sake of their proper spiritual goal – the contemplative search for God.[9]

We do not know how many monks were living in that community at any one time. The list that names the monks who are said to have accompanied Columba from Ireland mentions only thirteen men in total. All of those were Irish and several of them were related to each other. However, as Richard Sharpe has pointed out, Adomnán also mentions at least one Briton – almost certainly someone who spoke a P Celtic language, two English men – probably from Northumbria, and a Pictish monk.[10] All of those seem to have been part of the Columban community during the saint's lifetime. In other words, the monastery on Iona seems to have drawn its membership from all the various population groups or 'nations' that inhabited Britain at the time. Sharpe also tells us that Adomnán names about twenty monks who belonged

[9] MacDonald, 'Adomnán's Monastery', 25.
[10] Sharpe, *Adomnán*, 21.

to the monastery of Iona during the lifetime of Columba.[11] Again we know from Adomnán that other postulants from Ireland tried to join the monastery after its foundation. Of course we also read that some of the twelve who went with the saint initially, as well as others, spent some time in the associated monasteries both in Ireland and Scotland and in the other islands of the Hebrides. Some of those monks acted as *praepositi* or priors of the associated or dependent monasteries.

Aidan MacDonald argued that the communal style of living of the monks would probably have been reflected in the disposition of the various buildings within the monastic enclosure and in the internal arrangements of those buildings. Within the enclosure there was what Adomnán calls the *plateola*, a 'courtyard' or central open space. This may have been paved or otherwise surfaced in order to keep it dry. Perhaps the major communal buildings of the monastery were arranged around this space, although not necessarily in accordance with a definitive repeatable plan in the way that the great stone-built abbeys of later medieval times were arranged.

The most important building would have been the church, perhaps on the east side of the *plateola*. This was a wooden building, although there is no reason to assume that this meant that it was also primitive. Great buildings in timber are known from Irish contexts as far back as the Iron Age and before. Neither is there any reason to assume that the building was not richly decorated just because evidence of that does not survive. Carvings, painted walls and ceilings, and draperies of various forms could have been used to embellish the church in the way we read about in the roughly contemporary descriptions of Saint Brigid's church at Kildare.

The Iona church would have been aligned east-west and probably had a door at its west end, possibly opening out onto the 'courtyard'. There may have been a porch around this doorway. There was probably a window of some kind at the east end above the altar and possibly others, almost certainly at a high level, along the long side walls – maybe particularly on the south side where sunlight could enter. MacDonald shows us that there was a small extra chamber opening off one side of the church, probably towards the east end, but it is not clear whether this was on the south or the north side of the main building. This additional chamber may have had no proper door but could have been screened off by a curtain or other temporary partition from the main part of the church. The *exedra*, as Adomnán called that chamber, was itself internally partitioned, and a lockable door led from the outer to the inner compartment. The outer part of this chamber may have served as a small chapel while the inner section may have been a sacristy.

[11] *Ibid.*, 74.

Perhaps opposite the church on the west side of the *plateola* was the 'great house'. This seems to have been a relatively large building and was also built of timber. It could have been rectangular or curvilinear – even circular – in plan. Adomnán seems to suggest that an equivalent building in Durrow was round. As we have seen above, there is evidence of a large circular wooden structure on Iona, although the precise nature of that building has not been established and it was located to the southwest rather than west of the church. The 'great house' may have functioned as a general living space for the indoor activities of the monks such as assembly, study, teaching and recreation. It is not clear if it was also used for dining. Wherever the monks ate there had to be also a nearby kitchen, although whether that was a separate building is not clear. Fire was a particular hazard in medieval times and measures to protect the main buildings, all of which would have been constructed of timber, would have been uppermost in the minds of the monks.

Aidan MacDonald suggests that the main meal of the day would have been eaten around three in the afternoon. There was probably an earlier meal on most days, except on the two weekly fast days – Wednesday and Friday – and perhaps during Lent and other periods of abstinence such as Advent. On Sundays and feast days there seems to have been an additional meal. However, monks who were engaged in heavy work could have extra food and rest if they needed it. The arrival of guests sometimes interrupted the normal monastic eating regime. In terms of food, Adomnán mentions only bread, fish, fruit and milk. A baker is mentioned on one occasion, as is a gardener who may have supplied the monastery with fruit, vegetables and herbs. The latter, of course, would have been used for medicinal purposes also. As we have seen above, meat bones were found in the excavations and the killing of animals is described occasionally by Adomnán. The latter, however, does not mention meat being eaten as a normal part of the monastic diet and it is possible that it was allowed only to guests or perhaps to those monks who were ill.

Based on the general communal nature of the monastery, MacDonald has argued that most of the monks would have slept on beds in a dormitory of some sort, perhaps singly in cubicles opening off a larger communal space. That building could have been either circular or rectangular and may or may not have been identical with the 'great house'. It seems, however, from Adomnán's words that Columba himself may have slept in a separate cell, what is called the *hospitiolum,* implying a small space of some kind.

Nearby was the *hospitium* or 'guest house'. Various guests, both lay and clerical are mentioned as visiting the monastery, not to mention the famous story of the exhausted crane that is given 'hospitality' on the island after flying all the way from Ireland. Hospitality was an important duty in the monasteries as it appears to have been also in secular Irish society at the time. It may be, based on references found widespread in medieval Irish literature, that there was an obligation to offer guests a minimum of three days and three nights of hospitality. The guest house may have functioned also as an infirmary, and Aidan MacDonald also thinks that it was where new postulants would have been received.

MacDonald has shown us that Columba does not seem to have adopted a major pastoral or a missionary role. He was primarily, in Adomnán's phrase, the 'father and founder of monasteries'. At least as depicted by Adomnán, MacDonald argued that Columba was 'only conventionally an ascetic ... and in no sense a solitary'. There is a late text known as the 'Rule of Colum Cille' but it is very unlikely that it derives from the saint's own period. Rather than making regulations for the behaviour of a monastic community like that on Iona the rule is addressed to a hermit such as Virgno, whom we hear of living for twelve years at the beginning of the seventh century 'in the place of the anchorites, in *Muirbolc Mar*,' on the island of *Hinba*.

> Be alone in a separate place near a chief monastery, if your conscience is not prepared to be in common with the crowd. Be always naked in imitation of Christ and the Evangelist ... A few religious men to converse with you of God and his Testament; to visit you on days of solemnity; to strengthen you in the Testaments of God and the stories of the Scriptures ...[12]

The principal daily duty of the monks was the worship of God through participation in the various liturgical observances, together with private meditation and prayer. Mass seems to have been said only on Sundays and feast days rather than daily. Singing, especially of the Psalms, is mentioned repeatedly by Adomnán, including the 'miraculous' power of Columba's own voice to be heard at great distances. Later poets celebrated that talent in a little verse in Irish:

> The sound of Colum Cille's voice,
> Than every cleric's sweeter;
> It was audible at fifteen hundred feet;
> And, sometimes, it was even greater.[13]

Study and writing were also of great importance although possibly not for all the members of the community. One modern translator of Adomnán remarked that Columba always seemed to have been surrounded by books,

---

[12] Full text with translation printed in W. Reeves, *Acts of Archbishop Colton in his Metropolitan Visitation of the Diocese of Derry* (Dublin 1850), 109–12. For more recent references, see T. Clancy, 'Díarmait *sapientissimus*: the career of Díarmait, *dalta* Daigre, Abbot of Iona', *Peritia* 17–18 (2002–2004), 215–32, pp 225–6.

[13] Lacey, *Manus O'Donnell*, 36.

inkhorn and vellum.[14] The monks of course had to provide for their own domestic needs, erecting the various buildings and cultivating and walling-off the fields on the *machair*. There are numerous references in the *Vita Columbae* to boats and boating as we would expect for such island-dwellers. The monks themselves, their animals, visitors to the island, bulky building materials and other supplies would have had to be transported frequently across the sound from Mull or from the Scottish mainland which was even further away.

Besides Iona, Columba and his monks established a number of dependent centres and churches on some of the other islands in the Hebrides and on the adjacent parts of the western side of Scotland. One of these was at a place called *Campus-* or *Mag-Luinge* on the island of Tiree, where there were at least two further monasteries – *Artchain* and *Bledach*. There was a monastery on the unidentified island of *Elena* and another at *Cella Diuni* near Loch Awe on the mainland. A monastery which figures several times in Adomnán's Life – and which was certainly founded before about 574, was at the unidentified *Hinba*; this seems to have been associated particularly with penitents or lay people who came to shrive their sins by living according to a particularly strict regime under the supervision of the monks. As well as the main monastery at *Hinba* there was also a hermitage nearby, at the place called *Muirbolc Már*.

In the *Vita Columbae* we read of frequent comings and goings by boat between all these places as well as to others in Ireland and Britain, both during Columba's time and that of Adomnán. Columba and his monks travelled fairly widely among the western islands and on the Scottish mainland, going to Skye, Eigg and Ardnamurchan; journeying to the other side of the highlands across the *Druim Albain* or 'Spine of Britain' up the Great Glen into the lands of the Picts and seemingly to the vicinity of Inverness, as well as further north as far as the Orkneys. They also, as we have seen, received many visitors from Ireland and elsewhere, both on Iona and at some of the dependent monasteries.

[14] J. Marsden, *The Illustrated Columcille* (London 1991), 53.

'The Fifth of the Ides of June': Columba's Death

I commend to you, my children, these last words, that you shall have among yourselves mutual and unfeigned charity, with peace.

Columba,
quoted in Adomnán's *Vita Columbae*

In the second preface to the *Vita Columbae*, which of course is a work of unashamed hagiography, Adomnán tells us that it is his intention to describe his subject's 'holy way of life' and 'some instances of his miracles'. The *Vita* is divided into three 'books' or parts: 'prophetic revelations', 'divine miracles effected through him' and 'appearances of angels, and certain manifestations of heavenly brightness above the man of God'. Throughout these 'books', he is referred to always as *Sanctus Columba* – holy or Saint Columba.

Adomnán tells a story which is said to have occurred four years before the saint's death. Two men, an Irishman named Lugne moccu-Blai and Pilu who was a Saxon, were watching Columba in his hut when they saw his face light up with joy but then turn to sadness. After they had pressed him for some time, Columba explained to the two men the reasons for the change in his expression. He said that he had seen a vision in which angels were on their way to accompany his soul to heaven but that God had changed his mind at the last moment 'answering in preference the prayers of many churches for me'.

Adomnán concludes his Life with a chapter that allegedly details the last days of the saint, his death and the events surrounding his burial. It is not at all clear, of course, how accurate this description actually is or the degree to which it is invented hagiography. Some historians have suggested that Adomnán's account bears similarities with formulaic descriptions of the deaths of other saints. In other words, this is how Adomnán would have expected the final days of a saint – his saint – to have been. Richard Sharpe has shown how Adomnán, particularly in this section of the work, quotes a number of times from the Life of St Anthony by Evagrius.[1] Evagrius was a Syrian historian of the early church who, as it happened, lived around the same time as Columba. Notwithstanding this scepticism, it has to be said that Adomnán's account of the events contains a surprising amount of charming detail, some at least of which is likely to have been preserved, or at least believed, in the traditions of the monastery of Iona.

Adomnán starts the account by telling us that one day, probably late in the month of May 593, the aged and weakened Columba was taken in a wagon across the island to visit the monks who were working in the *machair* in the western part of Iona. The old man told his monks that at Easter time, during the previous month, he had desired to die but that he had put off his departure from this world for a little longer so as not to spoil for them the celebration of what was the greatest of all the Christian festivals. The monks grew very sad on hearing these words but Columba attempted to comfort them. Then still sitting in the wagon, he turned towards the east, facing back into the interior of the island, and blessed it and its inhabitants. Afterwards he was brought back to the main monastic enclosure on the opposite side of the island.

While attending Mass on Sunday a few days later, the abbot's face was seen to glow again with joy. Adomnán tells us that again the saint had seen an angel who had been sent to bring him into the presence of the Lord. On the following Saturday Columba along with his devoted attendant Diormit went to the monastery barn and blessed the building and the two heaps of grain there, saying that he was thankful that his monks would have enough food for the coming year in the event of his departure. Columba then confided to Diormit that he would die later that night.

Leaving the barn, the holy man walked back towards the monastery but stopped about halfway to sit down and rest for a while. As he sat there a white horse, which carried the milk vessels between the cow pasture and the monastery buildings, came up to him and put its head on the saint's bosom. Adomnán, betraying a very personal affection, says of this incident that the horse was 'inspired, as I believe, by God, before whom every living creature has understanding'. Prophetically, the horse began to mourn the imminent death of his master and his tears fell freely onto the saint's clothes and body. Diormit started to drive the horse away but Columba stopped him and instead blessed his 'servant', the horse.

The holy man then went to the top of a small hill that overlooked the monastery and, promising that Iona would be a place of special honour in future times, blessed it. He returned to his hut and resumed copying a Psalter. When he reached the thirty-fourth Psalm and the verse 'But they that seek

[1] Sharpe, *Adomnán*, 58.

the Lord shall not want anything that is good', he stopped and famously said 'Let Baithín write what follows'. Afterwards he went to the church for vespers. When this was finished the saint returned to his lodgings and lay down on the bare rock with its stone pillow. While lying down he communicated to Diormit his last instructions to his monastic brothers, including that they should have 'mutual and unfeigned charity, with peace' among themselves. These were to be his last quoted words.

He rested for another while but when the monastery bell sounded the hour of midnight he rose immediately and ran to the church, reaching it before the other monks. At the altar he sank down on his knees in prayer. As more of the monks arrived Diormit and a few others saw the holy man illuminated by an 'angelic light' that quickly faded, leaving them to grope for him in the darkness. On finding him, Diormit lifted the holy man's head onto his lap. The other monks arrived with lamps and seeing their beloved abbot about to die they all began to weep. Columba's face was filled with joy and Diormit raised the saint's right hand to help him bless his brother monks. With this gesture he 'breathed out his spirit' and the church resounded to the lamentations of the whole community. Almost certainly, it was the first few minutes of Sunday 9 June 593.

The office of matins was sung by the monks and then they carried the body of their late abbot back to his lodgings. Over the following three days and nights the funeral rites were observed. All the time these were being performed, a storm 'of wind without rain' raged about the island. The sea was so rough that it was impossible for anyone to cross the narrow sound between Mull and Iona. Only Columba's own 'family' of monks was present at the ceremonies, just as he was said to have foretold. When the obsequies were ended, the body was wrapped in fine cloths and laid to rest in a grave. When the burial of the holy man was completed the storm abated and the sea became calm once again. What was believed to have been his former pillow stone was subsequently erected beside his grave as a monument, and was still to be seen there in Adomnán's time. Adomnán also says that visions continued to be seen at that graveside after his death. What is believed to have been that grave marker – the 'pillow stone' – is now preserved in the Iona Abbey stone museum.

At the time that Columba died it is said that various extraordinary visions were seen in Ireland. For example Ernéne moccu Fhir-róide, who was later buried in the border monastery at Drumhome in south Donegal, claimed to have seen such a manifestation. As a very old man he himself told Adomnán, who at that time was a young man, about what he had seen. On the night of 8 until the 9 of June 593, Ernéne, along with some other men, was fishing on a river called the Finn in Donegal, almost certainly in territory that had been or would be shortly conquered by Columba's own people the Cenél

Conaill.[2] Suddenly the heavens were lit up. What seemed like 'a very great pillar of fire' appeared in the northeast 'in the region of the rising sun', and rose up into the sky illuminating the earth as if it was midday in high summer. The pillar pierced the sky and then darkness followed. Other fishermen at other parts of the river are said to have reported seeing the same sight. It should probably be said that in reality at such northern latitudes, complete darkness at that time of the year is very short-lasting.

Near the beginning of his Life of the saint, Manus O'Donnell quotes a 'prophetic' verse about Colum Cille said to have been composed by Saint Mochta of Louth:

> A boy will be born in the north,
> He will come after so many years;
> Ireland he'll set alight, and
> His death will leave Scotland in tears.[3]

The traditional site of Columba's grave with a small, greatly restored chapel – Saint Columba's Shrine – built over it, is still pointed out on Iona. That building, as Finbar McCormick following Ian Fisher has pointed out,[4] is definitely older than the late medieval Abbey and, whatever its origins, it was considered important enough to be respected and preserved when the latter building was being laid out and constructed in the early thirteenth century. Tomás Ó Carragáin argues that it must have been built before 849.[5] The same author adds that it might have been the first such structure – that is a mortared stone chapel – built anywhere in an Irish context.

> Though not possible to prove, it is tempting to suggest that, as in so many other areas, Iona was where the original innovation took place: that Columba's was the first shrine chapel to be built, perhaps when he was first translated in the mid-eighth century.[6]

However, there is a lot of confusion in the medieval sources about the location of the saint's body. It is believed that the remains were 'translated' to an elaborately decorated shrine (which may have been housed, originally, in an earlier shrine chapel at the same site) before the second half of the eighth

[2] That river is usually identified as the River Finn in east Donegal. However, recently Tomás Ó Canann has suggested the Finmore in south Donegal as an alternative – Máel Coba Ua Gallchobair and his early family background, *Journal of the Royal Society of Antiquaries of Ireland* 134 (2004), 42. As the latter river, unlike the Finn, is fairly close to what appears to have been Ernéne's monastery at Drumhome, Ó Canann's identification makes much more sense.
[3] Lacey, *Manus O'Donnell*, 19.
[4] McCormick, 'Iona: The Archaeology'.
[5] Ó Carragáin, 'The Architectural Setting', 136.
[6] *Ibid.*, 144 and 150–2.

century.[7] Raghnall Ó Floinn has pointed out that a note in the *Additamenta* in the Book of Armagh seems to suggest that by the early ninth century at least some 'of the bones of Columb Cille from Britain' were at Saul, now in County Down.[8] A legendary story telling how the saint's body came to be buried in Downpatrick (County Down) – in the same grave as Patrick and Brigid, is narrated by Manus O'Donnell.

> Mandar son of the King of Lochlainn [Scandinavia] came with a warfleet to the monastery [of Iona] and plundered it and its graves, and tore up its tombs and lifted its coffins to search them for booty. And they took away with them the wooden coffin in which was the body of Colum Cille. And they thought it was a chest in which there was gold and silver or other treasures of the world, so they took it to their ship without opening it. But when they were out at sea they opened the coffin and finding only the body of a man they shut it again and cast it into the sea. And by God's miracle and the grace of the blessed body that was in it, the coffin did not stay still until it reached Downpatrick. And the abbot of Down[Patrick] went out one morning and saw the coffin that had been cast ashore by the sea. He opened it and found the body inside. And he recognized that it was the body of Colum Cille. When he realised that, he kissed the holy body and gave glory and praise to God who had sent it to him. He washed it and then put it in the tomb where Patrick and Brigid already were.[9]

The Welsh–Norman chronicler Giraldus Cambrensis, writing fairly close to the event, tells how in 1185 the bodies of the three saints, with Patrick in the middle, were found 'in a cave that had three sections'. John de Courcy, who had led the Normans into Ulster, was said (conveniently?) to be present at the scene at the time and 'took charge when these three noble treasures were, through divine revelation, found and translated'.[10] A text known as the *Office of the Translation of the Relics of SS Patrick, Colum Cille and Brigid,* printed in various editions in the early seventeenth century, claims to give a detailed account of this incident.[11] Several decades before de Courcy came to Ireland, Saint Malachy – who died in 1148 – was said to have 'miraculously identified' the site of the burials inside the cathedral in Downpatrick. After

[7] See Fisher, 'The monastery of Iona', 47; R. Ó Floinn, 'Insignia Columbae I', in Bourke, *Studies in the Cult,* 136–61, p. 136; Ó Carragáin, 'The Architectural Setting', 134, as well as further references noted there.

[8] R. Ó Floinn, 'Insignia Columbae I', in C. Bourke (ed.) *Studies in the Cult of Saint Columba* (Dublin 1997), 136–7.

[9] Lacey, *Manus O'Donnell,* 213–14.

[10] J.J. O'Meara, *The First Version of the Topography of Ireland by Giraldus Cambrensis* (Dundalk 1951), 89–90.

[11] Discussed by John O'Donovan (ed.), *Annála Ríoghachta Éireann: Annals of the Kingdom of Ireland by the Four Masters from the earliest period to the year 1616,* 7 vols (Dublin 1848–51, reprinted 1998), note under the year 1185, vol. III, 456–9.

his arrival, de Courcy applied to Pope Urban III for permission to translate them, that is to move them honourably to a better and more visible location. The pope sent as a legate to the ceremony Vivian, the cardinal priest of the church of Santo Stefano Rotundo in Monte Caelio in Rome, and the translation took place appropriately on 9 June 1185.

However, a totally different story is told in the native Irish sources, as recorded in the Annals of the Four Masters for the year 1293.

It was revealed to Nicholas Mac Máel Íosa, the successor of Patrick (Archbishop of Armagh) that the relics of Patrick, Colum Cille and Brigid were at *Sabhall* (Saul) about two miles from Downpatrick. They were exhumed by him and great wonders and miracles were afterwards worked by them. And after having been honourably covered, they were deposited in a shrine.

Stripped of their miraculous and propagandistic elements, there is no need to dismiss the historicity of these separate accounts. Presumably the genuine discovery of the bones of some person or persons lies behind each of these descriptions, although it is extremely unlikely that these were the remains of the three saints.

Colum Cille was remembered in Irish tradition as the poet saint *par excellence*. The story about his intervention on behalf of the professional poets of Ireland at the Convention of *Druim Cett* celebrates that reputation, even if it dates to long after the time of the saint's life. It was believed that he himself had composed several Latin prayers or poems such as the *Noli Pater Indulgere* ('Father do not allow').[12] The litany-like *Adiutor laborantium* ('Helper of workers') is also attributed to him and its most recent editors found no reason to dismiss that association.[13] That short poem has twenty-five lines all of which end with the syllable '*um*'. It is composed in the abecedarian form; that is each following line of the poem begins with the next letter of the alphabet. This apparently 'lost' poem was, relatively recently, tentatively identified in an Anglo–Saxon manuscript from Winchester.[14] The author, 'a little man trembling and most wretched, rowing through the infinite storm of this age', appeals to Christ to protect him.

Very ancient tradition also believed that Colum Cille was the author of the well-known poem, *Altus Prosator* ('Father most high'):

---

[12] Recent scholarly editions of the three Latin poems mentioned here can be found in Clancy and Márkus, *Iona.* I have preferred, however, to use an older, rhyming translation by M.F. Cusack of the *Altus Prosator*, of which only the 'A' and 'Z' verses have been quoted here.

[13] Clancy and Márkus, *Iona*, 69–70. However, subsequently Gilbert Márkus argued that the poem may have been composed by Adomnán – *Adiutor Laborantium*: a poem by Adomnán, in J.M. Wooding (ed.), *Adomnán of Iona: Theologian, Lawmaker, Peacemaker* (Dublin 2010), 145–61.

[14] Clancy and Márkus, *Iona*, 69–70. See also Markús *Adiutor Laborantium*, 145 and references cited.

Ancient of days, Father most high,
Who art, and shall be, as the ages go by.
With Christ and the Spirit, in glory supernal,
Who art God evermore, unbegotten, eternal.
We preach not three Gods, but the unity, One,
The Father, the Spirit, and co-equal Son.
...

Zeal-kindled fire the unjust shall destroy,
Who deny the Lord Jesus, our hope and our joy.
And the good shall be raised in the heavenly choir,
As our merit and glory have made each one higher.

This relatively long poem is also abecedarian, with each new stanza beginning with the next letter of the alphabet. It is rhythmical and the line endings rhyme. It has been described as a 'kind of early "Paradise Lost"'. The author deliberates on the nature of God, supernatural beings, creation, the nature of the world, the final judgement and other similar topics. What are obviously fictional stories about the poem say that Colum Cille composed it in return for gifts sent to him by Pope Gregory the Great. Gregory, however, is said to have been critical of some of the theology of the poem, particularly the playing down of the Holy Trinity. Despite the ancient traditions surrounding it and the views of some modern writers, it would be difficult to prove that the historical Columba was the author. However, whoever composed it was imbued with ideas that seem to have been common among the monks of the saint's monasteries. The poem's most recent editors suggest that it was composed by some Iona monk before the end of the seventh century, and Dr Jane Stevenson concluded that it dates to around the same time as Adomnán.[15]

We have to be even more sceptical about the large collection of poems or verses in the Irish language that are attributed to the saint.[16] These often purport to express his views about the individual sites and monasteries associated with him, or else his thoughts on leaving Ireland. For example:

How rapid the speed of my currach,
With its stern turned upon Derry;
I am sad as I travel by water
On my mission to raven-filled Scotland.

[15] Clancy and Márkus, *Iona*, 40, referring to J. Stevenson, 'Altus Prosator: a Seventh Century Hiberno–Latin Poem', Cambridge University Library (unpublished PhD thesis).

[16] Many of these are incorporated into Manus O'Donnell's *Betha Colaim Chille*. J.R. Kenney, *The Sources for the Early History of Ireland* (New York 1929, reprinted Dublin 1979), lists seventy-nine such poems of various lengths, together with references to editions published prior to 1929.

Sad is the grey-green eye,
That glances back upon Ireland;
No more will it see in my lifetime,
Her men nor their beautiful women.

These poems and verses are invariably more recent literary works from as late as the eleventh and twelfth centuries, often composed with deliberate propagandistic intentions on behalf of the places where they were, or on whose behalf they were, composed. We do know that writing and the copying of other writings formed an important part of the activities of at least some of the monks in the monastery on Iona. In fact, as we have seen, one of the last acts reported of Columba himself was his copying of the Psalms. It is generally agreed now that the underlying record that forms the essential structure of the various collections of annals, from which the chronology of early Irish and Scottish history up to about the 740s can be established, derives from documents kept at Iona from its earliest days – the so-called 'Iona Chronicle'.[17] Indeed Columba was almost certainly centrally involved in the beginnings of that record-keeping enterprise himself. In that sense it can be argued that the very idea of Irish and Scottish 'history' – the factual recording of the pasts of both countries as distinct from the elaboration of legend and myth – is an Iona or a Columban invention. We can see that sensitivity to the historical record, to some extent at least, displayed in the work of Adomnán. When writing his spiritual Life of Columba he was at pains like any modern historian to demonstrate the sources of information about his subject although, of course, he was engaged in hagiography rather than history writing.

From very early in the history of the monastery on Iona, almost certainly as far back as Columba's own time, a record of significant contemporary events had been kept there. Initially this practice may have originated in the simple desire to keep abreast of events 'back home'. However, at some point other retrospective records of events prior to the foundation of the monastery, possibly based on even earlier records all of which are now lost, were also entered into this evolving chronicle. The Iona Chronicle, however, was the foundation on which all the later Irish annals (or at least all those that have survived to us) would be based. Various attempts have been made in modern times to analyse the surviving annalistic compositions with a view to reconstructing the story of the development of the earlier versions. Some authors have suggested that these initial records may have begun as jottings

[17] For a summary of views on the origins of the annals see N. Evans, Annals and Chronicles, in S. Duffy (ed.), *Medieval Ireland: an Encyclopedia* (New York 2005), 20–3 and refs therein; by the same author, *The Present and the Past in Medieval Irish Chronicles* (Woodbridge 2010). See also T. Charles-Edwards *The Chronicle of Ireland*, Liverpool 2006, esp. pp 7–16 and most importantly D. Mc Carthy *The Irish Annals*, (Dublin 2008), esp. chs 5 & 6.

on the tables used to calculate the annually changing date of Easter. However, Dr Daniel Mc Carthy has suggested that the story of the Irish annals began with even earlier events in continental Europe. He has drawn our attention to a chronicle compiled between 403 and 410 by Rufinus of Aquileia, which was:

> slightly extended in *c.*420 by Sulpicius Severus in Gaul and then transmitted to Ireland ... In the later sixth century St Columba had used this text as the basis for his compilation of the *Iona Chronicle* wherein he extended the chronicle up to his own time ...[18]

Dr Mc Carthy argued further that that chronicle had been 'maintained and continued in Iona after Columba's death' but revised fairly extensively 'at a date not long after the Paschal [Easter] reform in 716'. The various reforms and controversies surrounding the calculation of the date of Easter in the early church in Ireland and Britain will be returned to below. At any rate a copy of that extensively revised and continued text of the annals was then brought to Ireland about 740 where it continued to be copied, added to, moved around and further revised and amended. The analogy of a modern scrapbook has often been used to explain the evolution of the Irish annals.

Iona may or may not have been the earliest centre in an Irish or Scottish context for the compilation of such records but it is certainly the earliest such place for which we now have substantial evidence. The Iona Chronicle grew over time and, as we have seen, by the mid-eighth century a copy had been brought to Ireland where it continued to evolve and be developed. That text, which is also missing, is usually referred to as the 'Chronicle of Ireland'. Almost certainly the Iona Chronicle continued to be added to and developed in Scotland but, unfortunately neither that manuscript nor any copy of it is known to have survived to the present. On the other hand, the Chronicle of Ireland was later copied further and those copies were distributed to various other centres of annalistic compilation until, eventually, the whole country more or less came within the 'coverage' of the annals. These later texts continued to be moved around the country and to influence each other, making it difficult for us now to be precise about the origin of some portions of the surviving annals. In addition, some of the people who kept those later records were not content only with recording the events of their own time. Instead, they continued to add information and sometimes whole entries for events that had happened before (sometimes a very long time before) their own day. Many of those additions had a deliberate 'agenda' behind them, but it is often possible after close study to recognise and thus discount such later propagandistic elements.

[18] D. Mc Carthy, 'The Original Compilation of the Annals of Ulster', *Studia Celtica,* xxxviii (2004), 69–95, p. 84.

There is considerable debate still as to when those records began to be kept on Iona as a contemporary chronicle. Some scholars claim, as we have seen above, that this began as early as the abbacy of Columba himself while others would argue for a date in the early or middle part of the seventh century. In addition some authors have noted that from the 670s and 680s onwards entries in the annals become more frequent and much fuller. That expansion seems to coincide with the abbacy of Adomnán which began in 679. As we have seen, Adomnán definitely seems to have had a sense of 'history' which is almost (but not quite) modern in its understanding of the importance of evidence. Whatever the outcome of this debate, what is not in dispute is that, at the very least from the earliest days of the monastery on Iona, notes were kept for future reference of events that were deemed to be important or relevant. In that sense these records began not as a form of history-writing but as a chronicle of current affairs.

Adomnán tells a story that incidentally describes one such episode when the monk Colcu son of Cellach was in Columba's hut studying beside him. The holy man turned to Colcu and told him about the death at that very moment of a chieftain from the latter's district which he had miraculously learned about. At once Colcu wrote down on a waxed tablet the date and the hour at which he had heard this news. He was able to confirm that the details had been correct when he later returned to his home. Whatever about the historicity of the story, stripped of its miraculous character it clearly demonstrates the process by which at least some aspects of the 'Iona Chronicle' might have evolved.

Adomnán claims on a number of occasions that books and the pages of books written in the hand of the saint had miraculous powers. Among those he mentions is a 'book of hymns for the week'. None of these manuscripts is known to have survived despite the fact that several of the later great illuminated Gospel books, such as the Book of Durrow and the Book of Kells, were subsequently claimed as having been made by the saint himself. Indeed a colophon or tail-piece in the clearly much later Book of Durrow actually asserts that it is the work of the saint. As we will see that possibly means that the gospel text in the Book of Durrow was copied from an exemplar that may have actually been written by Columba.

One manuscript could possibly be the original work of the saint. The *Cathach* is a copy of the Psalms, which has been dated by modern scholars to the end of the sixth or the beginning of the seventh century. Each page measures about 9 inches by 6 inches but only 58 of an estimated original 110 vellum leaves have been preserved. It is probably the oldest surviving illuminated Irish manuscript. The mainly black ink lettering of the *Cathach* in an already developed 'Irish hand' is particularly beautiful, while the initial letters at the beginning of each Psalm are sparingly but brilliantly decorated with motifs taken from the La Téne art of the Iron Age. Some words and decorative details were also added in a limited range of other colours.[19]

Tradition has it that this was the Psalter that became the subject of the dispute between Colum Cille and Finnian ultimately leading to the famous 'copyright' judgement and the battle of *Cúl Dreimne.* A recent study has also suggested that the *Cathach* is the apparently lost manuscript known as the *Soiscél Martain* or 'Gospel Book of Saint Martin' which was one of the great treasures of Derry in the middle of the twelfth century.[20] It is probably impossible to prove or, indeed, to disprove any of this but the possibility still remains that the *Cathach,* which is one of our most beautiful and oldest manuscripts, and is certainly of roughly the appropriate date, might well be the work of one of our greatest saints.

Until recently the poem known as *Amrae Coluimb Chille* or 'eulogy' of the saint was thought to be one of if not *the* oldest, surviving poems in Irish and a, more or less, contemporary witness to the saint's life. Scholars generally dated at least some of the very difficult language of the poem to around the year 600, which is in keeping with the tradition that it was composed by the so-called chief poet of Ireland Dallán Forgaill as a tribute shortly after Columba's death.[21] It has been pointed out, however, that – despite the fact that it is in the normal native tradition of praise-poetry – the *Amrae* is greatly influenced by Latin learning such as that it might have been composed by a cleric; Prof. Máire Herbert has suggested that it may have been composed by a Columban monk.[22] As it happens Dallán Forgaill was believed to have been a cleric and was himself later revered as a saint. His genealogical connections link him with the Airgiallan kingdoms in what is now County Derry but he is said to have been buried on the monastic island of Inishkeel in Gweebarra Bay in southwest Donegal.[23] One line of this fairly long poem tells us that it was Áed who caused it to be made 'once the warrior [Colum Cille] should go to heaven'. This Áed was generally believed to have been Áed mac Ainmirech, the powerful and

---

19 M. Herity and A. Breen *The Cathach of Colum Cille: An introduction* (Dublin 2002), 15–7.
20 Raghnall Ó Floinn, 'Sandhills, Silver and Shrines – Fine Metalwork of the Medieval Period from Donegal', in W. Nolan, L. Ronayne & M. Dunlevy (eds), *Donegal History and Society* (Dublin 1995), 85–148.
21 But see the cautionary note about the date by E. Bhreathnach, Review article: 'Medieval Irish history at the end of the twentieth century: unfinished work', *Irish Historical Studies,* Vol. XXXII No. 126 (November 2000), 265; and see below.
22 M. Herbert, 'The Legacy of Colum Cille and his Monastic Community', in James P. Mackey (ed.), *The Cultures of Europe: The Irish contribution* (Belfast 1994), 4–20, p. 10.
23 For his genealogy see Ó Riain, *Corpus,* 64: 426 and B. Lacy, 'The Ui Meic Cairthinn of Lough Foyle', *Derriana, The Journal of the Derry Diocesan Historical Society* (1979), 3–24, p. 9. For a description of Iniskeel see Lacy, *Archaeological Survey,* 271–4.

ambitious Cenél Conaill king who eventually became king of Tara and died in 596. In legend, Áed is credited with being the king who donated the site for the foundation of the monastery of Derry. There are good reasons for believing that this may well have been the truth.[24] As suggested above, he might also have been involved in the foundation of the monastery of Durrow.

However, recently Dr Jacopo Bisagni who studied the *Amrae* in great detail has turned the long-accepted view about its date on its head.

> On the one hand, textual evidence suggests that an elegy in honour of Colum Cille may have been composed in the late 6th or early 7th century' by an Irish monastic scholar belonging to a foundation of the Columban *familia*. On the other hand while no trace of an E[arly] O[ld] I[rish] linguistic layer is discernible in the text, linguistic evidence does indicate that this hypothetical original composition was re-elaborated and enlarged by a 9th century reviser, whose degree of intervention on the earlier material cannot however be determined with exactness.
>
> On the whole, it seems quite possible that large sections of the second half of the *Amrae* were actually composed in the Late Old Irish period [i.e. after AD 800] by an author who was eager to highlight Columba's family connections with the Uí Néill, and more specifically with the Cenél Conaill. This redaction of the text may be what we know as *Amrae Coluimb Chille*.[25]

In other words it would be unwise to accept that the *Amrae*, at least as we now have it, is any older than about AD 800.

Whatever its date, the *Amrae Coluimb Chille* heaps praises on the holy man but gives us virtually no biographical details about him. It stresses his moderate asceticism and his intellectual skills and knowledge, and tells us *ba dín do nochtaib/ ba did do bochtaib* – 'he was a shelter to the naked, he was a teat to the poor.'[26]

> … Colm rises into high heaven
> At the coming to him of the angel of God, –
> A beautiful attendance.
> He made a vigil of his life.
> Short was his time.
> Paltry his sustenance.
> Everywhere a pillar of learning.
> An authority in the strict books of the law.

---

[24] Lacey, *Cenél Conaill*, 128–30.

[25] J. Bisagni, 'The Language and Date of *Amrae Coluimb Chille*', in *Kelten am Rhein: Akten des dreizehenten Internationalen Keltologiekongresses – Proceedings of the Thirteenth International Congress of Celtic Studies* (*Beihefte der Bonner Jahrbücher*, Band 58, 2) (Main am Rhein 2010), 1–11, p. 10.

[26] Clancy & Márkus, *Iona*, 110–11.

Light of the North,
Who brightened the West
And enflamed the East
...[27]

The poem celebrates Colum Cille as a Christian warrior and hero. It emphasises his secular and sacred learning as well as his charity. It tells us that 'for fear of Hell' he went to Scotland [Albu; perhaps literally 'to Britain']. According to the poem 'he was the guardian of a hundred churches' and 'his blessing turned them, the mouths of the fierce ones who lived on the Tay [the Picts], to the will of the King [God]'.

What age was Columba at the time of his death? Various estimates are given in the ancient sources: some of the annals suggest seventy-five, while Bede and other sources suggest seventy-seven. Prof. Pádraig Ó Riain has argued recently that the latter figure:

> broken down into forty-three (4+3 = 7) years in Ireland and thirty-four (3+4 = 7) in Scotland, though still widely accepted as genuine, were designed to make as much use as possible of the numerologically 'perfect' digit seven.[28]

If Daniel Mc Carthy's revisions of the chronologies of the annals are correct then in June 593 Colum Cille would have been 72 years of age.

---

[27] Clancy and Márkus, *Iona*, 96–128, provide full, scholarly text, translation and discussion. See also Chapter XV '*Amra Choluim Chille*', in P.L. Henry, *Saoithiúlacht na Sean-Ghaeilge* (Dublin 1976), 191–212, where there is a translation into modern Irish with scholarly introduction and notes. The excerpted version used here is my own, based on a combination of both of those works. See also the beautifully illustrated version *Amra Choluim Chille: Dallán's Elegy for Columba*, with texts in old Irish, modern Irish, English and Scottish Gaelic which was published by Colmcille: Èirinn's Alba in 2006.

[28] Pádraig Ó Riain, *A Dictionary of Irish Saints* (Dublin, 2011), 211–12.

Successors of Columba: Later Abbots of Iona

This we know for certain, that he [Columba] left successors distinguished for their purity, their love of God and their observance of monastic rule.

Bede,
Historia Ecclesiastica (731)

Baithín

When Columba died he was succeeded as abbot of Iona by his first cousin Baithín whom he himself had named as his successor. This was to set something of a pattern with many of the subsequent abbots coming also from Donegal, although the traditional assertion that they came from the saint's own kin-group – the Cenél Conaill – can no longer be accepted as proven.[1]

Baithín had been an *alumnus*, a pupil or foster-son of Columba, and, prior to his master's death, he had previously been superior of the daughter-house monastery of *Mag Luinge* on the island of Tiree. However, he had returned to Iona to be close to Columba as the founder's last days approached. There is also a late legend that Baithín succeeded Colum Cille in the abbacy of the monastery of Derry. But, as the latter was probably never abbot there himself, it is unlikely that Baithín ever held that position either. There is certainly no historical evidence for it and he died long before Fiachra, the 'alius fundator' of Derry.

Baithín did not survive Columba for very long. The records of the date of his death are confused. 600 is given in some sources but it is more probable that he died in 596. The Annals of Tigernach claims that he was sixty-six years of age at his death but this may have been confused with the age of another

[1] There are detailed discussions about the subsequent abbots of Iona in Andersons, *Columba*; Sharpe, *Adomnán*; and esp. Herbert, *Iona*. However, for the probable non-Cenél Conaill origins of some of these abbots see Lacey, *Cenél Conaill*, 98–9.

cousin, the king Áed mac Ainmirech, who died the same year. If the estimate is correct however, Baithín would have been about nine or ten years younger than Columba. Whether correctly or not, Baithín's feast day (what was believed to be the actual day that he died) was commemorated on the same date as that of Columba, 9 June. A Latin Life of Baithín has survived although, in the form in which we have it, it is much later in date and has been characterised as containing not much more than a series of conventional miracle stories. The name Taughboyne (*Tech Baithín*, 'Baithín's church' – now St Johnstown, County Donegal, seven miles southwest of Derry) is said to derive from a dedication to him. As we have seen above the legends associating Colum Cille with Saint Mo Bhí of Glasnevin may have derived from (or been confused with) stories about Baithín, the hypocoristic version of whose name was Mo Bhí also.

Laisrén

The third abbot of Iona was Laisrén son of Feradach. Almost certainly Laisrén belonged to the Cenél Duach dynasty. These were rulers of what was a petty kingdom in the northwest of Donegal, based around the Rosgill and Horn Head peninsulas.[2] The tradition asserted in the genealogies that Laisrén was actually more closely related to Columba is probably false. We know that Laisrén had previously spent some time in Scotland prior to his appointment as abbot, as he appears in one incident recorded by Adomnán when Columba was making a journey through the district of Ardnamurchan on the mainland. However, on another occasion we hear of Laisrén in a position of authority (probably as abbot or prior) at the monastery of Durrow in the midlands of Ireland. Columba, who was himself on Iona at the time, is said to have been aware miraculously that Laisrén was working the monks at Durrow too hard and was greatly relieved when he allowed them to rest. We know very little else about this man or about Iona and the other Columban churches during his period of office. Laisrén died in 603, probably on 16 September which was kept as his feast day.

Virgno

Laisrén was succeeded as abbot of Iona by Virgno also known by the Irish form of his name as Fergna. Virgno's genealogical background is not clear. Some later sources suggest that he belonged to the Cenél mBógaine, which was another small kingdom in southwest Donegal at the heart of which is *Gleann Cholm Cille*.[3] However, it is also possible that he was British. In some other sources he is described as Fergna Brit, and there is some other evidence

[2] Lacey, *Cenél Conaill*, 96–101.
[3] *Ibid.*, 76–84.

that might support the suggestion that he was not Irish. James Fraser suggests that he might have been a Pict.[4] Adomnán tells a hagiographical story about Virgno when he was a young monk on Iona. One winter's night while the other brothers slept, Virgno went to the church to pray. After he had been there for about an hour, Columba entered the church bathed in an angelic light. The following day the abbot forbade Virgno to tell anyone what he had seen the previous night until after he, Columba, had died. Much later when Virgno himself had become the abbot of Iona, he told the story of that night to his sister's son, the priest Commán, who later told it to Adomnán. It might be pointed out here that early Irish literature often treats 'sister's sons' as if they were somehow ritually special.

In 615, during Virgno's period in office, the annals describe 'the burning of Donnán of Eigg on the fifteenth of the Kalends of May [17 April] with one hundred and fifty martyrs'. Eigg is a small island to the north of Iona and the Ardnamurchan peninsula. We are not sure what connections there were between the churches on Eigg and Iona at the time of this catastrophe. Adomnán mentions that on at least one occasion before 593, Baithín 'was detained on the island of Eigg by contrary winds'. However, we do not know if he was carrying out some sort of business there or if he was simply sheltering from a storm. Neither is there any adequate explanation for the slaughter of Donnán and his 'martyrs' – probably his monks, although one hundred and fifty seems like a very large monastic community at that time. However, the story does indicate the sort of dangers that these 'pilgrim' monks could encounter. Donnán is said to have been Irish and a number of late sources, such as the Martyrology of Óengus under the 17 April, purport to give an account of his death.

> Tis this Donnán that went to Colum Cille to get him for a soulfriend, and Colum Cille said to him, 'I will only be a soulfriend,' quoth he, 'to folk of white martyrdom, i.e. I will not be (thy) soulfriend, for thou and the whole community with thee will go to red martyrdom.' And this was fulfilled.
>
> Then Donnán with his community goes into Galloway and takes up his abode where the queen of the country's sheep used to be. That is told to the queen. 'Let them all be killed', she says. 'That is not pious,' says every one. So men come to them to slay them. The cleric was then at mass. 'Grant us a respite till the mass ends,' says Donnán. 'It will be granted,' they say. The whole number is at once slain.[5]

There are a number of references in the annals to clerics on Eigg in the eighth century, implying the continuation of some kind of church presence there despite the attack in 615.

[4] *From Caledonia*, 110–11.

[5] W. Stokes, *Félire Óengusso Céli Dé: The Martyrology of Óengus the Culdee* (London 1905, reprinted Dublin 1984), 117.

In 619 the annals record the death of Fiachra son of Ciarán, son of Ainmire, son of Sétna. Fiachra belonged to the Cenél Conaill. He was a nephew of that dynasty's powerful king Áed mac Ainmirech and a distant cousin of Columba. In some of the sets of annals (specifically those associated with the monastery of Clonmacnoise rather than with any centre of annalistic compilation in the northern parts of Ireland) Fiachra is further identified as the 'other' founder of the monastery of Derry.[6] It is not clear if 'other' in this context is intended to mean 'alternative to' or 'in addition to' although the former seems more likely. The confusion results from what we might call subsequent interference with, or even censorship of, the historical record. In later times references to Fiachra must have constituted an embarrassment to those promoting what had become the official version of the story of the foundation of Derry by Colum Cille. There is no mention of Fiachra in the late legendary stories about that event which circulated from at least the middle of the tenth century. Despite the fact that, at the very least, he must have played some sort of significant role in the foundation of one of their most important monasteries, Fiachra is not listed either in the catalogue of often extremely obscure Cenél Conaill 'saints' preserved by the 'historians' of that dynasty.

Although they record his name and the year of his death, neither the Annals of Ulster nor the Annals of the Four Masters, both of which ultimately derive from Cenél Conaill sources, record the additional information about who Fiachra was or why he was important enough to have his death recorded. It is only by accident that those details were preserved in the various sets of annals compiled in the south of Ireland and in the midlands, away from the influence of the Derry and Cenél Conaill propagandists of later times. It is very difficult to resist the conclusion that those responsible for preserving the history of Derry, from at least the tenth century onwards, were extremely reluctant to give Fiachra the credit he was due, whatever his precise role. Fiachra is the forgotten hero of Derry's history. The historical evidence that exists for the identity of the founder of that monastery – as opposed to the legends – supports Fiachra's claim, not Columba's.

Two years after Fiachra's death the Annals of Tigernach records the construction of a church on Tory island. The monastery of Tory on the dramatic-looking island nine miles off the northwestern coast of Donegal was, at least in later times, closely associated with the confederation of Columban churches. However, the earliest evidence suggests that in the sixth and seventh centuries that area was part of the sphere of interest of the Cenél nÉogain who were opponents – even enemies – of Columba's people the Cenél

[6] For a full discussion of Fiachra and the foundation of Derry see Lacey, *Columba, founder of … Derry*, and Lacey *Cenél Conaill*, 128–31 and 200–2 respectively.

Conaill.[7] Although there is no evidence that the historical Columba (as distinct from the legendary Colum Cille) ever visited the island or indeed had any influence there, the folklore of Tory and the Cloghaneely area on the adjoining Donegal coastline are full of stories relating to the saint.[8] At least some of those seem to be Christianisations of stories originally told about the pagan god Lugh.

Colum Cille and his brother saints Beaglaoch, Dubhthach and Fionán are said to have been on *Cnoc na Naomh* (Hill of the Saints) above *Machaire Rabhartaig* (Magheraroarty) where the ferry now leaves for the island. They agreed that whichever of them could throw their crozier to Tory (nine miles away) that person would have the honour of converting its people to Christianity. Beaglaoch's crozier fell on the mainland at the spot where he subsequently founded the church at Tullaghabegly, Dubhthach's reached Inishdooey – one of three small islands between Tory and the mainland, while Fionán's split a rock on the mainland shore so that a waterfall thus named *Eas* ['waterfall'] *Fionáin* gushed out. Nearby he is said to have founded the church at Ray, nowadays remarkable for the magnificent twenty-foot high, plain ringed cross there. Although that cross is devoid of decoration which would help us to date it, it seems to show connections with some of its counterparts on Iona – such as St John' Cross – and other parts of western Scotland.[9] In the story, Colum Cille's crozier was the only one to reach Tory Island and to him, therefore, fell the task of converting its pagan inhabitants. That story seems to be a Christian reflex of the local legend of the god Lugh killing his evil grandfather Balor who lived on Tory, with a rod.

It is not clear if the 621 reference to Tory in the annals is to a new monastery on the island or merely to the reconstruction of an older one as the 'slaughter' of Tory – whatever that implies – was recorded for 615. A little over a century later in 733 the Annals of Ulster records that 'Dúngal son of Selbach profaned Tory when he forcibly removed Bruide from it'.[10] The use of the word 'profaned' seems to imply that it was an ecclesiastical centre there – a monastery? – that was the place in question.

Paradoxically, although this incident happened on an Irish island it came about largely as a result of internal Scottish affairs. Bruide was a son of the

---

[7] For the foundation of the monastery on Tory, see Lacey, *Cenél Conaill*, 89–91, also Lacey, *Lug's forgotten Donegal kingdom: the archaeology, history and folklore of the Síl Lugdach of Cloghaneely* (Dublin 2012), 118–21.

[8] See for example C. Ó Searcaigh, *Tulach Beaglaoch inné agus inniu* (An Fál Carrach – no date), Cumann Staire is Seanchais Chloich Cheann Fhaola.

[9] Fisher, *Early Medieval Sculpture*, 15 and 22; Lacey, *Cenél Conaill*, 99–100; and Lacey, *Lug*, caption to pl. 5.

[10] There is a full discussion of the local implications of this incident in B. Lacey, 'Fahan, Tory, Cenél nÉogain and the Picts', *Peritia* 20 (2008), 331–45; Lacey, *Cenél Conaill*, 284–5, and Lacey *Lug*, 120–1.

powerful Óengus (Onuist) who was the king of the Picts between about 729 and 761. The reason for Bruide's presence on a remote Donegal island is not at all clear but he may have been given refuge there because of internal problems in Scotland or, alternatively, he may have been a hostage-guarantee for a possible alliance between his father and the Cenél nÉogain who probably had overall control in that area at the time.

Dúngal son of Selbach belonged to the Cenél Loairn of the Scottish Dál Riata and had been king of those people between about 723 and 726. During his career he was subjected both to internal opposition from within his own people and also external attack from the Picts. In Donegal that year – as they frequently were – the Cenél nEógain were at war with their traditional rivals the Cenél Conaill. We know that the latter were allied with the Dál Riata, possibly in accordance with a treaty made as far back as the Convention of *Druim Cett.* Although we have no specific evidence for it, it seems that the Cenél nÉogain must have had some sort of parallel alliance with the Picts. That would be a sufficient explanation for a Pictish prince being forcibly removed from an Irish island which was almost certainly under Cenél nÉogain control at the time.[11]

Ségéne

Virgno died as abbot of Iona in 624; his feast day was 2 March. He was succeeded by abbot Ségéne of whom a lot more is known. Ségéne almost certainly belonged to the Cenél Duach of northwest Donegal also; in fact he was a son of a brother of Laisrén, the third abbot. Under Ségéne's guidance the network of Columban monasteries continued to expand. The annals say that he himself was responsible for the founding of the church on *Rechru* in 635. *Rechru* was the name of at least two islands off the coast of Ireland: Rathlin off County Antrim and Lambay off north County Dublin. A third possibility – now known as Rathlin O'Birne, lies off the southwest coast of County Donegal close to *Gleann Cholm Cille.* Based on later traditions it is likely but not certain that Lambay was the place referred to.[12] A recent geophysical survey by Prof. Gabriel Cooney has identified evidence of a possible enclosure there that might have been the site of the monastery in question. The location of that site, on the lower slope facing the mainland, is broadly comparable to the location of other 'Columban' island monasteries such as Iona, Tory and, to a lesser extent, Derry.

[11] See Fraser, *From Caledonia*, 295–7, for a more complex interpretation of these events.

[12] E. Bhreatnach, 'Columban Churches in Brega and Leinster', *Journal of the Royal Society of Antiquaries of Ireland*, 129 (1999), 5–18, pp 7 and 16, note 28; M. Byrnes, 'The Árd Ciannachta in Adomnán's "Vitae Columbae"' in Smyth, *Seanchas*, 127–36, pp 132–3.

Perhaps more importantly, during Ségéne's abbacy the influence of Iona began to be consolidated and extended in the north of England. Christianity had, of course, been introduced to what we now call England during the Roman period. Saint Patrick was a product of that church. However, with the departure of the Romans and the arrival of the Anglo–Saxons and the other pagan Germanic peoples, Christianity had retreated for the most part to the 'British' areas of the country.

In 597 Pope Gregory I – Gregory the Great – had dispatched a mission to England led by the man who would become known as Saint Augustine of Canterbury. Although Augustine was a monk, as indeed was Pope Gregory himself, there were still various differences of practices between this 'Roman' church and the 'Celtic' monastic traditions emanating from Ireland. Although those differences have often been exaggerated, some of them, such as the manner in which the monks of the distinct traditions were tonsured – that is had their heads ritually shaved in order to show their homage and submission to God – were of relatively superficial concern. However, none of the differences was so controversial or important as the conflict over the methods for calculating the moveable feast of Easter. Unlike most Christian festivals the dates of which are based on the annually recurring solar calendar, the date of Easter and its related commemorative events are based on the more variable lunar cycle.[13] Broadly speaking the Irish retained an older method of calculating the date of the festival when much of the rest of Christendom had adopted a newer form of calculation. Pope Honorius (who had been elected in 625) had written to the Irish (including the Scottish) church on this matter warning them as Bede tells us, 'not to imagine that their little community, isolated at the uttermost ends of the earth, had a wisdom exceeding that of all the churches, ancient and modern, throughout the world'.

A synod of the Irish church at which this matter was discussed had been held about the year 630, at *Mag Léne* near the Columban monastery of Durrow in the midlands. The outcome of that debate was that some of the leading churches in the southern half of Ireland accepted the 'universal' or 'Roman' view. The churches of the northern half, perhaps taking their lead from Iona, refused to change. An Irish delegation to examine this complicated matter was sent to Rome in 631. They were there at Easter-time when their own calculations differed from the local practice by a whole month. A bitter letter on the subject from a certain Cummian, which was written in 631–2 after this debacle, survives. One of those to whom it was addressed was Ségéne, abbot of Iona. Precisely who this Cummian was is not certain. Some have suggested that he was the abbot of Durrow although the most recent

[13] See for example, Ó Carragáin, 'The Architectural Setting', 171, note 111 and more detailed reference there.

editors of the letter tend to think that he should be identified with Cummíne Fota of the non-Columban monastery at Clonfert in County Galway.[14]

Cummian wrote his letter to try to encourage Ségéne to adopt the Roman practice on Easter. He was concerned that documents had been issued 'excommunicating, expelling from the church and anathematising those who go against the canonical statutes of the four apostolic sees – Rome, Jerusalem, Antioch and Alexandria – when these agree on the unity of Easter'. He sends a warning specifically to the monastery of Iona on account of the influence it enjoys over others: 'for you are the heads and the eyes of the people, and if they are led into error because of your obstinacy you shall answer according to Ezechiel, for the blood of each soul to the strict judge'.

However, Ségéne was not persuaded by these arguments or warnings. He appears to have been one of the churchmen who wrote to Pope Severinus about this matter and received a reply in 640 – actually from the new pope-elect, John IV, following the former's death. Bede has preserved large portions of the reply if not its entirety. It is addressed to eleven named clerics including Ségéne 'and the other Irish teachers and abbots'. As well as dealing with the Easter question, the Pope, inaccurately, accused the Irish of reviving the long-since dead Pelagian heresy. He begs those to whom he addressed his letter: 'not to rake up the ashes of controversies long since burned out'. However, notwithstanding the intervention of the papacy, the churches in the northern half of Ireland – especially those influenced from Iona – controversially maintained their longstanding method of calculating the date of Easter for at least another fifty years.

As well as Ségéne, Cummian's letter was also addressed to Beccán 'the hermit'. This was almost certainly the Beccán associated with the Scottish island of Rum whose death is recorded in the annals in 677 and who may have been born sometime around 600. His feast day was the same as Saint Patrick's, 17 March. If the two Beccáns were the same, then Beccán of Rum must have been allied with the 'conservative' side on the question of the dating of Easter and, although he was a hermit, he must also have been an important associate if not actually a member of the Iona or Columban community. Adomnán mentions certain songs of praise to Columba in the Irish tongue which by definition must have been composed before the end of the seventh century. He may have been alluding to two praise poems in Irish in honour of Colum Cille that are attributed to Beccán mac Luigdech of the Cenél nÉogain. Beccán of Rum can almost certainly be identified as that person and, therefore, as the author of the poems.[15] These relatively long poems –

[14] M. Walsh and D. Ó Cróinín (eds), *Cummian's Letter De controversia paschali, together with a related Irish computistical tract De ratione conputandi* (Toronto 1988). See also Review by T.M. Charles-Edwards, *Peritia,* Vol. 8 (1994), 216–20.

[15] Scholarly text, translation and full discussion in Clancy and Márkus, *Iona,* 129–63, from which the quotations used here have been taken.

(i) *Fo réir Choluimb* ('Bound to Colum') and (ii) *To-fed andes* ('He brings northward') – have some of the same themes as in the *Amrae Coluimb Chille* but go further in developing the idea of Colum Cille as a protecting saint:

> Colum Cille, while I live,
> will be my chant, till the grave's tryst;
> in every risk I'll call him,
> when I'll praise him with my full strength.
>
> (from *For réir Choluimb*)

> Leafy oak-tree, soul's protection, rock of safety, the sun of monks, mighty ruler, Colum Cille.
>
> (from *To-fed andes*)

Notwithstanding the difficulties over the Easter controversy, according to Bede when Oswald became king of Northumbria in 634 he invited the monks of Iona 'to send a bishop to teach the Faith of Christ to himself and his people'. Adomnán says of this:

> for up to that time all the land of the English was shadowed by the darkness of heathenism and ignorance, excepting the king Oswald himself, and twelve men who had been baptised with him, while he was in exile among the Irish.

Oswald's father, who had been a previous king of Northumbria, was defeated and died in battle in 616. His sons fled to take refuge among the Scottish Dál Riata and Oswald spent some time on Iona where he was baptised a Christian. Oswald defeated Cadwallon 'the most powerful king of the Britons' in a battle near Hexham in 634. According to the legend which seems to be modelled to some degree on the story of the Roman emperor Constantine, Oswald attributed his victory to a vision of Saint Columba that he had seen on the night before the battle; but he also had the more practical assistance of the fighting men of Dál Riata. He is said to have used a Christian cross as his standard for the battle. His subsequent victory in the battle brought him to power in Northumbria. He may also have gained the allegiance, in a more indirect way, of all the various kingdoms of Scotland. Indeed, Adomnán grandiosely and somewhat exaggeratedly claims that 'afterwards he was ordained by God as emperor of the whole of Britain'. On a subsequent occasion, probably while on another visit to Iona, the king gave an account to the abbot Ségéne of the vision of Columba that he had seen before the decisive battle. This account was given in the presence of the monk Failbe who himself would become abbot of Iona in 669. Failbe, who would be succeeded in 679 by Adomnán, told the story to the latter and thus it was included in the *Vita Columbae.*

Bede gives an account of what happened (or what he wanted his readers to believe happened) when a missionary from Iona was sent to Northumbria in response to Oswald's request. At first a man of 'austere disposition' was sent but he had no success there and returned to Iona. He informed his superiors that he had been unable to achieve anything with the Northumbrians 'because they were an ungovernable people of an obstinate and barbarous temperament'. A conference on the matter was organised because, while it was regretted that this first mission to the English had been unsuccessful, the Columban monks still wished to meet the Northumbrian 'desire for salvation'. One of those present, Aidan, spoke up and remonstrated with his unsuccessful colleague about the latter's harsh methods. Aidan said that the example of the apostles should have been followed and a more simple and gentle approach to the pagans should have been adopted initially, before leading them to 'the loftier precepts of Christ'. At this, all eyes in the conference turned towards Aidan and everyone began to pay close attention to what he had to say. All those listening agreed that here was the ideal person for the task, so Aidan was consecrated a bishop and sent to King Oswald.

Oswald granted Lindisfarne – close to his own fortress at Bamburgh on the mainland, to Aidan when he arrived in 635. Lindisfarne is attached to the mainland but cut off twice each day by the rising tide. Bede was fulsome in his praise of Aidan although he pointed out that Aidan was not a fluent English speaker, and remarked on how delightful it was to see the king, who himself had a perfect command of the Irish language, translate for the new bishop.

> From then on, day by day, many Irish arrived in Britain and preached the word of God with sincerity throughout all the territories under Oswald's rule, while those of them that were priests baptised those who were converted. Churches were built in many places and the people joyfully gathered to hear God's word, while the king generously gave lands and endowments for the foundation of monasteries, and the English nobles and commoners were instructed by their Irish teachers in the monastic way of life.

Although retaining his criticism of Aidan's method for the calculation of the date of Easter in accordance with the custom of Iona, Bede nevertheless extolled the bishop's humility, friendliness and charity, his disinterest in worldly wealth and his devotion to the Scriptures. Bede also tells us that, for solitude, Aidan withdrew to a tiny hermitage on the nearby Farne Islands that would later become famous as the home of Saint Cuthbert.

Fragments of a decorated, early seventh-century copy of the Gospels or New Testament, known by its catalogue reference as A.II.10, survives in the library of Durham Cathedral. Some scholars have suggested that this manuscript could have been made on Iona and brought by Aidan with him to Northumbria when he went there in 635, or else that it was made in the monastery of Lindisfarne shortly after its establishment.[16]

[16] Sharpe, *Adomnán*, 34; N. Edwards, *The Archaeology of Early Medieval Ireland* (London 1990), 150.

Aidan is said to have introduced the Northumbrians to the Irish practice of fasting on Wednesdays (*Céadaoine*, literally 'first fastday'), and Fridays (*Aoine*, literally 'fastday'), and when invited to dine with the king he himself would eat 'sparingly'. On one such occasion at the feast of Easter, when the king and the bishop were just about to eat from 'a silver dish of rich food', a servant came in to report that a crowd of needy people were sitting on the road outside begging alms of the king. The king immediately ordered the food that he was about to eat to be distributed and the silver dish to be broken up and distributed likewise. Aidan, who was sitting beside Oswald, is said to have been moved deeply and, taking the king's right hand, he said, 'May this hand never wither with age.' Bede goes on to tell us that this prayer was heard and that even when the king was subsequently killed in battle, his arm remained uncorrupted. The arm was preserved as a relic in a silver casket at the church of Saint Peter in Bamburgh at the time that Bede was writing in 731.

Aidan died on 31 August 651. He was staying at one of the king's rural lodges as was his practice when he moved around the English countryside preaching and converting the people. His remains were taken across to his island monastery and buried in the monks' cemetery there. When a larger church dedicated to Saint Peter was erected at Lindisfarne much later, Aidan's bones were translated to the new building and put in an honourable place at the right-hand side of the main altar. That church had been built in 'the Irish manner' (not of stone but of hewn oak, thatched with reeds) by Aidan's successor, bishop Finán who had also been sent from Iona. However, a later bishop of English origin removed the thatch and covered the roof and the walls with sheets of lead.

Many miracles were believed to have occurred through the intercession of Bishop Aidan. The Life of Saint Cuthbert, written by an anonymous monk from Lindisfarne about 699, tells us about a vision which that important English saint had as a young man, on the night of the death of Aidan.

> Cuthbert, along with other shepherds, was tending his master's sheep in the hills above the River Leader. As usual, he was spending the night in vigil praying without cease, with great devotion and single-minded faith ... The heavens opened and he saw angels descending and ascending ... with the soul of a saint carried towards heaven in their hands ... a few days later he heard that news of the death of our holy bishop Aidan had been announced at the same time of the night that he had seen the vision.

Bede in his separate Life of Cuthbert – written about twenty years later, claims that that vision was instrumental in Cuthbert's decision to enter monastic life. He chose the community of Melrose – now in the Scottish Borders which had been founded around 640 by the monks of Lindisfarne; it was one of several such monasteries which had been established throughout Northumbria and which were strongly influenced by the Irish form of monasticism.

On a number of occasions Adomnán speaks about descriptions of incidents in the life of Columba or testimony about his spiritual influence, being given in the presence of the abbot Ségéne. This has led some authors to conclude that Ségéne must have made a systematic attempt to compile biographical material about the saint by collecting the memories of those older monks who had lived directly under Columba's own abbacy.[17] As we have seen, Ségéne was associated with Beccán, the hermit who was probably the author of the two mid-seventh-century poems about Colum Cille quoted above. In our oldest manuscript of Adomnán's Life, the scribe Dorbéne has inserted a quotation from another biographical work about the saint which otherwise does not survive. This was the *liber de virtutibus sancti Columbae*, 'book on the miraculous powers of Saint Columba', the author of which was the monk Cummeneus albus (in Irish, Comméne Find).

The quotation from Cumméne's book used by Dorbéne refers to the battle of *Mag Roth* which took place in the year 639, and goes on to talk about 'from that day to this'. The *liber de virtutibus sancti Columbae* was written therefore after 639, but how much later is not clear. Some authors have suggested that the work was written subsequent to its author becoming abbot of Iona in 656, but Máire Herbert has argued that it is more likely that it was composed while Cumméne was a younger monk under the direction of his uncle Ségéne who was probably abbot at the time.

Suibne moccu Urthri and Cumméne Find

Ségéne died in 652, probably on 12 August – his feast day – and was succeeded as abbot by Suibne moccu Urthri. Suibne does not appear to have come from Donegal and very little is known about him. He died in 656, probably on 11 January – his feast day, and was followed as abbot by Cumméne Find who was following in a distinguished family tradition. He too seems to have belonged to the Cenél Duach of northwest Donegal, and both his uncle Ségéne and his great-uncle Laisrén had been abbots of Iona before him. From around the time of Cumméne's accession to the abbacy, perhaps reflecting his own literary and historical interests, we begin to have much greater detail recorded in the so-called 'Iona Chronicle' – the missing document that underlies all the early entries in the later sets of Irish annals. Cumméne made a visit to Ireland in 660 and seems to have spent a considerable length of time there, perhaps making a formal visitation of the monasteries of the Columban confederation.

It was during his abbacy that the Columban community experienced one of its greatest setbacks since the time of its foundation. This resulted when

[17] Herbert, *Iona*, 24–5.

the still-simmering controversy about the calculation of the date of Easter came to a head. The Columban mission to Northumbria had been a tremendous success. So successful was the work of Bishop Aidan and his colleagues that one Scottish author has written:

> from the mid-seventh century onwards Northumbrian Christianity became profoundly imbued with the best aspirations of Irish monasticism. From the Tweed to the Solway, hermits with English names but authentically Irish spirituality brought a general shift in the values of society and gave to northern England its 'Age of the Saints'.[18]

When Oswald died in 642 he was succeeded as king of Northumbria by his brother Oswiu. Oswiu had a number of Irish connections too. He had spent some time as a refugee in Ireland. At least some of that time was probably spent in Donegal because he is said to have had a son, Aldfrith, with Fín the daughter of the Cenél nÉogain king Colmán Rímid, who died in 602.[19] Aldfrith, who also spoke and perhaps wrote in the Irish language, was known in Irish tradition as Fland Fína. In turn he would become king of Northumbria and also, as we will see, a friend of Adomnán.

Oswiu's daughter and Aldfrith's half-sister, Alchfled, married Peada the son of the king of the Middle Angles following the latter's conversion to Christianity. Peada was baptised by Finán, Aidan's successor at Lindisfarne. The facts are not crystal clear but Finán may have been a son of Colmán Rímid[20] and, if so, would have been, therefore, a brother of Fín, a sort of brother-in-law of Oswiu and an uncle of Aldfrith.

After Finán had baptised him, Peada brought back with him to his own kingdom four priests of whom one was the Irishman Diuma. Diuma was later consecrated Bishop of the Middle Saxons and Mercians by Finán. When Diuma died, he was succeeded by another Irishman, Ceollach. Soon afterwards, Ceollach retired back to Iona and was replaced by an English bishop who, nevertheless, had been consecrated, as Bede tells us, by the 'Irish'. These Irish almost certainly had Lindisfarne or Iona connections. Thus the influence of the Columban church continued to be spread throughout the northern and midland parts of England. James Fraser points out that Bede recorded that Oswiu gave the Iona *familia* a lot of land in Northumbria for the establishment of monasteries: six estates in Deira and another six in Bernicia.[21]

[18] George Henderson, *From Durrow to Kells: The Insular Gospel-books – 650–800* (London 1987), 13.
[19] Fraser, *From Caledonia*, 217, thinks the relationship unlikely.
[20] Lacey, *Cenél Conaill*, 208–10.
[21] *From Caledonia*, 187.

Éogan *from whom descended the Cenél nÉogan*

I

Muiredach

I

Muircertach (532)

I

Báetán (571)

I

Colmán Rímid (602)

I

?Máel Mbracho (622) ?Finán (659) Fín=====Oswiu (670), *king of Northumbria*

I

Aldfrith (703), *king of Northumbria*

Table 3: Alleged relationships between some Northumbrian kings and the Cenél nÉogain

Bede tells us that Oswiu had nothing but praise for the Irish, having been taught and baptised by Irish men and 'having a complete grasp of their language'. We are also told that while Aidan was still alive the differences about the date of Easter had been patiently tolerated by everyone out of respect for the undoubted piety of their bishop. However, Oswiu married a Kentish princess, Eanfled, who followed the 'Roman' practice. Bede says the confusion was so great that 'Easter was sometimes kept twice in the one year, so that when the king had ended Lent and was keeping Easter, the queen and her attendants were still fasting and keeping Palm Sunday.' This was of more than theological and theoretical importance at a time when, for example, sexual relations between husband and wife were restricted during Lent.[22]

Another son of King Oswiu, Alchfrid, had been educated by Wilfrid who had been trained in the 'Roman' practice for calculating the date of Easter. Alchfrid had attempted, without success, to wean the Irish monks away from what he saw as their eccentric practices by offering them land for a monastery at Ripon. In 664 it was decided to hold a synod to resolve once and for all –

[22] Clancy and Márkus, *Iona*, 14.

at least in Northumbria – the Easter controversy. Bede gives us a detailed description of what happened. The synod was held at Whitby, at a monastery presided over by the abbess Hilda who, together with her community, supported the 'Iona' side in the debate. King Oswiu and Alchfrid were there as of course was bishop Colmán, together with his clergy from Lindisfarne. Colmán was the successor of bishop Finán. A number of English clerics who favoured the 'Roman' practice were present but so also was a venerable bishop Cedd, bishop of the east Saxons, who although an Englishman had been ordained by the Irish and favoured the system used by the Irish. In fact, Bishop Cedd is said to have acted as the interpreter between the Irish and the English at the synod.

King Oswiu opened the proceedings, stressing the importance of the unity of the church. He stated that the task of the synod was to establish which tradition was 'truer'. He called on Colmán, his own bishop, to explain the origin of the customs that he practised. Colmán spoke and defended the practices that he and his predecessors in Iona had observed for over a century. He claimed that they derived their authority from Saint John, the evangelist and 'beloved' apostle. Then Wilfrid spoke. He explained that the custom he practised was the one observed in Rome, throughout Italy, Gaul, Africa, Asia, Egypt and Greece. He argued that this was, in fact, the practice of the universal church and that:

> the only people who contend against the whole world are these Irish and their partners in obstinacy, the Picts and the Britons, who inhabit only a portion of these, the two uttermost islands of the ocean.

Technical arguments about the precise method for the dating of Easter followed and finally Wilfrid summed up, addressing Colmán directly:

> For although your Fathers were pious men, can you imagine that they, a few men in a corner of a remote island, are preferable to the universal church of Christ throughout the world. And even if your Columba – or, if I may say so, ours also – if he was the servant of Christ, if he was a saint who could perform miracles, can he take precedence over the most blessed Prince of the Apostles, to whom our Lord said: 'Thou art Peter, and upon this rock I will build my church, and the gates of hell shall not prevail against it, and I will give to thee the keys of the kingdom of heaven.'

When Wilfrid had finished speaking the king asked Colmán if it was true that the Lord had said these words to Peter. When Colmán replied that it was, the king asked again if similar authority had been given to Columba. Colmán merely said 'no'! With this the king indicated that he would not contradict Saint Peter who held the keys to the gates of heaven, lest when he himself should turn up there 'he who holds the keys has turned away'.

Ironically nearly a thousand years later, but perhaps somewhat tongue-in-cheek, Manus O'Donnell would 'get his own back' on the issue of the superiority of Saint Peter over Colum Cille.

> Colum Cille was similar to Peter in terms of the enormous love he had for his own Lord, that is, Jesus Christ. Further we could say that he exceeded Peter ... in his love for the Lord for this reason; because Peter denied Christ three times at the time of the passion. But Colum Cille did not deny him from the time he began to serve Him until he died, but he bore every discomfort, trouble and sorrow that he got for His sake.[23]

The matter was settled at Whitby. Having had his views rejected, Colmán, together with his followers who included 'all the Irish whom he had gathered together on the island of Lindisfarne and also about thirty men of English race', returned to their mother-house on Iona. An Englishman called Tuda took Colmán's place as bishop at Lindisfarne. Ironically Tuda had been trained and consecrated a bishop in the south of Ireland where the 'Roman' practices had already been adopted. Colmán took away with him from Lindisfarne, as relics, some of the founder bishop Aidan's bones. Some of Colmán's monks remained at the island monastery under Eata who had formerly been abbot of the daughter-house at Melrose and who was now appointed abbot of Lindisfarne. Many years previously, Eata had been one of the twelve original English boys to whom Aidan had taught the Christian faith when he had first become a bishop at Lindisfarne. Bede, who obviously rejoiced in the triumph of the 'Roman' customs, nevertheless speaks well of the charity and piety of the Irish monks. He says that so simple was their existence that when they left the island 'there were very few buildings except the church; indeed, no more than met the bare requirements of a seemly way of life'.

After spending some time on Iona Colmán and his followers crossed over to Ireland, The Annals of Ulster records for the year 668: 'the voyage of bishop Colmán, with the relics of the saints to Inis Bó Finne [off the coast of County Mayo], where he founded a church.' He is also credited with founding a monastery later at the village of Mayo, on the mainland, for the English monks who had followed him from Lindisfarne. There were many English monks there in the time that Bede was writing around 731 and the annals for 732 record the death of Gerald, 'the pontiff [bishop?] of *Mag Eó na Saxan* ['Mayo of the English']'.[24] Colmán's death as 'bishop of Inis Bó Finne' occurred in 676, and his feast day according to the Martyrology of Óengus was 8 August.

[23] Lacey, *Manus O'Donnell*, 219.

[24] For a full discussion of the history of this monastery see V. Orschel, 'Mag nEó na Sacsan: an English colony in Ireland', *Peritia*, Vol. 15 (2001), 81–107.

A group of important manuscripts, which are thought to have originated in Lindisfarne somewhat later than Colmán's withdrawal but showing undoubted contacts with the Columban world, still survives.[25] The Durham Gospels is a manuscript measuring about 13½ inches by 10½ inches. It now consists of 108 folios but many of its pages are missing. It was damaged considerably at some point in its history. It is close in style to the Book of Durrow and the so-called Echternach Gospels now preserved in Paris. The latter manuscript is about 13 inches by 10 inches, comprising 223 folios. It is often claimed that the Echternach Gospels had connections with Lindisfarne but a recent study points out the strong connections between the monastery at Echternach (now in Luxembourg) with the monastery of *Rath Melsigi*, identified as Clonmelsh, County Carlow.[26] The Lindisfarne Gospels, now in the British Library, containing 258 folios each page about 13½ by 9½ inches, is one of the greatest masterpieces of medieval insular art. Between the original lines of the Latin Vulgate text, which are written in majuscule script, there is a translation into Old English that was added-in around the end of the tenth century. A note written in the same hand as the translation tells us that 'Eadfrith Bishop of the church of Lindisfarne, originally wrote this book for God and for Saint Cuthbert and jointly for all the saints whose relics are in the island.' This was probably between 687 and 721 or, as George Henderson has argued, no later than 698 when Eadfrith became bishop.

Like the Durham Gospels, the Lindisfarne Gospels was preserved in Durham Cathedral during the later Middle Ages. In 875, fearing Viking attacks, the monks of Lindisfarne moved to Chester-le-Street on the English mainland. From there they moved to Durham before the end of the tenth century, bringing with them their surviving Columban traditions. Durham claimed to have bones and relics of 'Columkelle' as late as the fourteenth century. Other texts associated with Colum Cille were also preserved in Durham, such as the exemplar and the so-called B manuscripts of Adomnán's Life of the saint, as well as the lists of his relatives and the monks who accompanied him to Iona. However, Raghnall Ó Floinn has argued that as the cathedral also had relics of other Irish saints, including Patrick and Brigid, it does not seem that there was a particular devotion to Colum Cille in Durham.[27] Whether that is true or not, it has to be said that Durham must figure very highly in the list of places where evidence for the medieval

[25] There is a vast and argumentative literature on this subject. See Henderson, *Durrow*, and, for an 'Irish' perspective, Bernard Meehan, *The Book of Durrow* (Dublin 1996).

[26] For an examination of the relevance as well as all the evidence surrounding this issue see D. Ó Cróinín, 'Rath Melsigi, Willibrord, and the earliest Echternach manuscripts', *Peritia*, Vol. 3 (1984), 17–49.

[27] Ó Floinn, 'Insignia Columbae', 144.

traditions about Saint Columba were preserved down to our own time. Some of those materials were unique to Durham and without them there are some things about the saint that we simply would not know.

Cumméne Find had been abbot of Iona throughout the course of the Easter controversy in Northumbria. We are not sure how the 'Irish' churches in England related to the mother foundation on Iona; certainly Cumméne himself does not seem to have become involved directly in the Easter dispute. However, one of the principal results of the Synod of Whitby was the loss of the monastery of Lindisfarne to the Columban confederation as well as the considerable reduction of the influence and status of Iona in the north of England.

In the year that the Synod met or possibly the year after, the annals, which were being compiled at Iona at the time, recorded a series of strange natural phenomena. There was an eclipse of the sun about five o'clock in the afternoon of 1 May, 'and in the same summer the sky seemed to be on fire. The plague reached Ireland on the Kalends [1] of August'. That plague had devastating results throughout the country continuing for about four years. But it does not seem to have affected Iona or the major part of Scotland to any significant extent, otherwise its effects would presumably have been recorded in detail in the 'Iona Chronicle'.[28]

Failbe

Cumméne died on 24 February 669 and was succeeded by Failbe who was a distant cousin. As a young monk Failbe had been present on Iona when King Oswald had come to visit the monastery there. During his abbacy he seems to have spent about three years (between 673 and 676) in Ireland. Although it is not explicitly recorded, he undoubtedly spent this time making a visitation of the Irish Columban churches as seems to have become a general practice for the abbots of Iona. Those visitations would have helped to bind the Columban confederation together. In the year that Failbe went to Ireland the annalists recorded a fire at *Mag Luinge*. This must surely be the monastery of that name on the island of Tiree frequently referred to by Adomnán. Three years after returning from his long sojourn in Ireland, on 22 March 679, Failbe died.

[28] See also the quotation on this matter from Adomnán's *Vita Columbae* on page 119 below.

Adomnán and the Vita Columbae

The ray of light, the flame, the precious stone, and brilliant lamp ... that is Saint Adomnán, that is the noble and holy priest, Adomnán.

Betha Adomnáin (mid-10th century)

Shortly after the death of Failbe, Adomnán, who would later write the *Vita Columbae*, became the ninth abbot of Iona. Some authors have suggested that during the 673 to 676 period that his predecessor Failbe had spent in Ireland, Adomnán, who was possibly still living there at the time, was identified as a suitable candidate for the abbacy of the chief monastery of the Columban monks. The holder of that position was also, *ex officio*, the head of the whole Columban *familia* or confederation of churches throughout Ireland and Scotland. A Life of Adomnán in the Irish language – *Betha Adamnáin* – was written in the middle of the tenth century but gives us virtually no real biographical information about its subject. As we will see below, the work has been shown to be more useful as a reflection of the times in which it was written.[1]

Adomnán himself gave us the Latin form of his name as Adomnanus. The name was often understood later in the medieval period to have been Adamnán (that is, with the second vowel written as an 'a') and treated as if it was a gaelicised diminutive of the biblical name Adam, meaning something like 'little' or 'dearest' Adam. At least two other relevant Adamnáns in that form are known from roughly the same period. Adamnán of the church of *Ráith Maige Enaig* (or *Oenaig*) in east Donegal will be discussed further below but Bede also tells us about an ascetic Irish monk of that name who belonged to the monastery of Coldingham in what is now Berwick in northeastern England. However, it is clear that the name Adomnán (with an 'o') actually derives from an entirely different Irish language root word and seems to mean something like 'man of great dread'.[2]

[1] M. Herbert and P. Ó Riain (eds.), *Betha Adamnáin: The Irish Life of Adamnán* (London 1988).

[2] Andersons, *Columba*, 92–3. It has been suggested, however, that the name 'can be understood to mean "little Adam" and equated with the Latin word *homunculus*' – Márkus, *Adiutor Laborantium*, esp. 157–60.

The Annals of Ulster has an entry for Adomnán's birth at the year 625 but when he died in 704 (a much more reliable entry) it says that he was seventy-seven years of age. His feast day (the day he was believed to have died) was 23 September. That would mean that his birth, as Richard Sharpe has pointed out, almost certainly took place sometime between 24 September 627 and 23 September 628.[3] His father was said to have been Ronán son of Tinne of the Cenél Conaill – the same people to which Columba belonged; his mother, Ronnat, was believed to have belonged to the Cenél nÉnnai. Those people inhabited the good lands of east Donegal north of the ruling Cenél Conaill kingdom. The territory of the Cenél nÉnnai probably extended originally from the area around Raphoe northwards as far as Derry. In fact Derry was probably a Cenél nÉnnai secular site (a royal caput?) when their whole kingdom was conquered by the Cenél Conaill around the last quarter of the sixth century.[4]

Some authors have suggested that Adomnán's family may have been settled in south Donegal in *Tír Áeda* (Tirhugh), but for a variety of reasons this now seems unlikely.[5] He is also often associated with the monastery of Raphoe in the territory of his mother's people, but it now seems that that monastery may not have been founded for around a century or so after Adomnán's death. Paradoxically, an Adamnán (with an 'a') died as bishop of the monastery of *Ráith Maige Enaig* – close to Raphoe – in 731. As we have seen above, a story in the twelfth-century Irish Life of Colum Cille tells how when he was a small boy that saint went with his foster father the priest Cruithnechán and took part in the Christmas ceremonies at *Ráith Maige Enaig*.

It seems very probable now that some of the traditions about Adamnán of *Ráith Maige Enaig* have become confused (either accidentally or more likely deliberately) with those associated with the earlier Adomnán of Iona. Despite these reservations it may well be that the latter Adomnán was born and grew up close to Raphoe, near the border between the homelands of his mother's people and his father's people. There is a hint in some of the early legendary material for County Donegal that it was customary for aristocratic children to be born in their mother's territory as distinct from the lands of their father's people.

Adomnán of Iona also seems to have definitely spent some time when a young man, a *juvenis*, close to or even at the monastery of Drumhome in south Donegal. He was certainly familiar with that monastery. It has also been speculated that he spent some time at the monastery of Durrow. However, in reality we know virtually nothing about his life until he took over the

[3] Sharpe, *Adomnán*, 44.

[4] For an outline of the early history of the Cenél nÉnnai, see Lacey, *Cenél Conaill*, 120–31.

[5] *Ibid.*, 242–6, and B. Lacey,' Adomnán and Donegal', in J.M. Wooding (ed.) *Adomnán of Iona: Theologian, Lawmaker, Peacemaker* (Dublin 2010), 20–35.

leadership of the Columban church in 679 when he was already over fifty years of age and a very 'senior citizen' in the context of the time. Obviously his adult life had been spent in a monastery (or monasteries) somewhere in an Irish context but we have no real evidence as to where that might have been. There is no evidence that he was ever even on Iona until the period of Failbe's abbacy when he would have been already well over forty years of age. However, wherever he pursued his youthful preparations for his later clerical life, the Life of Columba that he wrote shows that he must have studied a wide range of Latin texts as well as the Scriptures and the usual liturgical works.[6]

The first time we read about Adomnán in the annals after his appointment to the abbacy of Iona is in 687. In that year he returned to Ireland bringing with him the sixty captives who had been held prisoner by Ecgfrith, king of Northumbria, since they had been captured in a raid on *Brega* (roughly equivalent with County Meath) in 685. Ecgfrith died shortly after this raid and was succeeded by his half-brother Aldfrith, whose relationship with the Irish as we have seen above was very different.

Aldfrith was the son of the former king Oswiu who, sometime during the years 616 to 633, is said to have met Fína the daughter of the Cenél nÉogain king Colmán Rímid. Aldfrith was said to be their son but he was considered illegitimate according to English law. Aldfrith also had (or was later given) an Irish name, Fland Fína, and he knew the Irish language in which he was believed to have composed poetry.[7] The nineteenth-century Irish writer James Clarence Mangan made a metrical version of the following poem about Ireland, alleged to be by Aldfrith, from the unrhymed translation of John O'Donovan.

> I travelled its fruitful provinces round,
> And in every one of the five I found,
> Alike in church and in palace hall,
> Abundant apparel, and food for all.
>
> I found strict morals in age and youth,
> I found historians recording truth;
> The things I sing of in verse unsmooth,
> I found them all – I have written sooth.
> ...

Although a Northumbrian prince, Aldfrith had probably spent at least two periods of his younger life in Ireland or with Irish people. His first stint

[6] See Sharpe, *Adomnán,* 57–9.

[7] *Ibid.*, 350–1. See also: Henry, *Saoithiúlacht,* 96, 98 and 217 and further references cited there; C. Ireland (ed.), *Old Irish Wisdom Attributed to Aldfrith of Northumbria: An edition of* Bríathra Flainn Fína maic Ossu (Tempe Arizona, 1999).

among the Irish may have been as a baby and perhaps as a small boy. He lived with the Irish again as an adult when he was a fugitive from his brother Ecgfrith. Bede tells us that he studied among the Irish as well as the English. Some late sources claimed that he had been one of Adomnán's pupils; he certainly became a friend of Adomnán at some stage. Aldfrith, whom James Fraser characterises as having been a monk at the time, was actually at the monastery on Iona the same year that Ecgfrith had taken his Irish captives.

In 686 Adomnán was sent as an ambassador to the newly-installed King Aldfrith to seek the release of the Irish captives. Adomnán must have been almost sixty years of age if not older when he undertook what must have been an arduous journey from Iona, across southern Scotland and the north of England to Northumbria. In 687, having got them released, he brought the prisoners back to Ireland himself. In 688 he returned to Northumbria. While there he visited the important conjoined monasteries at Monkwearmouth/Jarrow and saw their outstanding library. He discussed the Easter controversy there with the abbot Ceolfrith and may even have met a young monk who would later become famous as the Venerable Bede. Bede would eventually write about Adomnán. On one of his visits to Northumbria Adomnán presented King Aldfrith with a copy of his other famous book, *De Locis Sanctis.*[8]

Adomnán's account of 'the holy places' – one of if not *the* oldest such work in existence – was based on the descriptions given to him allegedly by a Gaulish bishop named Arculf, who had travelled to Jerusalem but later found himself on Iona. Arculf has sometimes been tentatively identified with a man called Arnulf who was bishop of Châlons-sur-Marne in northern France around the year 682 but this is far from certain. Bede, who made his own version of Adomnán's work on this topic, described how he understood the original book had come to be written:

> After touring the Promised Land, Arculf travelled to Damascus, Constantinople, Alexandria and to many islands; but while returning home, his ship was forced by a violent storm on to the west coast of Britain. After many adventures, he went to see Christ's servant, Adomnán, who, recognising that he was learned in the Scriptures and was well acquainted with the Holy Places, was delighted to welcome him and even more to listen to him. Accordingly, [Adomnán] quickly wrote down everything of interest that Arculf said that he had seen at the Holy Places. By this means, he compiled a useful work for a great many, especially those who live far away from the places where the patriarchs and Apostles lived, and whose only source of information about them come from books.

[8] Denis Meehan (ed.), *Adamnan's De Locis Sanctis* (Dublin 1983). See also the three essays on that book – by R. Aist, T. O'Loughlin and D. Woods – and, separately, B. Yorke, Adomnán at the court of King Aldfrith, in Wooding (ed.), *Adomnán of Iona.*

Through whatever circumstances, a copy of *De Locis Sanctis* reached northern France by the middle of the eighth century; that text is probably the origin of all the later copies that have survived.[9]

It seems that it was during his second visit to Northumbria that Adomnán accepted (if he had not already done so before) the 'Roman' calculation for the date of Easter. However, on returning to Iona he failed to convince the monks of his own community. He may have been more successful in converting the Columban churches in the northern part of Ireland on some of his return journeys there.[10] It would not be until 716 that the Iona community would conform with the rest of the 'universal church' on this most controversial of issues.

In 692 the annals say that Adomnán visited Ireland. This was most likely a formal visitation of the Columban churches throughout the country similar to that made on several occasions by his predecessors. He may have had to deal with the sort of problem adverted to by Tírechán who, writing about the same time, mentions a dispute between the communities of Colum Cille, of Patrick in Armagh and of Eógan of Ardstraw (County Tyrone), about the control of the monastery of *Rath Cunga* in south Donegal which was very close to the Columban church at Drumhome. Adomnán is likely to have returned to Iona for the following year when we are told that the king of the Picts, Brude mac Bile – the victor over Ecgfrith at *Nectansmere*, was buried on that island. Two short ironic verses commemorating this event are attributed, probably inaccurately, to Adomnán:[11]

> Great wonders are worked
> By the king born of Mary,
> To Scuabán on Mull he gives life,
> But death to Brude mac Bile.
>
> It must be, at least, unexpected,
> For him who was king of a *tuath*[12]
> That an old, hollow trunk of an oak-tree
> Should enclose him, the king *of Ail Cluaith.*

Short as it is, this little poem presents us with a number of problems. *Ail Cluaith* was the Rock of the Clyde or Dumbarton where the king of the Strathclyde Britons lived. However, here for whatever reason it seems to be cited as a residence of the king of the Picts. It's not clear either what the

[9] Picard, 'The Cult of Colum Cille', 6.

[10] See C. Stancliffe, '"Charity with peace": Adomnán and the Easter question', in Wooding (ed.), *Adomnán of Iona*, 51–68.

[11] See Herbert and Ó Riain, *Betha Adamnáin*, 58–9, on which the following is based.

[12] The word in Irish for a tribal kingdom.

reference to 'Scuabán on Mull' means. It seems as if Scuabán was 'at death's door' but was subsequently reprieved 'by the king born of Mary'. On much less authoritative grounds one of Brude's predecessors, Brude son of Maelchú, the contemporary of Columba who visited him at his fortress in the vicinity of Inverness, is also sometimes said to have been buried on Iona – around 581. However, for a variety of reasons, that seems unlikely.

Adomnán visited Ireland again in the spring or early summer of 697 in order to lead the Synod of Birr (Birr – now in County Offaly) and, as the annals say, to give 'the Law of Innocents to the peoples'. The Law of Innocents, *Lex Innocentium*, was designed to protect clerics, women and children from combat and to take them under the protection of the monastery on Iona. It also became known as the *Cáin Adomnáin* – 'the Law of Adomnán', by which name it is referred to in the Irish secular law tract *Crith Gablach* as 'a law of religion that inspires'. The text of the Law of Adomnán does not survive except in a later expanded version (although it is probably possible to separate the later material from the original); however, a contemporary list of those said to be its guarantors, that is those who agreed to make sure that it was enforced, does survive.[13] That list includes leading churchmen and lay rulers from all parts of Ireland, and from both the Dál Riata and Pictish territories in Scotland. It also, perhaps surprisingly, includes figures from both sides of the Easter calculation dispute. The list is headed by the Cenél Conaill king of Tara, Loingsech son of Óengus, a distant relative of Adomnán who had probably come to power in 695. Many commentators have pointed out that Adomnán's Law and his role at the Synod of Birr is a clear indication of the enormous prestige and eminence that he had achieved in both Irish and Scottish church circles as well as in the secular political sphere in both countries.

As Máire Herbert has said, it is probably highly significant that the Law of Adomnán was proclaimed at a synod held in what was possibly thought to be (most likely inaccurately) the year of the centenary of Columba's death. Richard Sharpe draws attention to a story told by Adomnán about himself and his companions when they were returning to Iona, almost certainly from the Synod of Birr. Having reached the unidentified Scottish island of *Saine* by 8 June, the eve of Saint Columba's (and Báithín's) feast day, contrary winds forced them to halt their journey. They were anxious to be back in Iona for the joyful festival on the following day. Adomnán prayed to his predecessor

[13] Máirín Ní Dhonnchadha, 'The Guarantor List of *Cáin Adomnáin*, 697', *Peritia*, Vol. 1 (1982), 178–215. See also G. Márkus, *Adomnán's Law of the Innocents* (Glasgow 1997); M. Ní Dhonnchadha, 'Birr and the Law of the Innocents, and, The Law of Adomnán: a translation', in T. O'Loughlin (ed.), *Adomnán at Birr, AD 697: Essays in Commemoration of the Law of the Innocents* (Dublin 2001), 13–32 and 53–68.

and, on rising at first light on the next morning, he found that the wind had dropped so that he and his companions could set out and sail back to Iona safely. They arrived about 9 in the morning and, having washed themselves, were ready to celebrate 'the holy ceremonies of the mass' at noon, in honour of Saints Columba and Baithín, the first and second abbots of their beloved monastery. Adomnán clearly believed that the timely change in the weather had been a miracle wrought through the intervention of Saint Columba.

We cannot be certain that the custom of specially commemorating centenaries was practiced by the monks at this time although it does seem likely; we know that anniversaries definitely were remembered. Adomnán must have been working on his other masterpiece, the *Vita Columbae* or 'Life of Columba', around this same time. Whether this too was a conscious effort to commemorate the centenary of its subject's death is often debated. Certainly it must have been written close to the appropriate date as Adomnán himself died only a few years later, in 704.

In the Life, the author appears to collect all the evidence available to him about his subject from both written and oral sources. The work mainly deals with the saint's life in Iona and Scotland. Events in Ireland are included but not to the same extent. Unfortunately, from our point of view, Adomnán did not write anything like a modern chronological biography. Frustratingly he hints at topics we would like to know more about and avoids others we might consider to be of great importance. He may also have deliberately ignored evidence that cast his subject in a bad light. Instead, he compiled a work of hagiography to extol and venerate the spirituality of his subject.

The *Vita* is set out in three sections or 'books', dealing with examples of Columba's 'miraculous' powers, his 'prophetic foreknowledge' and his 'angelic visions'. Adomnán says that he wrote the work at the request of his own monks but clearly he also envisaged a much wider readership.[14] Writing in Latin and almost certainly slightly tongue-in-cheek, he apologises in the first of two prefaces for his necessary use of Irish language words and names, 'words that, I suppose, are held to be of no value, among other different tongues of foreign peoples'. It is apparent, however, that the very opposite is the real truth; Adomnán clearly loved playing with the unusual words and the variety of languages that were relevant to his theme.

Some authors have stressed Adomnán's special interest in promoting the memory of his predecessor in Northumbria, particularly following the loss of Columban influence there in the aftermath of the Easter dating controversy and the debacle of the Synod of Whitby. He is said to have

[14] For a discussion of this topic see J. Picard, 'The Purpose of Adomnán's *Vita Columbae*', *Peritia,* Vol. 1 (1982), 160–77 and T. Charles-Edward, 'The structure and purpose of Adomnán's *Vita Columbae*', in Wooding (ed.), *Adomnán of Iona,* 205–18

attempted to do this by demonstrating that Columba was on a par with other great saints of the church such as Martin of Tours, and even with some of the original apostles. One translator has gone so far as to describe the *Vita* as nothing less than the 'Gospel of Colum Cille' written principally for the Northumbrians.[15]

The oldest manuscript of the *Vita Columbae* we have was transcribed by a cleric called Dorbéne who asks us to pray for him in a little colophon attached to the end of the Life. He has been identified as the Dorbéne whose death as abbot of Iona, after only five months in office, is recorded by the Annals of Ulster for 28 October 713. Dorbéne was said to be another member of the Cenél Conaill and thus a distant relative of Adomnán (and of Columba). He could have made his copy while Adomnán was still alive and even have shown it to the author before his death in 704. The manuscript, which consists of 68 pages of goatskin parchment, each almost 11 inches by 9 inches, is now preserved in the public library in the small town of Schaffhausen in Switzerland. It formerly belonged to the nearby monastery of Reichenau on an island in Lake Constance but had arrived in Schaffhausen by the end of the eighteenth century. Reichenau, as we will see, had many Irish connections in the early Middle Ages. Dorbéne's manuscript was almost certainly taken to the continent in the eighth century but probably took some time to reach its destination at Reichenau. Three much later copies of Adomnán's *Vita,* the so-called B manuscripts, also survive. The best – B1, emanated in the late twelfth century from the scriptorium of Durham cathedral where we know a devotion to Colum Cille survived into late medieval times. The other two manuscripts, B2 and B3, are clearly related to B1 in terms of their text. The B manuscripts preserve a slightly different version of Adomnán's original work to the one copied by Dorbéne. One suggestion is that Dorbéne may have copied an early draft of the Life, whereas the B manuscripts represent a slightly later version, possibly one corrected by Adomnán himself.

Another important Columban manuscript, possibly of around the same date as the Schaffhausen *Vita,* is the richly ornamented Book of Durrow which has 248 folios each page about 9½ inches by 5½ inches.[16] The book, which is now in the manuscript collection of Trinity College Dublin, contains a copy of the Vulgate version of the four Gospels, together with some prefatory material. It is written in a beautiful large clear script known as Irish majuscule. The date and place of origin of this manuscript, like that of its 'sister' codex the Book of Kells, is still the subject of much scholarly debate. Between the years 877 and 916 the king of Tara Flann son of Máel Sechnaill had a

[15] Marsden, *Illustrated Columcille,* 181.

[16] Meehan, *Book of Durrow.*

somewhat too small *cumhdach* or shrine-box made for the book. Some damage was caused to the manuscript when it was squeezed into the box. A secondary note entered about the late eleventh or early twelfth century in a blank space on the last page of the book makes it clear that the book was in the Durrow (Co. Offaly) area at that time.

Around the beginning of the seventeenth century the 'Book of Colum Cille', as the Book of Durrow was by then called, was known to and studied by a number of antiquarian scholars. Also, water in which the book, or at least several pages from it, had been dipped was known to local farmers in the Durrow area as a 'cure' for their sick cattle. In the later seventeenth century the book came into the possession of the library at Trinity College Dublin. It was there in 1689, when the college was temporarily occupied during the Williamite wars, that its *cumhdach* was lost or stolen.

Experts have argued for a long time – as they do about many of the related manuscripts – about where and when the Book of Durrow was made. Northumbria, Iona, Derry, somewhere in the Pictish territories, as well as Durrow itself, have all been suggested as its place of origin. What is common to each of these is that they were all part of, or considerably influenced by, the Columban form of monasticism. The book displays some similarities with the fragments of a manuscript of the Gospels preserved in Durham which is conventionally dated to about 650. Until recently many scholars accepted a late seventh-century date for the Book of Durrow, making it one of the earliest of the illuminated 'insular' Gospel books from either Britain or Ireland. However, recent studies would suggest a slightly later date – in the early eighth century, about the same time that Dorbéne was copying Adomnán's *Vita Columbae.*[17] A somewhat erased and over-written colophon at the end of the book says:

> I ask your beatitude, holy presbyter Patrick, that whoever holds in his hand this little book may remember [me] Columba the writer who wrote this Gospel book for myself in the space of 12 days by the grace of our Lord.

Clearly the book is not as old as Colum Cille himself but Bernard Meehan has suggested that it may be that it is a copy of a Gospel book that actually had been the work of the founder saint. In that scenario the scribe of the Book of Durrow would simply have copied an original colophon written by Columba at the end of the latter's own manuscript.[18]

[17] *Ibid.*, 17–22. Subsequent to Meehan's book, an article on the topic of, The Book of Durrow, originally published in 1967 was reprinted with an updated appendix, in L. De Paor, *Ireland and Early Europe* (Dublin 1997), 125–33. In 1967 De Paor had argued for a date of between 660 and 675 but in his 1997 appendix he altered this to the 630s. The most recent account of the debate with extensive bibliographical references can be found in C. Newman, 'St Matthew's cloak, Durrow fol. 21', in T. Condit and C. Corlett *Above and beyond: Essays in memory of Leo Swan* (Bray 2005), 219–26.

[18] Meehan, *Book of Durrow*, 26–8.

Various other literary works are attributed to Adomnán.[19] While it is probable that he did write more than the two well-known works, it is also likely that several of those that are now associated with his name were written by other authors at much later dates. A set of dietary laws known as Adomnán's Canons list the animal foods that may or may not be eaten. A commentary on Virgil's *Bucolics* and *Georgics* is likewise attributed to him. The *Fís Adamnáin* is a text of about the eleventh century professing to describe a vision that Adomnán is said to have seen at the time of the Synod of Birr. In fact, it is a later literary description of heaven and hell, perhaps composed by a cleric who belonged to the Columban community. A number of poems are also attributed to Adomnán, one of which – the *Féilire Adamnáin* – is a prayer addressed to saints whose festivals were celebrated throughout the year. As we saw above, Gilbert Márkus now believes that the poem *Adiutor Laborantium* was composed by Adomnán. The prayer of Saint Adomnán, a short poem of fifteen lines in Irish, is included in the eleventh-century *Liber Hymnorum.*

> Colum Cille,
> To God, please commend me.
> When the time comes to die,
> May I not die too soon
> . . .

Adomnán died in 704. His feast day was commemorated on 23 September. Although almost certainly he was buried in Iona, a later tradition claimed that his relics were kept at *Scrín Adamnáin* 'the shrine of Adomnán – now Skreen in County Sligo. This belief is difficult to explain although in the early eleventh century Máel Coba Ua Gallchóir of the Cenél Conaill – to which Adomnán had belonged – was said to be *comarba* there.

An early eighth-century collection of Irish church laws, known as the *Collectio Canonum Hibernensis,* is attributed to Ruben of Dairinis (who died in 725) and to Cú Chuimne – a monk of Iona who died in 747.[20] Cú Chuimne's death notice in the Annals of Ulster, which refers to him as *sapiens* – 'the learned', has a little poem in Irish added in the margins of the manuscript, said to have been composed by his foster-mother. The witty translation of the poem by John V. Kelleher picks up on the tradition that Cú Chuimne may not have always practiced the highest ideals of monastic celibacy.[21]

> Cú Chuimne in youth
> Read his way through half the Truth.

---

[19] Kenney, *Sources*, esp. 283–7 and 444–5.

[20] See R. Flechner, *A Study, Edition and Translation of the Hibernensis, with commentary.* Scriptores Latini Hiberniae Series, Dublin Institute for Advanced Studies (Forthcoming).

[21] Quoted in Dáibhí Ó Cróinín, *Early Medieval Ireland* (London 1995), 216, from John V. Kelleher, *Too small for stove wood, too big for kindling* (Dublin 1979), 12.

> He let the other half lie –
> While he gave women the try.
>
> Well for him in old age.
> He became a holy sage.
> He gave women the laugh.
> He read the other half.

The *Collectio* quotes from, among others, the writings of Adomnán. Cú Chuimne may have become a monk on Iona during Adomnán's abbacy after he had renounced the sort of secular life referred to in the poem. The two oldest manuscript copies of the *Collectio* come from northern France – an area where there were lots of Irish connections – and date to the second half of the eighth century.[22] As we have seen above, Adomnán himself had something of a reputation as a jurist and a maker of laws and continuing research seems to be adding to that claim. In this regard it may be relevant to note also that in 724 the annals record the death of Caech Scuili the *scriba* of Derry. A *scriba* was not a lowly copyist but – in the biblical sense – a senior ecclesiastical scholar and jurist. The recording of his death in what would have been the original Iona Chronicle is surely indicative of a high reputation within the *Familia Columbae.* Perhaps he too was associated with the compilation (or at least with those involved in the compilation) of the *Collectio Canonum Hibernensis.*

The beautiful rhyming hymn in Latin *Cantemus in omni die* ('Let us sing every day') is said in the introduction to it in the *Liber Hymnorum* to have been composed by Cú Chuimne

> to praise the Virgin Mary in the time of Loingsech son of Óengus [the king of Tara who died in 703 and who was also a relative of Adomnán] and of Adomnán ... The cause of its composition was to free [Cú Chuimne] from the evil life in which he lived, for he had a wife and lived a bad life with her.

> *Cantemus in omni die*
> *concinentes varie*
> *conclamantes deo dignum*
> *ymnum sanctae Mariae*
>
> Let us sing every day,
> harmonising in turns,
> together proclaiming to God
> a hymn worthy of holy Mary.
> ...[23]

[22] Picard, 'The cult of Colum Cille', 6–7.
[23] Clancy and Márkus, *Iona*, 182–3.

There is some confusion in the sources regarding the succession to the abbacy of Iona in the years immediately following the death of Adomnán.[24] Some authors have suggested that this comes about because of the internal controversies regarding the Easter date issue. It may be that there were rival candidates for the office, some of whom supported the traditional Iona view and others who were more in tune with the 'Roman' position – the position held by Adomnán himself.[25] By 713 Dorbéne, the *Vita Columbae* copyist, had become abbot but, as his death notice records, he held that position for only five months. By 716, however, the Easter issue was effectively settled. That year, the Annals of Ulster records that the date of 'Easter is changed in the monastery of Iona'. The Venerable Bede tells us that:

> the most reverend and holy father, Bishop Egbert, an Englishman, who had spent many years of exile in Ireland for the love of Christ, and was most learned in the scriptures, and renowned for lifelong holiness came and corrected their error.

Egbert was from an Anglo–Saxon noble background and as a young man he had gone to pursue religious studies in the southeast of Ireland at the important monastery of *Ráith Melsig*.[26] He spent a lot of his life in Ireland but later planned to go and preach to the German peoples. All his preparations had been made for the voyage and he had chosen his companions for the journey when he received a visit from a monk who told him about a vision he had seen in his dream. The vision had indicated that Egbert should go instead to 'instruct the monks of Columba'. The vision was repeated a few days later but Egbert still continued with his preparations for the journey to Germany, however, a storm destroyed his ship. He finally accepted these omens as a sign that he was not to go to the Germans. Instead, in 716 he went to Iona and persuaded the monks there to adopt the 'canonical rite of Easter and style of tonsure'. Bede describes what happened, using the opportunity to praise the Irish for bringing the knowledge of Christ to the English and simultaneously condemning the Britons for not being so generous with their knowledge:

> Being a very persuasive teacher who carefully practiced what he taught, Egbert was listened to by all, and by his continual, pious preachings he drew them

[24] Herbert, *Iona*, 57–9.

[25] For a discussion of these issues see Sharpe, *Adomnán*, 74–5. For a less complicated explanation, see Clancy, 'Díarmait *sapientissimus*', 221. The latest commentator on the subject, James Fraser, suggests that pressure of responsibility may have resulted in a splitting of the workload and hence of offices – *From Caledonia*, 260–2

[26] See Ó Cróinín, Rath Melsigi, 23; T. Fanning, Appendix: 'Some field monuments in the townlands of Clonmelsh and Garryhundon, Co. Carlow', *Peritia*, Vol. 3 (1984), 43–9.

> away from the obsolete traditions of their forefathers ... This occurred through a wonderful manifestation of God's grace, so that the nation which had willingly and generously laboured to pass on its own knowledge of God to the English nation might later, through that very same English nation, come to the correct knowledge which they had not previously possessed. In contrast the Britons, who had not shared their knowledge of Christ's Faith with the English, continue even now, when the English nation does believe, and is fully instructed in the teachings of the Catholic Faith, to be stubborn and crippled with error, going about with their heads incorrectly tonsured, and keeping Christ's [Easter] ceremonies without unity with the Christian church.

Bede goes on to tell us that Egbert remained a further thirteen years on Iona and died there, paradoxically on Easter Sunday (according to the Roman calculation), 24 April, 729. As Bede's text was written only two years later in 731, we can be fairly confident that he had accurately recorded the dates of those events.

Notwithstanding the changeover to the 'correct' method for the calculation of the date of Easter in 716, the following year the annals record 'the expulsion of the community of Iona beyond the *Dorsum Britanniae* [the Spine of Britain or the Grampian Mountains] by king Nechtan', the ruler of the Picts. The precise meaning of this event is not clear.[27] It seems to mean that some of the Columban monks operating in the territories of the Picts were slow to change and hence were expelled by Nechtan who had his own direct lines of communication and information on this matter with what was considered to be the more orthodox church to the south, in Northumbria. It was not until the following year, 718, that the issue of the correct tonsure was settled at Iona.[28] It appears that the conservative Irish tonsure required that the head be shaved from the forehead to the crown, rather than in the approved 'Roman' manner, in which the crown only was shaved.

According to the annals, in 727 'the relics of Adomnán [were] brought over to Ireland [from Iona] and the Law [of Adomnán was] promulgated anew'. One explanation of this is that even by that early date Adomnán himself was being treated as a saint. However, an alternative interpretation is suggested by the ancient notes to the Martyrology of Óengus. There it is suggested that the relics in question were those of other saints which had been collected by Adomnán. Whatever the explanation, the relics were probably brought to Ireland by Cilléne Droichtech of the southern Uí Néill, who had recently succeeded to the abbacy of Iona. According to a twelfth-century note they may have been used in an attempt to make peace between the two leading

---

[27] See short discussion in M. Carver, *Portmahomack: monastery of the Picts*, Edinburgh 2008, 24.
[28] See Herbert, *Iona*, 60 note 14; E. James, 'Bede and the tonsure question', *Peritia*, Vol. 3 (1984), 85–98.

Donegal dynasties – Cenél Conaill and Cenél nÉogain – who were at war with each other again that year.[29] The relics remained in Ireland until 730 when, in the month of October, they were returned to Iona. Whenever the process began, Adomnán did eventually come to be treated as a saint and there were many churches dedicated to him in both Ireland and Scotland, including a number known as *Scrín Adomnáin* or 'Adomnán's Shrine'. In the anglicised form of the local dialectical version of his name, 'Eunan', he is the patron of the Catholic diocese of Raphoe, and the Catholic cathedral in Letterkenny is dedicated to him.

Sometime about 740, a copy of the document containing our very earliest annalistic entries – the so-called 'Iona Chronicle' – was brought over to Ireland. There is no agreement among scholars as to where it was brought. The famous monastery at Bangor in County Down has often been suggested. So also are various monasteries in *Brega* – the area between the River Liffey and the Boyne. Another suggestion for the destination of the Iona text is the monastery of Clonard, now in County Meath, and also the monastery at Armagh. Dr Daniel Mc Carthy has recently made persuasive arguments for the monastery of Movilla in County Down.[30] Wherever it was brought to, from then on a new phase in Irish record-keeping commenced. Máire Herbert has suggested that likewise, about the same time, a list of the abbots of Iona up to that point together with their anniversary dates may have been brought to Ireland. Such a list could later have formed the basis for the compilation of the native Irish martyrologies or 'calendars' of the saints.[31]

Cilléne Droichtech continued as abbot of Iona until his death in 752 when he was succeeded by Slébéne of the Cenél Conaill. At some point during his term as abbot of Iona, Slébéne went to Ripon in England and in the course of his visit examined the historical records of that monastery. The twelfth-century Life of Saint Kentigern – written by Jocelin of Furness (who also wrote a Life of Saint Patrick) – records that a crozier of Colum Cille was preserved as a relic in Ripon. The story claims that Colum Cille went to visit Kentigern (also known as Mungo) at his monastery at Glasgow. 'Before bidding each other farewell they exchanged pastoral staves in pledge and testimony of their mutual love in Christ.' Colum Cille's stave or crozier was said to have been brought later to Ripon, which had been founded originally by Irish monks. But a more believable explanation might be that the crozier was brought there directly from Iona as a gift by Slébéne.

[29] Sharpe, *Adomnán*, 77. See also Stokes, *Félire Óengusso*, 211.
[30] D.P. Mc Carthy, *The Irish Annals: Their genesis, evolution and history* (Dublin 2008), esp. ch. 6.
[31] Herbert, *Iona*, 62. For a fuller discussion of the Irish martyrologies see, P Ó Riain, *Feastdays of the Saints: A History of Irish Martyrologies* (Bruxelles 2006).

In 753 the 'Law of Colum Cille' was enforced by the king of Tara Domnall Mide. It may be relevant that in the following year, 754, Slébéne came on a visitation to Ireland. We do not know what aspect of life the Law of Colum Cille actually dealt with but presumably it must have been similar in type and effect to the Law of Adomnán. Those 'Laws' would have been brought around the country and displayed in solemn visitation ceremonies, accompanied by relics of the saint in question. Presumably offerings and fines for the breaches of their ordinances would be collected during such events. Slébéne promulgated the Law of Colum Cille again in 757, and died sometime between then and 766 when his successor Suibne came on a visitation to Ireland. Suibne died in 772.

It had been during his abbacy that the Irish scholar-monk Dicuil was present on Iona. Dicuil who would go on to work on the continent of Europe as a teacher at the courts of Charlemagne and Louis the Pious wrote a number of important scientific works of which the most significant is probably his *Liber de mensura orbis terrae*, a compendium of the geography of the then known world. Dicuil tells us himself that he was on Iona when a monk returned there from a pilgrimage to the Holy Land, and it was also at the island monastery that he acquired some of his knowledge of the geography of the northern and western islands.[32]

King Domnall Mide who enforced the 'Law of Colum Cille' had come to power in 743. He belonged to the Clann Cholmáin of the southern Uí Néill and was the first of that dynasty to reign as king of Tara. As F.J. Byrne says, Domnall's reign of twenty years was extraordinarily peaceful and the king himself was more than nominally Christian. On at least two occasions he retired to a monastery to enter 'clerical life'.[33] One of those episodes occurred in 744, the year after his installation as king of Tara. As he was buried in Durrow on his death in 763, it is sometimes suggested, logically, that this was the monastery in which he had sought retreat earlier in his life.

There were clearly excellent relations at this time between the Clann Cholmáin dynasty and the community of Colum Cille, especially the monastery of Durrow. Domnall Mide's son, Donnchad who became king of Tara in 770, promulgated the Law of Colum Cille again in 778 along with the abbot of Iona – Bresal – who had come across to Ireland for the occasion. On Donnchad's part this may have been a sort of payment for the support of the community of Durrow when he had fought 'a destructive battle' with the Munstermen two years earlier. The participation of the monastery of Durrow in the battle is not too surprising. In 764 there had been a battle between the monasteries of Durrow and Clonmacnoise themselves, at an unidentified

[32] A. Breen, Dicuil, in S. Duffy (ed.) *Medieval Ireland: An encyclopedia* (New York 2005), 128–9.
[33] Byrne, *Irish Kings*, 156.

place called *Argaman.* We do not know the reason for the battle but apparently two hundred of the community of Durrow fell and Clonmacnoise took the victory. Instead of the withdrawn cenobitic communities of earlier times, it seems as if at least some of the Columban monasteries, as well as others associated with separate saints, were embracing secularisation and full engagement with the political world around them.

Other Columban Monasteries and Dedications in Scotland

The islands of the Ocean, namely Ireland and Britain, were twice ravaged throughout by a terrible pestilence, excepting two peoples only, that is the population of Picts, and of the Irish in Britain [the Dál Riata], between which peoples the mountains of the spine of Britain are the boundary. And although neither people is without great sins, by which the Eternal Judge is often provoked to anger, yet until now he has spared both of them, enduring patiently. To who else can this favour conferred by God be attributed, but to Saint Columba, whose monasteries, placed within the boundaries of both peoples, are down to the present time held in great honour by both of them.

Adomnán,
Vita Columbae (*c.* 700)

In 731 the Venerable Bede claimed that Columba 'came from Ireland to Britain to preach the word of God in the provinces of the northern Picts'. Most modern commentators would refute this, arguing that there is no contemporary evidence for it. The fact that no such assertion is made in the *Vita Columbae* when Adomnán would almost certainly have cited it if it had been correct is seen as particularly indicative. Indeed, some evidence is beginning to emerge that Christianity may have been already present among the Picts by the time of the saint's arrival in Scotland, as it certainly was among the petty kingdoms of Dál Riata.[1] Columba was certainly not a significant missionary to the ancient peoples of Scotland – many other clerics were involved in such activity, records of whom unfortunately are not as well preserved as for the founder of Iona. Nevertheless, the activities of the saint's followers ensured that his cult became widespread in all parts of that country.

[1] See G. Márkus, 'Iona: monks, pastors and missionaries', in D. Broun and T. Clancy (eds), Spes Scotorum, *Hope of Scots: Saint Columba, Iona and Scotland* (Edinburgh 1991), 115–38.

In 1857 William Reeves, one of the greatest Columban scholars, published his extraordinary work on the *Life of St Columba.* The book is mainly an edition of the Schaffhausen text of Adomnán's *Vita Columbae* but the enormous amount of additional notes and appendices makes it an indispensable source – an encyclopaedia – for the study of all the other aspects of the cult of Saint Colum Cille as well as of the churches associated with him in both Ireland and Scotland. Among the copious appendices, Reeves' book contains a section on the *S. Columbae Ecclesiae Britannicae*, 'Saint Columba's British churches', in effect, the churches associated with the saint in what is modern Scotland. In his introduction to that section Reeves tells us that:

> The following catalogue of Columbian [*sic*] foundations in Scotland admits of considerable enlargement, but it is sufficient to show how widely the veneration of St. Columba was extended in his adopted country.

Reeves divided this catalogue into two sections: those churches that were *Inter Scotos* – 'among the Scots', or the territories originally ruled by the Dál Riata; and those that were *Inter Pictos,* 'among the Picts'. He listed thirty-two sites in the former category and twenty-one in the latter but, in an appendix, he later added another three sites all in former Pictish territories. That made in all a total of fifty-six establishments throughout various parts of Scotland. Reeves also tells us that these lists included not only churches which were actually founded by Columba himself but also those established by his followers and those which 'professed subjection to the mother church of Hy [Iona]'. But he also pointed out that some of the latter churches 'ceased in after times to bear any trace of their original relation [to Columba or Iona], and became distinguished only by the names of the immediate founders, under whose patronage they were built'. As an example of that sort of process he mentioned that 'St Dochonna's church, for instance, was probably at first subject to Hy, though afterwards independent when known as St. Machar's of Aberdeen.'

The name originally associated with that church, Dochonna ('Thy Conna'), is of course a hypocoristic or endearing form of the name Colum. So also is its equivalent Mochonna ('My Conna'). There is a lot of confusion in the sources and legends about these various names and the persons who held them, and there is a good chance that, in fact, the real historical person behind most of them is Columba himself. Reeves tells us that the Calendars list two Dochonnas or Mochonnas both of whose feast days fell on 8 March which was, in addition, the feast day of two even more obscure saints also called Colum. One of the two 8 March Mochonnas was associated with Assylin on the Boyle River in County Roscommon, in an area where Columba is said to have at least visited according to Adomnán. All of this supports the view that despite the differences in names and feast days all of these characters can probably be identified with Columba.

Manus O'Donnell tells us that Dachonna or Mochonna of Aberdeen, whose feast day was 12 November, had two other names: Machar (latinised as Macarius) and as Mauricius.[2] The latter name was said, in legend, to have been given to him by Pope Gregory the Great.[3] O'Donnell twice mentions a Life of Mochonna which he refers to or quotes from, 'but we have omitted much of what [it says] because of the length it would take to copy it'. O'Donnell's decision was unfortunate for us as, regrettably, the Life of Mochonna appears not to have survived to the present. The alleged biographical information given about that Mochonna by O'Donnell does not make much sense in the context of what we know about the time, although he is said to have been a 'close kinsman' of Colum Cille. The latter is said to have consecrated Mochonna a bishop:

> He [Colum Cille] gave him [Mochonna] a ring and a crosier and every other instrument needed by a bishop in serving the church. And he gave him twelve men as loyal followers that were diligent in the service of the church of God. And he told him to go to the province of the Picts and to dwell there in the place where he would find a river in the form of a crosier. And he said that it was there that God wished him to live, passing his days.
>
> Macarius and his community set out bidding farewell to Colum Cille, and went to the province of the Picts. He found a river [the Dee] in the shape of a crosier just as Colum Cille had told him. He founded a church in a certain place [Aberdeen] beside that river. But there was a poisonous serpent in the place that belched out fiery flames from his throat, killing many of the local people. Seeing that, Macarius wished to injure it. He cursed it and, by the power of God and the miracles of Colum Cille, he turned it into a pillar of stone. For Colum Cille had sent Macarius to that location, instead of to any other place in the province of the Picts, in order to destroy that beast which had been destroying the people, once its existence was revealed to him in spirit. Many were the miracles then that Macarius worked in that province and many were its hosts and its forces that he brought to the faith. Many were the churches he founded there. And he ended the diabolical sacrifices and destroyed the images of the devilish gods that the people believed in.[4]

This is the legend of the foundation of St Machar's church at Old Aberdeen but, if there is even a 'germ of truth' in it, there is a strong likelihood that the real story actually refers to the genuinely historical Columba, slightly obscured by the hypocoristic version of his name. This is not to assert that this church was founded by Columba but that it was probably part of the *Familia Columbae* from the outset or from early in its history.

---

[2] For a legendary account of Machar's life see Lacey, *Manus O'Donnell*, 134–7.
[3] *Ibid.*
[4] *Ibid.*

Adopting a somewhat different approach from Reeves and based mainly on place names, Nollaig Ó Muraíle, again stressing that his lists were not definitive, came up with a total of about one hundred and forty Columban churches or probable sites of churches in Ireland and Scotland.[5] All of these included in their titles some variation of the name Colum Cille or the simpler Colum. No less than twelve of these, for example, had the form *Cill Choluim* [or *Chaluim*] *Cille*, 'Church of Colum Cille'. About eighty on Ó Muraíle's list were in Ireland, the remainder were scattered throughout Scotland.

Ó Muraíle also suggested that, in addition, 'there must be – at a conservative estimate – dozens of holy wells dedicated to Columba throughout Ireland and Scotland.' Adomnán mentions one such well in Ardnamurchan which in his time was 'potent in the name of Saint Columba'. Another well, which caused injury to anyone who drank or washed in it, is described as being in the territories of the Picts. The local people venerated it as a god. Contrary to the expectations of the *magi* – the 'magicians' or 'druids', Columba washed in it and drank its waters, ridding it of its demons and turning it instead into a source of cures.

As well as the specifically Columban churches and sites, Ó Muraíle listed fourteen locations in Ireland and twenty-one in Scotland where the name of the place incorporated some variation of the element Adomnán whose cult was closely associated with that of his master. An additional list, originally made by the Scottish place names expert W.J. Watson, included the names of church sites derived from one of the hypocoristic versions of the name of Colum: Mo-Cholmóg, 'my little' or 'my young Colum'. Watson had listed five of these, all in Scotland but Ó Muraíle was able to add another two: one in Scotland and another in Ireland. There may well be other originally Columban church sites in Ireland and Scotland that are now concealed behind obscure versions of the hypocoristic forms of the saint's name, just as we have seen above for example in the case of Aberdeen. These might include, among others, churches dedicated to Cainnech, a name that is sometimes anglicised in Scotland as Kenneth but which Pádraig Ó Riain has suggested might have been anciently an alias of Columba. John Marsden listed Cambuskenneth, and Inchkenneth off Mull. Marsden also instanced additional examples of that saint's name being attached – apparently – to other places in Scotland, including Kilchenich (now 'Kilkenneth') on Tiree, which appears to be a direct equivalent of the anglicised Irish place name Kilkenny.

---

[5] Ó Muraíle, Onomastic Legacy. Very important work in this regard has also been carried out in Scotland by scholars such as Gilbert Márkus and esp. Simon Taylor. See for instance the latter's, 'Seventh-century Iona abbots in Scottish place names', in Broun and Clancy (eds) Spes Scotorum, *Hope of Scots*, 35–70.

On Colonsay island there is a hill called *Carn cul ri Erenn*, 'Mound of the back to Ireland'. A romantic tradition claims that on their original voyage from Ireland in 562 Colum Cille and his monks landed there but, as they were still able to see the land they had left behind from that hill, they continued their journey onward until they arrived at a place where they could no longer see their homeland. That place was Iona. There is a similarly named place in the southeast corner of Iona from where, of course, Ireland could not be seen thus confirming that island as the ideal location for the new monastery. *Cul ri Erenn* was also used as a nickname for Colum Cille himself because for the love of God he had turned his back on the land of his birth. A late poem, quoted by Manus O'Donnell, has the saint say:

> At dawn and at dark, I lament,
> 'Ochone', for the journey I take;
> From now on, to my shame, my name,
> Will be 'back turned against Ireland'.

There was also a church on Colonsay dedicated to Saint Oran who, although he is not listed among the twelve monks that are said to have accompanied Columba from Ireland, does figure in the legends associated with the saint's journey to Iona and the foundation of the monastery there.

The churches mentioned by Adomnán that may have been founded directly by Columba himself must have primary position in any list of the saint's establishments in Scotland. The monastery of *Campus* or *Mag Luinge* ['Plain of a ship'?] is mentioned several times in the *Vita Columbae.* Its name is probably just a poetic reference to the surrounding Atlantic Ocean. It is clear from Adomnán's references that this church was located on Tiree and that it was a daughter house of the monastery on Iona. As Richard Sharpe reminds us, *Mag Luinge* was about half a day's sail from the mother house, and travel between these two places, as described by Adomnán, seems to have been an almost daily occurrence. Baithín, Columba's nephew and *alumnus* and also his successor as abbot of Iona, was prior of the monastery at *Campus Luinge* but he had returned to Iona apparently shortly before his master's death.

Adomnán tells us that the monastery at *Mag Luinge* was also a centre for the penitents who came to seek forgiveness for their sins from the saint. It seems to have continued with that function even after Columba's death. There were several other monastic sites on Tiree, including *Artchain*, which was probably not originally a Columban foundation. *Bledach* a church associated with Saint Brendan 'the Navigator' was probably also on Tiree, as well as a church connected with Saint Comgal of Bangor in County Down. We do not know exactly where *Bledach* was. Two places on the island have been suggested as possible sites: Kirkapoll and Soroby, both of which had churches in medieval times dedicated to Saint Columba and both of which have sculptural evidence dating to early medieval times.

Reeves tells us that the island of Eileach an Naoimh, where it is said that the saint's mother – Eithne – was buried, also had a holy well dedicated to Colum Cille and a tradition that claimed that it was 'once the residence of the monks of Iona'. However, there are also strong associations with Saint Brendan. There are a number of remains of the early medieval period on the island including the ruins of a so-called bee-hive hut, which had a figure of eight plan and which is reminiscent of the similar huts found particularly at early medieval ecclesiastical sites on the islands and coastline of County Kerry.

Recent archaeological investigations on the island of Canna have uncovered a remarkable collection of sculptured stones of the early medieval period close to the location of a previously-known stone cross and the remains of the medieval parish church at A'Chill. That church does not survive but its existence is known from excavation. Other similar carved stones have been found elsewhere on the island, including three at the stone-walled enclosure known as *Sgorr nam bán-naomha*, 'cliff of the holy women'. The latter site has been interpreted as a possible hermitage or penitential station and it is claimed that it 'is the best preserved of several such sites in the Hebrides'.[6] Canna has often been suggested as the location of the unidentified monastery frequently mentioned by Adomnán called *Hinba*. However, as we have seen above, several other island churches have also been suggested and, at present, there is little to tilt the balance in favour of any of them.

Another unidentified daughter-house of Iona was at *Cell Diuni* near Loch Awe on the mainland, although Thomas Clancy has suggested its identification with Kilchrenan at the north end of the lake.[7] *Cell Diuni* was named after the brother of the prior of that church in Columba's time, a monk who was called Cailtan. A related church establishment at *Elena* (*Eilean* in Gàidhlig or, in Irish, *Oileán* – 'Island'?) is also still unidentified.[8] A man called Luigne, a younger contemporary of Columba, would become its prior later in his life.

One miracle story in the *Vita Columbae* relates to a follower of Columba, a young man named Finten whom the saint healed while they were journeying across the Grampian Mountains into the territories of the Picts. Finten afterwards founded the church of *Kailli au inde*. Richard Sharpe has noted that an older suggestion that this was possibly Killundine or *Cell Fhionntain*

---

6 Royal Commission on the Ancient and Historical Monuments of Scotland, *RCAHMS Broadsheet 5 – Canna: The Archaeology of a Hebridean Landscape.*

7 Referred to in Campbell, *Dunadd*, 25; T. Clancy, 'Annat in Scotland and the origins of the parish', *Innes Review*, 46 (1995), 91–115, pp 112–4.

8 As with *Hinba*, there have been many suggestions as to the location of *Elena*. For a full discussion of these see Sharpe, *Adomnán*, 325–6.

in Morvern has been strengthened by the finding there relatively recently of some early medieval cross-inscribed stones.[9]

The famous ancient monastery on the island of Lismore in the Firth of Lorne is often also claimed as a Columban church. However, its traditions attribute its foundation to a different saint – Mo Luag or Lugaid who was allegedly associated with the monastery at Bangor in County Down and whose death is recorded in the Irish annals in 590. According to the Martyrology of Óengus, his feast day was 25 June. The monastery of Lismore seems to have had a distinctly separate, non-Columban character and the occasionally-claimed association with the churches linked to Iona may have come about solely from its geographical location. The island of Lismore, of course, lies adjacent to the path of those travelling nowadays by boat to Iona from Oban on the mainland. A local legend seeks to explain the confusion about the two saints. Apparently Colum Cille and Mo Luag were racing, each by boat, towards the island. Whichever of them reached it first would have the honour of founding its monastery. Colum Cille was in the lead but, just in time, Mo Luag cut off his finger and threw it onto the island, thus claiming that he had reached it first and winning the right to found the monastery there!

There are several places on and around the Isle of Skye as well as in the various islands of the outer Hebrides or Western Isles that have churches of varying dates dedicated to Saint Colum Cille, under some variation of his name. Little or no historical evidence from the early medieval period survives for these sites making it impossible to be certain at what point they were founded or became associated with the Columban cult. Some of these may only date from Viking times when the Columban church was actively involved in the conversion of the Norse settlers.

William Reeves printed the current nineteenth-century story of the church dedicated to Saint Colum Cille at *Fladda Chuain* ('Fladda of the Ocean'), an island off the north end of the Isle of Skye, where a blue round stone 'which is always moist' was kept. The stone was used for swearing oaths, and anyone who wished to improve the weather would 'wash' it. The stone was also believed to be effective for 'curing' various illnesses. Those traditions recall the beliefs about the saint's 'red stone' at Gartan mentioned above which, at the end of the Middle Ages, was in the possession of the O'Nahan erenagh (hereditary steward) family. There was also 'a round green stone' from *Gleann Cholm Cille* in Donegal, which according to Manus O'Donnell was given to the saint by an angel so that he could use it to rid the valley of the demons that had congregated there. What was claimed to be that stone was in the valley as its 'chief treasure' in O'Donnell's time. In the early seventeenth

[9] Sharpe, *Adomnán*, 333 and other references cited there. See also Fisher, *Early Medieval Sculpture*, 11 and 124.

century a local informant said that it had been the custom of the MacSweeney Banagh (the lord of the area of Donegal in which *Gleann Coluim Cille* is located) to supply O'Donnell's army with 'a man to carry the breastplate and stone of Colum Cille'.[10] It is not clear from the text if the 'breastplate' was also a relic associated with the saint but the stone clearly was and was also obviously used as a battle talisman as we know other Columban relics were, both in Ireland and Scotland.

Adomnán also describes a miracle with a stone, allegedly performed by Columba in the 'district of the Picts' and in the presence of their king, Brude son of Máelchú. The saint took a white stone from a river and blessed it 'so that it should effect some cures'. Also according to Adomnán, when the stone in question was immersed in water it floated like an apple 'contrary to nature'. The king is said to have kept the stone among his 'treasures'.

Sites dedicated to Colum Cille are found widespread in the Gaelic, and formerly gaelicised, parts of Scotland and the Isles – as far away as St Kilda. Even further to the north, as we will see, there are said to have been sites in Iceland connected with the cult of the saint. Undoubtedly some of these dedications were propagated by the Viking settlers of those areas when they later became influenced and Christianised by the church of Iona. The conversion of these people, as also some of their counterparts around the Norse settlement at Dublin, was almost certainly carried out by clerics closely associated with the Columban *familia.*

Likewise, sites connected with the saint are found throughout the formerly Pictish areas of Scotland, as far north as the Orkney Islands. Adomnán shows Columba appealing to Brude, the king of the Picts, to order his subject king of the Orkneys not to interfere with 'some of our [Columba's] people', led by Cormac ua Liathán, who had sailed out into the ocean 'to find a desert place'. At least some of the churches in the Pictish territories may date back to the seventh or even, in some cases as we will see below, to the late sixth century. Adomnán tells us quite clearly that Columba had travelled from Iona across Scotland via the Great Glen and that he visited the Pictish king Brude son of Máelchú, possibly a number of times and possibly at the fortress of *Craig Phádrig* near Inverness or at some other nearby site.[11] We can read in the *Vita Columbae* about Columba preaching to the Picts through an interpreter but, although the Venerable Bede says that the saint converted those people to Christianity, modern scholars have been more reluctant to conclude that this was achieved so rapidly. However, without doubt over the succeeding century

[10] D. McGettigan, *Red Hugh O'Donnell and the Nine Years War* (Dublin 2005), 27 and 131.

[11] Sharpe, *Adomnán*, 335, discusses this identification, which was originally made by William Reeves. Foster, *Before Alba*, 16, however, has suggested the alternative identification of Castle Hill in Inverness.

and a half, Christianity was spread throughout the Pictish territories by monks, many of whom, but not all, were definitely associated with Iona. In 693 the Pictish king Brude son of Bile was buried on Iona and in 697 a successor of his, Brude son of Derile, was listed as one of the so-called 'guarantors' of the Law of Adomnán.

Reeves tells us that on or around the saint's feast day on 9 June, up to relatively modern times, St Colm Fairs were held at several of the church sites associated with Colum Cille in the former Pictish lands. Among those he listed were: Auldearn in Nairn; Kingussie in Badenoch, east Invernesshire; Kirktown in Daviot, Aberdeenshire; Drumhead, Belhelvie near Aberdeen; Muirs-keith, Cortachy in the northwest part of Forfarshire (now Angus); and Drymen in The Lennox in West Stirlingshire.

Many of the sites referred to above continued their Columban associations all the way through the later Middle Ages right up to the time of the Reformation, and some even later. One site where the cult of Colum Cille was preserved into much later medieval times was the island of Inchcolm, 'Colm's Island' in the Firth of Forth opposite Edinburgh. The origin of that monastery is said to have come about when, in 1123, the Scottish king Alexander I found his boat overtaken by a violent storm. He vowed that if he was saved from drowning he would found a religious house there, as Reeves tells us, 'to serve as an asylum and comfort to the shipwrecked'. He safely reached the island – then called in Latin *Aemonia* – where he and his retinue were entertained, frugally, by a Columban hermit. Later, the king established the Augustinian Abbey of Inchcolm on the island from where, among other things, the music and words of a delightful service of Lauds for the feast day of Colum Cille has been preserved.[12]

As we have seen, not all the sites associated with Colum Cille in the former Pictish territories are as easy to recognise from their modern place names.

One such site may be that at Tullich in upper Deeside near Ballater in Aberdeenshire. About fifteen cross-marked stones can be found within the suggestively, sub-circular churchyard there, which is reminiscent of similar period ecclesiastical sites in Ireland. The churchyard also contains the ruins of a medieval church associated with a Saint Nathalan. Ian Fisher has suggested that the site may have been originally a monastic centre with Columban associations and noted that the upright pillar stones with plain outline crosses are similar to those found at *Gleann Cholm Cille* and other sites in Ireland.[13] The same author notes that Fortingall in Perthsire may have

[12] Edinburgh University Library, Ms. 211. iv. See introductory notes by Isobel Woods Preece to CD album, *Scottish Medieval Plainchant: Columba, Most Holy of Saints*, sung by Cappella Nova conducted by Alan Tavener; also Broun and Clancy, *Spes Scotorum*, xiii–iv and 24–5.

[13] Fisher, *Early Medieval Sculpture*, 13 and 23.

been one of 'the unnamed Columban monasteries mentioned by Adomnán as existing among the Picts in the late seventh century'.

In the same connection, Fisher also mentions a site at Tarbat in Easter Ross in northeastern Scotland. There, in a fascinating major research exercise, archaeologists have been able to make some really remarkable discoveries. One of the sites, the name of which had been noted in the 1920s by the place names expert W.J. Watson as being derived from Mo Colmóg, the hypocoristic form of Colum, was Portmahomack – *Port Mo Colmóg* – on the Tarbat peninsula. The peninsula was already well known in modern times to scholars of the medieval period because of its three so-called Class II Pictish cross-slabs – at Hilton of Cadboll, Nigg and Shandwick – as well as fragments from Portmahomack itself. Class II sculptures are those which, unlike the 'earlier'(?) Class I examples, include depictions of the Cross. Although there are several fine Class I sculptures elsewhere in Easter Ross, they do not occur on the peninsula itself.

That peninsula, which is at the centre of what were the territories of the northern Picts at the time of Columba, protrudes out into the Moray Firth and, indeed, offers one of the best landing places in that area. Tarbat (with various alternative spellings) is a Gaelic word that seems to indicate a 'portage' or a relatively easy short overland route between two bodies of water. Among other things it was possible for boats to be carried or dragged over such routes thus shortening dangerous sea journeys. The name occurs in various forms in several places in Scotland and Ireland; for example, Belturbet in County Cavan.

Portmahomack is the name of a small village on the shore near the most northerly point of the Tarbat peninsula. On a slight rise just behind and above the village are a de-commissioned eighteenth-century church and a graveyard which was formerly dedicated to Saint Colmán. Colmán like Mo Colmóg is another hypocoristic version of the root name Colum. One hundred yards south of Saint Colmán's church is a holy well, *Tobar a' Bhaiseidh*, 'Well of [John] the Baptist'. There are other such wells in the vicinity and, within a mile's radius, another three churches existed in medieval times. One of these was dedicated to Saint Brigid and another to Saint John the Baptist.

Since the nineteenth century gravediggers and other people working at Saint Colmán's church had occasionally discovered pieces of early medieval sculpture in the churchyard and its surroundings.[14] A particularly instructive fragment of carved stone, that came from the garden wall of the adjacent manse one hundred and fifty yards north of the churchyard, had a portion of a Latin inscription written in the type of lettering known as Insular majuscule,

[14] J. Harden, 'A Potential Archaeological Context for the Early Christian Sculptured Stones from Tarbat, Easter Ross', in C. Bourke (ed.), *From the Isles of the North: Early Medieval Art in Ireland and Britain* (Belfast 1995), 221–7.

similar to that used in Lindisfarne Gospels and the Book of Kells as well as in other related contemporary manuscripts.[15] Even more interestingly, in 1984 archaeologists undertaking an aerial survey of the area had noted a large sub-rectangular cropmark that seemed to indicate a possible buried ditch that might have originally enclosed the site of the church. Radiocarbon analysis of material taken from this ditch during a small test excavation in 1991 produced a range of dates extending from the second to the sixth centuries. However, even at that stage of the research it had been noticed that the location and disposition of this ditch was somewhat similar to that at the early monastic site on Iona.

In 1994 a campaign of intensive archaeological research was initiated to investigate this fascinating area. The original idea for the work was proposed by the local Tarbat Historic Trust but the programme of research was eventually undertaken as a collaboration between that body, the Highland Council and, most importantly the Department of Archaeology of the University of York. An initial geophysical survey of the enclosure area, together with some additional test excavations, was followed by a major programme of excavations that got under way in 1995 and continued until 2007.[16]

The results of the excavations to date have been astonishing and have provided evidence for an important early medieval monastic site, which the director of the project, dared to call 'the Iona of the East'.[17] Indeed, because of the nature of the surviving buildings and monuments at Iona and their use in the present, it has not been possible to investigate that site to anything like the same degree as at Portmahomack. The excavation and examination of the present church there showed that it was effectively the eighth (or, depending on the interpretation, the seventh) stone church on the site. The earliest of these buildings has been dated to the eighth century but there could have been even earlier wooden churches that formed part of the original complex which have yet to be identified.

Within the outlines of the present church building two phases of burials were found. The first, appropriately, consisted of the burials of mainly middle-aged and elderly males, with the earliest radiocarbon date for any of these coming out at about 560 – apparently earlier than the foundation of Iona, although the margin is relatively insignificant. The burials were laid out in long slab-lined cists or in simple depressions in the ground but with stone

[15] See M. Carver, 'An Iona of the East: The Early-medieval Monastery at Portmahomack, Tarbat Ness', *Medieval Archaeology*, Vol. XLVIII (2004), 1–30, p. 4.

[16] M. Carver *Portmahomack: Monastery of the Picts* is a preliminary account of the work and discoveries, pending the completion of all associated analyses and a final report. The following section is based on Prof. Carver's publications.

[17] The same title is also used for Inchcolm.

'head supports' to each side of the skull. Similar types of burial are found on contemporary sites in Ireland. This range of burials is clearly consistent with a male only monastic community, although a small number of middle-aged and older women were also present who could have been domestic servants of some sort. The second phase of burials included a more balanced range of men, women and children of various ages. No stone settings as in the previous phase were present but there was evidence for the use of coffins and shrouds. These burials ranged in date from about the beginning of the twelfth up to the sixteenth century.

A large number of sculpted stone fragments were also found in the church and nearby workshop areas. These greatly expand the amount of such pieces known from the immediate vicinity. The stones ranged from simple grave markers with incised or relief crosses – several of which showed similarities with their counterparts from Iona, to relatively elaborately decorated architectural fragments and pieces of free-standing decorated cross slabs. The latter showed affinities with some of the types of decoration used in the Book of Kells and may, therefore, be dated to around the late eighth century, but they also showed parallels with the Pictish iconography on the still surviving standing slabs on the Tarbat peninsula. Prof. Martin Carver, who was director of the project, pointed out that the Pictish symbols on these stones may represent the names of actual persons, and he has summed up the importance of these finds as follows:

> The Tarbat sculpture allows us to imagine a community in which the secular and the religious were closely integrated, and where leading roles were being taken by individuals with Pictish names in the Moray Firth area on the eve of the 9th century.[18]

About fifty yards of a formerly stone-paved roadway, with stone-lined drains running along each side, were uncovered to the southwest of the church; on each side there were a series of rubble scatters. Together with the small finds that came also from these areas, the plan of these features allowed them to be identified as the foundations of a series of individual workshops. Metalworking was represented by the finding of a variety of crucibles and moulds as well as other objects used in the production of metal objects including, possibly, some that had been made of gold. A glass stud with inlaid wire and enamel, like those on the eighth- and ninth-century Ardagh and Derrynaflan chalices from Ireland, was found. Glass-working on the site was represented by waste lumps and droplets as well as by the moulds for producing escutcheons which could be paralleled by similar finds from Iona.

[18] Carver, 'An Iona of the East', 16.

Evidence for wood-working and the use of a lathe was found, as also evidence for leather-working. There were large quantities of cattle and sheep bones. What was presumed to have been a tanning pit was found, also evidence for the use of seaweed ash which could have been used to lighten the colour of some of the leather products such as the vellum for manuscripts. A typical crescent-shaped iron knife and bone needles possibly provide evidence for the cutting and stitching of the leather, while conical pieces of pumice stone were probably used to smooth and finish the fine leather surfaces. Most interestingly, and at first very puzzlingly, the excavators found rectangular settings of cattle metapodials, or foot bones, pushed vertically into the ground. These bones were associated with small round pebbles. These enigmatic features were later identified as the pegs attached to a wooden frame that had been used for stretching leather; that is they were possibly part of the equipment needed for preparing the calf-hide to turn it into vellum.[19]

The roadway mentioned above had passed over a bridge consisting of massive stone slabs. The bridge also formed part of a dam across a now buried stream. There was a mill-pond adjacent to the dam, and a gap in the dam wall was interpreted as the opening for a sluice gate for a mill-race. Five rotary quern stones were recovered from the pond area. The excavators believed also that a horizontal mill was likely to have been located downstream of the dam but, unfortunately, outside the excavation area. Evidence for early medieval ploughing was also found in this area in the form of marks in the soil.

As indicated above an aerial survey in 1984 had detected evidence for a ditch that enclosed the whole complex. In fact two ditches – an inner and an outer – were found at the southern end of the site during the excavation. The inner ditch had been backfilled with earth that contained eighth- to ninth-century objects but it was possible to conclude that the outer ditch definitely did not have a defensive function. Instead, it was dug and lined with wattle-work for the purpose of collecting water from the adjacent hillside. Between the two ditches evidence for a large 'bag-shaped' building was found. It was about thirteen yards long by about eight yards at its widest. It had a porch and timbers that seemed to support a (at least) partial second story. The walls, which were probably made of turf, would have been built on a foundation layer of beach stones. The building also had a hearth in which evidence of iron-smithing was found. The excavators interpreted the building as having been used mainly as a barn for the laying out, drying and malting of barley but which probably also served a secondary function as a forge in summertime before the harvest was brought in.

---

19 For additional information see E. Campbell, 'The archaeology of writing in the time of Adomnán', in J.M. Wooding (ed.), *Adomnán of Iona*, 139–44.

It seems clear from the excavations that between the sixth and the ninth centuries the site at Portmahomack functioned as a relatively important monastery. This was, as Martin Carver has said, 'a learned and literate community' with workshops in which metal ecclesiastical objects and sculpted stone items could be made that were the equivalent of similar objects from Iona and the contemporary monasteries in Ireland. Manuscripts could have been (and probably were) prepared from scratch there, that is from the first killing of the calves to the curing of the vellum and probably right through the whole process of book-making to the creation of the written word. The settlement had a 'strong economic basis, both agricultural and industrial, which, we can suggest, peaked in the eighth century'. The names in use at the site and its vicinity hint strongly at some connection, at least, with Colum Cille. The evidence of the excavation suggests that the monastery came to an end sometime between 800 and 1100, possibly from a large-scale destructive fire. Was that fire accidental or deliberate? While there can be no certainty about those responsible, Martin Carver has concluded that 'the Vikings must currently remain the prime suspects'.

The investigations of this site are far from over and we can expect as much interesting material to come from the excavations in the future as has appeared in the past. The director of the project, Prof. Martin Carver, has said:

> At present we are entitled to believe that Portmahomack was Columba's port, founded during his expedition in the 6th century on the nearest thing that the saint could find to an island at the opposite end of the Great Glen to Iona. This peninsula estate, with its landing beach and portage, developed over the next 250 years in close association with both Dalriada and Northumbria, while maintaining the substrate of Pictish culture that survived in its symbols. By AD 800, the peninsula was the object of massive investment in the form of some of the most impressive monumental sculpture known from Early-medieval Europe. Placed at the edges of the peninsula overlooking the surrounding seas, the huge and complex cross-slabs functioned as seamarks and portals to a famous if ephemeral ecclesiastical centre – an 'Iona of the East'.[20]

It seems clear that in the later sixth and seventh century, missionaries associated with Iona were extremely active in spreading the Christian faith and culture (with a distinctively Irish tinge to it) throughout the Pictish territories. At least to some extent, this seems to have originated with Columba himself. In the context of the aftermath of the Easter calculation controversy, and probably also as a reaction to what was seen as an excessive Dál Riata or Irish influence in those territories,[21] Columban influence seems

[20] *Ibid.*, 29.
[21] Smyth, *Warlords*, 178.

to have received something of a setback among the Picts in the early part of the eighth century under their king Nechtan. However, with the coming to power of Constantín son of Fergus as king of the Picts around 789 something of a Columban revival seems to have occurred.[22] Constantín, who died in 820, actually belonged to the Cenél Gabráin segment of the Dál Riata and became king of those people separately in 811. He was known in the Pictish king lists as Castantin son of Uurguist.[23] His brother Óengus or Unuist was also listed as a king of the Picts.

Several medieval traditions attributed to Colum Cille the foundation of the church of Dunkeld in Perthshire, although modern scholars tended to associate its establishment with the Dál Riata king, Cináed mac Ailpín who is credited also with uniting the Dál Riata 'Scots' and the Picts into the kingdom of Alba or Scotland, around 849. Cináed certainly did transfer some of the relics of Colum Cille to that church making of it what William Reeves called an 'inland Iona'. However, Alfred Smyth has pointed out that it is more likely that it was Constantín son of Fergus who re-founded the church of Dunkeld, probably having 'revitalized an older Columban monastery there'.[24] There are several references in the Irish annals to Dunkeld during the ninth, tenth and eleventh centuries, including the fact that in 1027 it was 'totally burned'. For the rulers of the new kingdom of Scotland, Dunkeld gradually assumed the former role that had been the prerogative of the monastery of Iona. This great change was partly brought about, at least at first, as a result of the Viking raids on Iona and later by the Norse settlements in the Western Isles.

Paradoxically Óengus son of Fergus, Constantín's brother, who died in 834 is credited with the foundation (or, more accurately, the re-foundation) of the church of Kilremonth (*Cinrigh Móna*) in Fife, later known more famously as St Andrews.[25] The death of an abbot of *Cinrigh Móna* is recorded in the Annals of Ulster as early as 747, underlying the fact that it existed in some form long before the time of Óengus. St Andrew, one of the apostles and a brother of Saint Peter, had, of course, no direct connection with Scotland but, following its introduction there, his cult would subsequently eclipse that of Colum Cille and the other local early medieval saints. Eventually, in the later Middle Ages, and for reasons arising from what we might call contemporary British ecclesiastical politics, Andrew – rather than Colum Cille – would become recognised as the official patron saint of Scotland.

---

[22] Henderson & Henderson, *The Art of the Picts*, 191: Smyth, *Warlords*, 186.

[23] *Ibid.*, 177.

[24] *Ibid.*, 186.

[25] *Ibid.* See also discussion about Constantín and Oengus in Clancy, 'Díarmait *sapientissimus*', 220–1 and further references cited there.

The Cult of Saint Columba on the Continent of Europe

> Although he lived in this small and remote island of the Britannic ocean, he merited that his name should not only be illustriously renowned throughout our Ireland, and throughout Britain, the greatest of all the islands of the whole world; but that it should reach even as far as three-cornered Spain, and Gaul, and Italy situated beyond the Pennine Alps; also Rome itself, which is the chief of all cities.
>
> Adomnán,
> *Vita Columbae* (*c.*700)

About twenty-five years ago I was visiting Dar Es Salaam, the capital of Tanzania in east Africa. There were several mosques in the immediate vicinity of where I was staying, however the nearest religious building was actually a Presbyterian church dedicated to St Columba. I am sure that similar dedications can be found in even the most unexpected of places around the world, particularly where Irish and Scottish missionaries or settlers have been active in the past.

Unlike from Adomnán himself,[1] we get very little sense of Columba's awareness of the wider world apart from Ireland and Britain except, of course, through his acquaintance with the Bible and other church literature. Adomnán tells a story about one of the monks on Iona who on one occasion saw the saint's face become very flushed and enquired from him what was the cause. The saint said that he had seen a vision of terrible retribution having been meted out 'in a distant part of the world'. He said that 'sulphurous' fire had been poured from heaven on a Roman city within the borders of Italy and that three thousand men as well as countless women and children had been killed there. He further predicted that Gaulish sailors would later come

[1] See, for example, Anderson & Anderson, *Columba*, 458–61 and 540–3.

'to the chief place of the district [near to Iona]' and confirm the story. Various historians have attempted to work out the identity of the city in question since Notker Balbulus writing about the 890s suggested 'the city in Italy which is now called "New"'. Richard Sharpe has reviewed the evidence pointing out that since the seventeenth century a favourite identification has been Citta Nuova in Istria (present-day Novigrad in Croatia) although there is nothing in the work of either Adomnán or Notker Balbulus to support that suggestion.[2] Sharpe himself thinks that Balbulus may have been referring to the 'new city' or *Neapolis* – known to us as Naples, and that the ninth-century writer may have assumed that an eruption of the Vesuvius volcano is what was intended. But, again, there is nothing in the *Vita Columbae* either to support or contradict such an identification.

We have seen above how the name and reputation of Colum Cille had been spread throughout Ireland, Scotland and the northern parts of England from the late sixth century onward. But despite Adomnán's understandable exaggeration in the quotation used above, it is quite unlikely that the saint's fame had spread widely in Europe by the time that the ninth abbot of Iona was writing his *Vita Columbae* around 700. It is clear, however, as we will see below that some awareness of the cult did arrive on the continent about or shortly after that date and that the situation would change in the century that followed.

Jean Michel Picard points out that the cults of the Irish saints Patrick, Brigid and Columbanus, were introduced to and spread throughout many parts of the continent of Europe in the seventh century, and have survived more or less down to the present day.[3] Colum Cille is in a somewhat different league; his cult is hardly known at present and even in medieval times it was not as widespread or as well known as the others listed above. In fact, it is clear that because of the alternative form of his name in Latin – Columba, the identity of Colum Cille was occasionally confused with that of the similarly named Irish saint Columbanus of Luxeuil and Bobbio, as well as with the female saint Columba of Sens. Sens is about seventy miles southeast of Paris. This confusion with a number of other persons may have contributed to the early disappearance of Colum Cille's cult in some parts of the continent where it had previously existed. However, a lot of sporadic evidence survives showing that the saint was known in several parts of what are now Austria, Belgium, France, Germany, Italy, Luxembourg and Switzerland as well as, in various transmogrified forms, in other parts of continental Europe.

---

[2] Sharpe, *Adomnán*, 289.

[3] Picard, 'The cult of Colum Cille in continental Europe', 2. That paper and also J. Picard, 'The Cult of Columba in Lotharingia (9th–11th Centuries): The Manuscript Evidence', in J. Carey, M. Herbert and P. Ó Riain, *Studies in Irish Hagiography: Saints and Scholars* (Dublin 2001), 221–36, form the basis of most of what follows in this section.

Prof. Picard tells us that the earliest trace of the cult of the saint on the continent occurs in a text known as the Calendar of Willibrord, which is found in a manuscript that dates to around or shortly after 700, about the same time that Adomnán was writing the *Vita Columbae*. The manuscript containing the Calendar of Willibrord originally came from the monastery of Echternach. Echternach is now in Luxembourg and we have seen above that the early medieval monastery there had several other connections with Ireland, as did Willibrord himself.[4] The Calendar correctly and unambiguously lists 9 June as the feast day of *Sanctus Columcilla*. From the outset it also listed Saint Patrick and Saint Brigid but, a few decades later, the name of Saint Aidan of Lindisfarne – another Irish Columban saint, was added. The citing of Colum Cille among the original listings in the Calendar demonstrates that already by that early date he was numbered as one of the three most important saints of Ireland along with Patrick and Brigid. Prof. Picard shows us that this trio continued to be revered as special, not least in the Irish monastery at Ratisbon or Regensburg on the Danube founded in the eleventh century.

The arrival of a copy of Adomnán's *Vita Columbae* on the continent was the next most important step in the diffusion of the saint's cult there. That copy was almost certainly the one made by Dorbéne before he died in 713. That particular manuscript, which still survives in the town library of Schaffhausen in Switzerland, appears to have been the source of all the other copies and abridgments of the saint's Life made on the continent in later times. Prof. Picard believes that it might have been brought from Iona to the continent very shortly after it was finished, almost definitely at some point in the eighth century.[5] He also suggested that it may have been originally taken to one or other of the monasteries associated with the Irish Saint Fursa in northern France and Belgium, such as Peronne or Fosses. It may even have been brought there as a result of a specific request for a copy from one of those monasteries where the cult of the saint already seems to have been known. The place most likely to have provided the common links between these various institutions could have been the monastery of Louth in Ireland, with which both Iona and Peronne had close associations. Other material relating to Adomnán and Iona seems to have passed to the continent by way of these monasteries also.

[4] Ó Cróinín, 'Rath Melsigi'.

[5] However Dr Picard's views have recently been challenged by Thomas Clancy who argues that the manuscript may have been brought from Iona to the monastery of Saint Gall in the middle of the ninth century by Díarmait, abbot of the latter monastery. Dr Clancy also suggests that, on the same occasion, Díarmait could have informed Walafrid Strabo about the martyrdom of the Iona monk, Blathmac, which Strabo would subsequently write about (see below) – 'Díarmait *sapientissimus*', 228–9.

A study of the provenance and context of the oldest known (mid-ninth-century) continental copy of the Dorbéne manuscript – from the monastery of St-Mihiel in Lorraine, France – also suggests that there was a connection with the Peronne or Fosses area, a region in which Irish monks of the period were particularly active. The cult of Saint Colum Cille was also known in the Metz area of Lorraine. However, around Metz there seems to have been some confusion with the cult of Saint Columbanus, arising from the fact that the latter had actually visited that area in 610 and there were consequently several monasteries in the surrounding district associated with him.

Prof. Picard tells us that the cult of Colum Cille seems to have been revived in the Metz area again in the middle of the tenth century with the arrival of a fresh wave of Irish monks to the region. Of particular interest in this regard is the Benedictine monk Cathróe who was abbot of the monastery of Waulsort for about three or four years before 950. The monastery at Waulsort on the River Meuse had originally been founded by the local lords as a refuge for Irish pilgrims travelling on the continent; it retained its distinctly Irish character for some time afterwards.[6] Cathróe must have acquired a reputation as an excellent abbot as he was later asked by the local bishop to move to the monastery of St Félix in Metz. Cathróe died in 978 and about four or five years later his hagiographical Life, the *Vita Cadroe*, was written at the monastery of St Felix by a monk called Hermann.

The Life tells us that Cathróe's parents lived in Scotland. At first his mother had been unable to have a child. Repeatedly she prayed to many saints in an attempt to become fertile but her petitions were unsuccessful. However, having made a pilgrimage to the tomb of Saint Colum Cille she became pregnant. The 'tomb' in question may actually have been a shrine of the saint's relics at Dunkeld in Scotland. Later Saint Colum Cille himself appeared in a vision to the lady and impressed on her that if she did become pregnant she was to dedicate her child to the service of God and the church. At last she gave birth to a boy, but when he eventually reached the appropriate age his father refused to let him enter the church as a novice. As a result, the father was himself struck down with illness in consequence of Colum Cille's anger. The mother was forced again to pray to the saint on behalf of her husband and Cathróe did eventually join the church, later going to the monastery at Armagh in Ireland for clerical training. Whatever about these legends, when the genuinely historical Cathróe eventually settled in the Metz area he seems to have brought with him his devotion to Saint Colum Cille which was subsequently reflected in some of the contemporary literature produced in that district.

[6] Picard, 'The Cult of Columba', 230.

About the same time that the Life of Cathróe was being written in Metz, a new version of Adomnán's *Vita Columbae* was also produced there. This is a shortened version which contains only about a sixth of the original text. However, unlike other abbreviated versions where a great deal of the Irish material – especially Irish personal and place names – is deleted, the Metz version was clearly written by an educated Irish person who lived about the year 1000. Prof. Picard has shown, for example, that the person in question was fully familiar with the changes that had taken place in the Irish language between Adomnán's time and his own day, particularly the changes that had occurred in the writing of names. It is also clear that instead of the St Mihiel copy of the *Vita Columbae* mentioned above, the compiler of the Metz version used as his exemplar a text very close to Dorbéne's copy – possibly even that manuscript itself. In turn, the Metz version was copied later into manuscripts of the eleventh, twelfth and thirteenth centuries although, again, there was frequent confusion with St Columbanus in some of those. This resulted in Colum Cille often being commemorated on 23 November – Columbanus's feast day – rather than on his own, 9 June.

A shortened version of the *Vita Columbae*, dating to the twelfth and thirteenth centuries but also based ultimately on the Dorbéne copy, circulated in northeastern France in the Cambrai and St-Omer region. That version was later attributed inaccurately to Cumméne, the seventh abbot of Iona who had died in 669. In fact Cumméne did write a study in Latin which Adomnán refers to as 'the book on the miraculous powers of Saint Columba', but that is not the text that circulated in the Cambrai and St Omer region. However, a quotation from Cumméne's book, the only portion that actually does survive, was inserted into Dorbéne's copy of the *Vita Columbae*, apparently on Iona, after that text had been completed. An appropriate gap had been left in the original text for the Cumméne quotation to be inserted later. This was clearly written by the same scribe as the main text but in much smaller lettering.[7]

Prof. Picard also outlines the evidence for the veneration of the name of Colum Cille in western France: in Normandy, Brittany, Anger, Le Mans and the Poitiers region, as well as in other places. Again there is occasional confusion with the French female saint Columba of Sens. In Brittany there is even a place called Plougoulm, 'the parish of Colum', which is almost certainly named after Colum Cille. Prof. Picard draws special attention to the celebrations for the feast day of Colum Cille at Trinity Abbey in Vendome. There the Irish monk is included along with several of the major saints of the universal church. At the monastery of St Évroult in Normandy, the twelfth-century chronicler Orderic Vital noted positively how Queen Margaret of

[7] Anderson & Anderson, *Adomnán*, 474, note 6.

Scotland had provided funds for the restoration of the ruined monastery on Iona, 'which the servant of Christ Columba had built'.

Perhaps in the second half of the ninth century, a little later than the time that the St-Mihiel version of the *Vita Columbae* mentioned above was being copied in the episcopal school at Reims – presumably from an intermediate copy now lost, another copy was being made directly from Dorbéne's manuscript in the Sankt Gallen area in present-day Switzerland. We know that Dorbéne's manuscript was in the relatively close by monastery of Reichenau by the tenth century. It is well known that the monasteries at all these places had numerous associations around that time with Ireland or with Irish monks. However, there seems to have been some knowledge of Colum Cille at the monastery of Reichenau before Dorbéne's manuscript arrived there. Walafrid Strabo, the German cleric who was born in 808 and died as abbot of that monastery in 849, had begun his studies there as early as 815. He became abbot of that monastery in 838. We know that during his varied career he met many Irish monks and learned a great deal about other Irish missionary saints such as Saint Columbanus and Saint Gall. He would eventually write a long poem in Latin about the martyrdom of Blathmac, a leading monk of Iona who was slain by the Vikings in 825. Of course the Vikings had raided Iona several times before that date, but in 825 they attacked the monastery again and slew Blathmac and his companion monks because the latter had refused to reveal the hiding place of the valuable ornamental shrine that contained the relics of their founder saint.

Walafrid Strabo was distinguished as a theologian and a man of letters, and had written poetry as well as various other pieces of Irish interest, especially a Life of Saint Gall and, in verse, the Life of Blathmac.[8]

> A certain island lies off the Pictish shores, floating above the billowy sea; known as Iona, there the saint of the Lord, Columba, rests in the flesh …
>
> The golden dawn shone forth, dissipating the dewy dusk, and the brilliant sun glittered with beautiful roundness, when this holy teacher, celebrating the holy service of the mass, stood before the sacred altar as a calf without stain, a pleasing offering to God, to be sacrificed by the threatening sword. The others of the community were prostrate, commending to the Thunderer, with tears and prayers, their souls that were about to depart from the burden of the flesh …
>
> The violent, cursed host came rushing through the unprotected buildings, threatening cruel perils to the holy men; then having slain with mad savagery the rest of the community they approached the holy father [Blathmac], to force him to surrender the precious metals wherein lay the holy bones of Saint Columba; but the monks had removed the shrine from its stand and placed

[8] Kenney, *Sources,* 550–1.

> it in the ground, in a hollowed space under a thick sod ... In this way he became a martyr for Christ's name; and, as rumours testify, he is buried in that same place, and there many miracles occur on account of his holy merits.

Jean Michel Picard notes how Walafrid Strabo's actual knowledge of Saint Columba, as indicated in the Iona poem, seems to be very meagre. The saint is mentioned only incidentally in relation to the concealed relics. Strabo shows none of the knowledge he would necessarily have had if he had been acquainted with the contents of Adomnán's *Vita Columbae.* Consequently it seems certain that Dorbéne's manuscript had yet to arrive at Reichenau when Strabo wrote there. Fifty years or so later, however, the manuscript seems to have been definitely in the region. This is revealed in the Martyrology written by another German monk Notker Balbulus, mentioned above, who died in 912 at the relatively nearby abbey of Saint Gall (Sankt Gallen). Under 9 June, the correct feast day, Balbulus gives a full entry on Saint Columba, or Colum Cille as he also calls him. He quotes liberally from Adomnán's *Vita Columbae* and includes a discussion of the mysterious city in Italy mentioned above on which sulphurous fire had rained. Almost certainly he was using Dorbéne's manuscript copy of the text. However, he incorrectly gives Colum Cille the credit for educating Saint Comgall of Bangor. This is probably because the latter, in turn, was said to have taught Saint Columbanus who was, of course, the master of Saint Gall who was the founder of Balbulus's own monastery. Balbulus was, in fact, drawing a kind of apostolic succession – inaccurately as it happens, from Saint Colum Cille down to Saint Gall.

A greatly shortened copy of the *Vita Columbae* was also produced at the monastery of Sankt Gallen between 841 and 872, under the abbacy of Grimoald. That text was later copied and circulated very widely in Europe throughout the whole of the Middle Ages, but it concentrated mainly on the miraculous deeds of the saint and largely ignored details about Iona and Ireland. As Prof. Picard points out, even proper personal and place names were deleted from that text later in its history, being seen as having little or no interest or relevance for its non-Irish and non-Scottish continental readership.

Prof. Picard also shows how, in the following centuries, the cult of Colum Cille spread widely in some of the German regions. He points to the evidence of calendars and martyrologies – even relics – in Swabia and Bavaria. There were said to have been bones of the saint at Sankt Gallen in the ninth and tenth centuries. The relics, allegedly of Saint Columba of Sens at the nearby monastery of Pfäfers, are more likely to have been originally associated with Colum Cille. That saint's relics were also to be found in the fourteenth century at the monastery of Hirsau in the Black Forest, west of Stuttgart. Colum Cille was also included in a list of saints venerated at the cathedral in Basel in

Switzerland and, along with other Irish saints, in litanies at the monastery of Mondsee in eastern Bavaria. In the later tenth century we find Colum Cille's name listed in ecclesiastical sources in Strasbourg. A century later he is listed in documents belonging to the cathedrals at Augsburg and Merseburg. Many of these later references seem to have originated in contacts with the monastery of Sankt Gallen. By the twelfth century the cult of Colum Cille was being commemorated at what is now Novacella in the Italian Tyrol.

A list of abbots of the monastery on Iona, preserved in the confraternity book of the abbey of Saint Peter in Salzburg in Austria, seems to have come from a somewhat different source. Around 742 an Irishman named Virgilius or Fergal, who had almost certainly been a monk at Iona, went to Gaul and Bavaria. Eventually he took charge of the diocese of Salzburg through his position of abbot at the monastery of Saint Peter there. He was consecrated as bishop in 755. A number of texts about him survive, including a letter from Pope Zachary that suggests that Virgilius was a believer in the heretical theory of the antipodes: 'that there are another world and other men under the earth'.[9] The Salzburg list of Iona abbots concludes with the name of Slébéne who died in 767 and, based on an analysis of the linguistic evidence inherent in the text, it is possible to see that it must have been drawn up by an Irish person around that time.

Ian Fisher has drawn attention to another possible connection between Virgilius and Iona. St John's Cross on Iona is a composite work made up from several pieces of carved stone. The four pieces that form the distinctive ring at the centre of the cross are made from a local stone, whereas the main elements were formed from a stone specially imported to Iona from the Scottish mainland. Fisher considers that the ring pieces were added to the cross later than its initial construction, possibly as a repair to an original ringless cross. A close visual parallel for the layout of the ornamental features on that hypothesised ringless cross would have been the metal-plated wooden example known as the Rupertus Cross from Bischofshofen in Austria, which was probably made by an Anglo–Saxon craftsman for Virgilius in the third quarter of the eighth century.[10]

In addition to the evidence for the cult of Saint Colum Cille on the continent that can be gleaned from medieval manuscripts, Prof. Picard has also discussed the evidence available in the folkloric sources. As we have seen above, Colum Cille appears as a character frequently in the folklore of Scotland and Ireland. What is slightly more surprising is the extent to which he (even if somewhat transmogrified) figured in folklore on the continent as

[9] Kenney, *Sources*, 523–6.
[10] Fisher, *Early Medieval Sculpture*, 15 and 22.

well. As in Irish folklore, and indeed as adverted to by Adomnán in the *Vita Columbae*, Colum Cille was believed to have had particularly effective powers for modifying or altering weather conditions. A fourteenth-century Munich manuscript contains the instructions for a charm in which a prayer to Saint Colum Cille has to be written on four sheets of paper and buried in the ground in the four corners of the district to be protected.

> Saint Colum Cille, take away all bad storms
> As when you recited the prayer sent to you from Heaven
> By the voice of Saint Michael when you departed this world.

The phrase, 'the prayer sent to you from Heaven', may be an indirect reference to the poem *Noli Pater Indulgere* discussed above. Prof. Picard draws attention to the similarity with traditions surrounding an allegedly female saint, Kakukilla (apparently, a corruption of the name Colum Cille), outlined in a manuscript of the sixteenth century from the monastery of Linköping in Sweden, who is called on to give protection against fire. The same saint (although sometimes regarded as a male rather than a female) was invoked against infestations of rats and mice in Sweden and Germany. This is paralleled, of course, in Irish Columban lore by the folk beliefs surrounding the Tory and Gartan Clays mentioned above, which are also used as a protection against rats and similar infestations. Paintings of St Kakukilla with rats or mice are found in some medieval churches in Sweden. Sometimes she is depicted as spinning, with a mouse running up the thread. In other places, such as over the pulpit in a fifteenth-century Swedish church at Kaga near Linköping, she appears as if she is being attacked by a group of rats. Whatever the origins of the cult of St Kakukilla in Sweden, it should be remembered that the cult of St Colum Cille himself may have arrived in Scandinavia also by means of the devotion to him among the Norse of the Hebridean islands. This became widespread following their conversion to Christianity. That conversion seems to have been carried out mainly by the monks of the Columban federation centred on Iona.

German folklorists had concluded that Kakukilla was an assemblage of disparate elements derived on the continent from both the cults of Colum Cille and Saint Gertrude of Nivelles, perhaps combined also with some aspects of the cult of Saint Columba of Sens. Saint Gertrude, although not Irish herself, was known to have had several Irish associations. Kakukilla also features in similar prayers in manuscripts from both Helmstedt in Germany east of Hannover, and Oxford. Prof. Picard suggests that the relics of Saint Kakukilla in the Holy Cross church at Schwäbisch Gmund, east of Stuttgart, were most probably those of Colum Cille in reality, as it was relatively close to the church of Hirsau where relics of the Iona saint were definitely kept in the later Middle Ages. Prof. Picard also tells us that invocations against the plague in the northwest of France may originally have involved prayers to Saint Colum Cille.

Despite these widespread manifestations of some awareness of the cult of Saint Colum Cille, Prof. Picard concludes that interest in that saint was developed mainly in areas of the continent where there were other concrete Irish associations. Unlike some other major Irish saints whose cults spread independently of the Irish themselves, veneration of Colum Cille seems to have been propagated in Europe mainly by travelling Irish monks. Other than among 'specialist' scholars of medieval times, the 'historical' figure of Columba had effectively disappeared on the continent by the late fourteenth century. It was subsequently replaced by the folk creation of Kakukilla. Only with the invention of printing and the early publications of versions of Adomnán's *Vita Columbae* in 1549 and 1604, as we will see below, did some knowledge of the saint of Iona begin to circulate in continental Europe once again.

The Comarb of Colum Cille and the Monastery of Kells

Beloved are Durrow and Derry,
Beloved Raphoe of no ills,
Beloved Drumhome of sweet acorns,
Beloved is Swords, as is Kells.

Attributed to Colum Cille
(*c.*11th or 12th century)

As we have seen above, the practice of Pictish kings being buried in a cemetery on Iona seems to have commenced from fairly early in its history. The same custom seems to have spread eventually among Irish kings. In 791 Artgal son of Cathal, king of Connacht, died on Iona. He was possibly on pilgrimage there or, alternatively, had retired to the island to live out his last days in retreat. Similarly Niall Frossach, who had been king of Tara until 770 when he retired to Iona, died there in 778. One wonders if the great flowering of sculptural and artistic activity on the island in the second half of the eighth century, which has given us the three magnificent crosses – St John's Cross, St Oran's Cross and St Martin's Cross and most probably the Book of Kells also – might in some way be connected with the patronage that must have accompanied the retired king of Tara. Unfortunately the close relationship between the Comarba of Colum Cille [literally the 'heir' or 'successor' of Colum Cille – the title used for the abbots of Iona] and the kings of Tara was to receive a major setback in 797.

In that year the then king of Tara Donnchad son of Domnall Mide died. Donnchad's family, who were based in what is now County Westmeath, had been very supportive of the Columban confederation or *familia.* They were especially connected with the monastery at Durrow which, up to that time, was probably the chief church in Ireland associated with the saint. Donnchad was succeeded as king of Tara by Áed Ingor ('Áed the Undutiful') of the Cenél nÉogain from Donegal. However, unlike their Cenél Conaill neighbours, the Cenél nÉogain generally supported the aspirations to superiority in Irish ecclesiastical matters of Saint Patrick's church at Armagh rather than the monastic confederation associated with Saint Colum Cille. As F.J. Byrne has noted, Áed also became known in the later lists of kings (but apparently not in the contemporary annals) 'as Áed Oirdnide, "the ordained", and he may possibly be the first king of Tara to have been inaugurated ecclesiastically'.[1] Several authors have pointed out that Áed's ordination ceremony may have taken place in 804 at a 'meeting of the synods of the Uí Néill in Dún Cuair [just to the north of Enfield, County Meath] presided over by Connmach, abbot of Armagh'.[2]

Other contemporaneous matters were bringing about major changes in the fortunes of the Columban *familia*, as well as to the monastery on Iona. In 795 the island was attacked by the Vikings for the first time as was, possibly, the Columban monastery on Lambay Island, just north of Dublin. The only doubt about this latter attack arises because, as we have seen above, the original name of Lambay – *Rechru*, was also the name of Rathlin Island off the coast of County Antrim and probably also of an island off the coast of County Donegal adjacent to *Gleann Cholm Cille*, the present Rathlin O'Birne.

In 802 Iona was attacked again and burned and, in 806, sixty-eight persons were killed on the island by the 'heathens'. Although we have no documentation describing it, it is apparent that the authorities must have decided that something had to be done about this change in circumstances.

A line from an eleventh-century poem, added in the margins of the Annals of Ulster for the year 804, says that Kells in present-day County Meath 'was given without battle to the melodious Colum Cille [*Colum Chille cheolach*] this year'. In 807 the annals record the 'building of the new monastery of Colum Cille at Kells'. Precisely how the Columban church acquired the site at Kells is not clear. Charles Doherty has suggested that the land was granted by the church of Armagh and that the so-called stone cross of 'Patrick and Columba' at Kells commemorates that event.[3] Doherty also points out that in the Book of Armagh which was also being written in Armagh that same year, 807, the name of the abbot of Iona, Cellach, written in Greek letters, is entered in the margin opposite the following passage from the Gospel of St Mark:

---

[1] Byrne, *Irish Kings*, 159.

[2] Annals of Ulster, 804.7.

[3] C. Doherty, 'The Vikings in Ireland: a Review', in H. Clarke, M. Ní Mhaonaigh & R. Ó Floinn (eds), *Ireland and Scandinavia in the Early Viking Age* (Dublin 1998), 310–11.

> For in those days there will be such tribulation as has not been from the beginning of the creation which God created until now, and never will be. And if the Lord had not shortened the days, no human being would be saved; but for the sake of the elect, whom he chose, he shortened the days. (13:19–20)

In 814 the annals say that 'Cellach the abbot of Iona, when the building of the church of Kells was finished, resigned the office of superior, and Díarmait, the *alumnus* of Daigre, was appointed in his place.'[4] This has usually been taken to mean that Cellach retired from the office of abbot of Iona and went to live in the new monastery at Kells. That monastery seems to have been built as a sort of refuge for at least some of the relics and the monks of Iona, its inland location safe from the attacks of the sea-marauding Vikings. Kells [in Irish *Cennanas*, 'head' or 'chief place'] had been referred to in ancient sources on several occasions prior to the construction of the monastery there. Its traditions claimed that it had been a royal site in prehistoric times. It seems probable that Áed the king of Tara at the time, who as we have seen came from what is now Inishowen in Donegal, was also involved in giving the site at Kells to the church – as it were, killing two birds with the one stone: that is he provided a site for the Iona monks and simultaneously deprived his southern rivals of an important royal centre. That sort of practice can be seen repeatedly in the behaviour of early Irish kings and, as has been argued above, may well explain the choice of Derry as the location for a Columban monastery in the sixth century.

It has often been asked why Kells was chosen as the site for this refuge from Iona. Surely if the traditions later claimed for it were correct, Derry, for example, would have been a more appropriate destination. But, despite the legends it is unlikely, as we have seen above that Colum Cille was the founder of the monastery of Derry. It was certainly not his first monastery nor indeed the one 'most loved by him'. Such a tradition dates to a much later period than the life of the saint and probably post-dates the foundation of the monastery at Kells. On the other hand Kells was located in territory controlled by the southern Uí Néill kings who had been well disposed to the Columban community for most of the previous century.[5] Moreover, as has been argued above also, that site, which was probably already some kind of existing 'royal enclosure', may have been given to the Columban community by the king of Tara in a sort of sleight of hand.

The monastery founded there is undoubtedly most famous because of its association with the Book of Kells – 'the most precious object in the western

[4] For a full discussion of Díarmait's career, see Clancy, 'Díarmait *sapientissimus*'.

[5] Herbert, *Iona*, chs 4 and 5. Most of what is written here is based on those chapters.

world' as the Annals of Ulster described it in 1007. The Book of Kells is the greatest of all the ornamented manuscripts from the early Christian period in these islands – an apotheosis; it is one of the world's greatest artistic achievements.[6] Basically it is an illustrated copy of the four Gospels. As we now have it there are 340 folios, each page about 13 inches by 10 inches. We know that originally there must have been about thirty more folios which probably included some of the more elaborately decorated pages. The folios are made from vellum, the prepared skin of very young – or even aborted – calves. Approximately one hundred and eighty animals were needed to make this one volume. It has been estimated that it would have taken a herd of about twelve hundred cattle to produce enough vellum to make the manuscript.

The decoration was not completed by those who originally devised it. Although it is a consummate work of art, the Book of Kells nevertheless contains several errors and corrections. In one instance a hole in the vellum has been repaired and the writing continued across the patch. We know that it is a collective work, although experts have differed about the precise number of contributors involved in its production. It appears that four separate scribes and two or three different painters or illuminators worked on it; some of the latter may have been responsible for parts of the calligraphy as well. Attempts have been made in modern times to estimate how much work was involved in making such a complex artefact and it has been suggested that even one major illustration – such as the fabulously intricate *Chi Rho* page, would have taken about a month to produce. The decorations and illustrations in the book draw from the full range of contemporary artistic traditions in these islands, as well as some from further afield. There is a definite decorative and iconographic plan for the book, with an apparent emphasis on Eucharistic themes.

Like the other related manuscripts – such as the Book of Durrow – there has been a great deal of discussion about when and where the Book of Kells was made. We know that it was in Kells in its ornamented *cumhdach* or shrine box when it was stolen in 1007. Like an old family Bible, it was used in the twelfth century to record permanently some of the property transactions of the monastery of Kells. These notes and entries – known as the 'Kell's charters' – are extremely informative about the life of the settlement at that time. Early in the second half of the seventeenth century the book was sent from Kells to Dublin 'for safety'. It was subsequently acquired by the library of Trinity College, where, displayed as a treasured 'icon' in formidable security and conservation conditions, it is still visited daily by thousands of people.

[6] There is, of course, a huge discursive literature about the Book of Kells. See esp. O'Mahony, *Book of Kells*. An excellent summary description and outline of some of the academic issues can be found in Bernard Meehan, *The Book of Kells* (London 1994, reprinted 1996). See also Bernard Meehan, *The Book of Kells* (London 2012).

Scholars disagree about the date of the book. That debate has a bearing on the identification of the place of its creation as the construction of the monastery of Kells does not seem to have been completed prior to 814. Most scholars now seem to accept that the manuscript was made in the scriptorium on Iona – conventionally around the year 800 although a much earlier date, *c.*750, has been suggested by Ian Fisher.[7] Some commentators have argued that it was made as a great display object – in effect an *hommage* in honour of the founder Saint Colum Cille around the time of the second centenary of his death in the 790s or, according to Fisher, for the occasion of the earlier enshrinement of his relics. Parallels are often drawn between the illustrations in the book and the designs on the three surviving, magnificent high crosses on Iona: Saint Oran's Cross, Saint John's Cross and Saint Martin's Cross. These are usually said to have been completed (in that order) from the middle to the end of the eighth century. Two of the crosses – Saint Oran's and Saint Martin's, have depictions of the relatively rare subject of the Virgin and Child, as does the Book of Kells. The same theme is also alluded to in the eighth-century poem mentioned above *Cantemus in omni die*, allegedly composed by the Iona monk Cú Chuimne. It is hardly coincidental therefore that one of the very few early medieval sculptural depictions of that subject in Ireland is on a later cross at another Columban monastery, Drumcliff in County Sligo. Among its other claims to fame, the Book of Kells also contains what is probably the oldest representation of the Devil in western art.

Giving an alternative opinion, Charles Doherty has suggested that the book may have been made on the occasion of the establishment of the new Columban church at Kells:

> The building of Kells was nothing less than the recreation of the Temple of the Lord upon the earth. Monastic churchmen schooled on the Psalter since childhood would have seen the Temple as the 'seat of justice for the oppressed'. Indeed it has been suggested that the 'Hiberno–Latin glosses on the Psalms in Codex Palatinus Latinus 68, the original text of which dates to *c.*700 AD, 'were of the *paruchia* [confederation of churches] of St Columba in Northumbria and Ireland, and possibly also in Iona'. There can hardly have been a more fitting time for the creation of a book such as the Book of Kells. It was surely created to adorn the altar of the new church, the *templum*, on its consecration in 814.[8]

The foundation of the monastery at Kells did not of course mean the end of its mother institution on Iona, although the monastery there did continue

[7] Fisher, 'The monastery of Iona', 47.

[8] Doherty, a Review, 311–12, where he refers also to M. McNamara (ed.) *Glossa in Psalmos: the Hiberno–Latin Gloss on the Psalms of Codex Palatinus Latinus 68* (Studi e testi, 310, Vatican City 1986), 76.

to suffer at the hands of the Vikings. In 825 they attacked Iona again and slew the monk Blathmac and his companions because they refused to reveal the hiding place of the valuable ornamental shrine that contained the relics of their founder. The story of that incident, as has been outlined above, eventually reached Walafrid Strabo. In 838 he became abbot of the monastery at Reichenau, now in southern Germany, where there were Irish monks as well as other Irish connections. For example, the library at Reichenau preserved Dorbéne's copy of Adomán's *Vita Columbae* until the seventeenth century, at least.

The relic shrine on Iona was not discovered by the Vikings in 825, unlike the shrine of Adomnán which was stolen by the 'heathens' in 832 from *Domnach Maigen* – possibly Donaghmoyne in present-day County Monaghan or alternatively some site near to Lambay Island. There must have been more than one collection or container of the relics of Colum Cille as, in 829, Díarmait the abbot of Iona is said to have taken them back with him from Ireland to Scotland. Two years later he returned with them to Ireland. His successor, Indrechtach ua Finechta, also brought relics of Colum Cille to Ireland in 849.

Relics of the saints in medieval times included – primarily – parts of their bodily remains as well as secondary items said to have been associated with them. A third category of relics included objects (very often of cloth) which had, at least, touched the primary relics. Adomnán mentions that Colum Cille's tunic and books in the saint's handwriting were used to end a drought and to obtain favourable winds in his own time.[9] Ian Fisher and Raghnall Ó Floinn suggest, however, that the primary relics must have been enshrined in a portable container by the second half of the eighth century when we hear of the Law of Colum Cille being proclaimed in Ireland.[10] Presumably those occasions were accompanied by ceremonies that would have included the solemn public display of the saint's relics. Ó Floinn also points out as we have seen that a note in the *Additamenta* in the Book of Armagh seems to suggest that by the early ninth century at least some 'of the bones of Columb Cille from Britain' were at Saul, now in County Down.

Around 849 Cináed mac Ailpín [Kenneth Mac Alpin] united the territories of the Picts and the Scottish Dál Riata into the kingdom of Alba or Scotland, and moved his own residence – apparently in Argyll in the west – to the eastern side of the country, possibly to Forteviot or Scone. He also transferred relics of Colum Cille to the church of Dunkeld which seems to have become his new royal church. The division of the relics of the saint between Ireland and

---

[9] MacDonald, 'Adomnán's monastery', 33.

[10] Fisher, 'The monastery of Iona', 47; Ó Floinn, 'Insignia Columbae', 136–7. See also Ó Carragáin, 'The Architectural Setting', 134.

Scotland was probably on the basis of some sort of agreed apportioning. The Columban relics may actually have come to Ireland from Dunkeld rather than Iona. However, as Máire Herbert has said, all these transfers inevitably inflicted damage on the influence and status of the monastery left behind on Iona. One of the relics taken to Dunkeld may have been the crozier later known as the *Cathbuaidh* – 'victory in battle', which was carried 'successfully' as a talisman by the Scots in a battle against the Norse in 918. As George Henderson points out, the *Cathbuaidh* is shown along with a gabled shrine-chest on a thirteenth-century seal of Dunkeld Cathedral chapter.[11] It has been suggested by a number of authors that the 'practical' use of relics in this and related ways was 'an innovation of the eighth century, initiated by the Columban federation, but soon imitated by Armagh and others'.[12]

Díarmait 'the alumnus of Daigre' had become abbot of Iona in 814 following Cellach's resignation. We don't know where Díarmait came from although Thomas Clancy (who examined his life in detail) drew attention to the involvement of an Ua Daigri family in the affairs of Derry and Iona in the 11th, 12th and 13th centuries.[13] Clancy tells us that Díarmait's career as abbot was marked by a number of important developments. These included 'the rise of a powerful and influential Pictish dynasty – which by 811 may have also extended its overlordship over Dál Riata' – as well as 'Viking raids, monastic and church reform, and a new wariness between rulers and clergy'. Clancy suggests that Díarmait may have been present when the Columban clergy went to Tara in 817 to excommunicate the high-king Áed Oirdnide in connection with the killing of the *princeps* (abbot) of Raphoe. That matter will be discussed further below. Díarmait himself seems to have died between 831 and 849, possibly on the continent.[14]

At any rate, by 849 when he 'came to Ireland with the halidoms [*mindaibh*] of Colum Cille' there was a new abbot in Iona – Indrechtach. In 854 Indrechtach 'the successor of Colum Cille [and] an excellent scholar suffered a violent death among the Saxons on 12 March'. The Annals of Innisfallen says that he was on his way to Rome. William of Malmesbury (1095–143), the great Anglo-Norman chronicler, wrote a Life of a Saint Indract, the son of an Irish king who was murdered along with his companions near Glastonbury while returning from Rome. William had very little real data about his subject and, although it is almost certain that he was writing about the ninth-century abbot of Iona, he placed the story in the late seventh and early eighth centuries. Cellach son of Ailill, Indrechtach's

[11] Henderson, *Durrow*, 190.

[12] Ó Carragáin, 'The Architectural Setting', 169, note 74 and further references cited there.

[13] Díarmait *sapientissimus*, 217.

[14] *Ibid.*, esp. 220, 222–3 and 229.

successor as abbot of Iona, died more peacefully in 865 – somewhere in the territory of the Picts. He was succeeded by Feradach son of Cormac who must have been responsible for the transfer to Ireland in 878 of more relics of Colum Cille – including the saint's 'shrine', 'which were taken in flight to escape the Vikings'. Feradach died in 880.

He was succeeded by Flann mac Maíle Dúin of the Síl Lugdach, a people who originated in west Donegal – in the *Fál Carrach* and *Gort A'Choirce* area.[15] With the decline of the fortunes of Colum Cille's own people the Cenél Conaill – especially from the end of the eighth century onwards – the Síl Lugdach took on much of the mantle of the latter. Eventually they went as far as to claim, falsely for propaganda purposes, that they were actually descended from the Cenél Conaill themselves.[16] The O'Donnells were the most famous medieval family to emanate from the Síl Lugdach and a number of them – such as Manus in the sixteenth century – would become strong devotees of Saint Colum Cille. In addition, many of the sites believed – rightly or wrongly – to have been associated with the birth and early life of Colum Cille were located in the territory controlled by the Síl Lugdach, probably from the ninth century onward. The clergy of the church at Kilmacrenan, as will be explained below, were the chief guardians of the lore of Colum Cille in that area.[17] Flann mac Maíle Dúin himself may have been connected with Kilmacrenan and may have been among those involved in the cultivation of the traditions about the saint – in what would have been the homeland of both of them – before he died as abbot of Iona in 891.

Unprecedentedly, as Máire Herbert points out, Flann was succeeded as the *comarba* or 'successor' of Colum Cille – a title that seems to have come into use about the middle of the ninth century – by Máel Brigte son of Tornán. Máel Brigte had become *comarba* of Patrick in 888, that title indicating that he was the most senior ecclesiastical official at Armagh. Máel Brigte's personal name meant 'devotee of Brigid'. Therefore, as *comarba* of Patrick and Colum Cille also, his name and titles included references to all three of Ireland's medieval patron saints. He belonged to the Cenél mBógaine of southwest Donegal and died in 927. There is no evidence that he was ever actually in the monastery of Iona. His appointment indicates, however, that significant changes were occurring in the relationship between the Columban churches in Scotland and Ireland. The most obvious of these was that the position of Successor of Colum Cille, previously reserved for the abbot of Iona, was no longer confined to the holder of that office. What did seem to be of continuing importance – although apparently not always absolutely

[15] Lacey, *Lug's forgotten Donegal kingdom.*
[16] Lacey, *Cenél Conaill*, 84–96.
[17] See also Lacey, *Lug's forgotten Donegal kingdom*, esp. ch. 4.

necessary – was that the holder should have some connection with Donegal. A church and a cross dedicated to Colum Cille in Armagh, which are mentioned in the annals during the eleventh and twelfth centuries, may have been erected during the time of Máel Brigte's abbacy in order to commemorate his joint Patrician and Columban 'successorships'.[18] However, the manner in which Máel Brigte unified these different strands of the Irish ecclesiastical tradition was probably really an example of what has been called 'the aggrandisement of Armagh'. For a very long time the Columban and Patrician churches had been in some senses in competition with each other. Máel Brigte achieved what many on the Armagh side had sought for centuries.

Despite these changes Iona maintained its role as an important monastery. The deaths of its officials continue to be recorded in the annals and it continued to be the burial place of Scottish kings – with some Irish kings and later some of Norse descent also being interred there. The death of the abbot of Iona, Fiachra Ua hArtacáin, is recorded in 976. He was almost certainly related to the 'chief' Irish poet of the time Cináed ua hArtacáin who was closely associated with Amlaíb Cuaráin ('Amlaíb of the sandal'), the Norse king of Dublin.[19] Amlaíb ended his life 'in penitence' in the monastery of Iona in 980 probably having been converted to Christianity by Columban monks. There is some evidence also, as we will see further below, that Amlaíb may have had a particular involvement with the foundation or re-foundation of a number of Columban churches in what is now north County Dublin (perhaps Dublin city itself?) and County Meath: Swords, Lambay and Skreen, as well as a few others. However, those connections with the Norse king did not prevent the monastery on Iona from being attacked by a separate group of Vikings on Christmas night 986, when the abbot and fifteen of the most senior monks were slain. The island monastery also continued to be a destination for pilgrims. Máel Ruanaid Ua Mael Doraid – Cenél Conaill 'king of the North' – went on pilgrimage to Rome in 1026 having gone first *en route* to Clonfert and from there to Iona.[20] Máel Ruanaid's ancestors would have had genuine genealogical links with Columba and he was probably the patron of the Columban church at Drumcliff as we will see below. The death of the bishop of Stackallan – now in County Meath, while on a pilgrimage to Iona is recorded in 1047. The Lector of Kells, Maicnia ua hUchtáin, was drowned with others coming from Scotland (presumably from Iona or, perhaps, Dunkeld) to Ireland in 1034 with relics, including what was known as the *Cuilebad* or 'Colum Cille's fan'.

[18] See Ann Hamlin, 'The Blackwater Group of Crosses', in Bourke, *Isles*, 187–96.
[19] Doherty, a Review, 299.
[20] S. Mac Airt (ed.), *The Annals of Innisfallen* (Dublin 1951).

Máel Brigte son of Tornán died in 927. The next occasion when the title of *comarba* of Colum Cille occurs in the annals is at the death in 938 of Dubthach, a cousin of Máel Brigte, who is styled successor of Colum Cille and Adomnán. Máire Herbert has shown that Dubthach was the abbot of Kells. The title *comarba* of Colum Cille and the leadership of the Columban *familia* that went with it had originated in Iona; it had then passed to Armagh under Máel Brigte and through him had been transferred to his cousin in Kells. It is not clear whether Dubthach was in Kells already or had moved there to take up his new appointment. The inclusion of 'Adomnán' in his title might suggest that he had been associated previously with some other church connected with that saint.

Around this time a collection of the genealogies of fourteen so-called Uí Néill successors of Colum Cille was compiled in Kells, using sources mainly derived from Iona. The purpose of that compilation was probably to demonstrate the historical continuity of the successorship of the saint despite the change of its geographical location. It is also probable that some other historical sources relating to Adomnán, originally compiled not too long after his death, were transferred to Kells around this time as well. These would be used later as sources for the *Betha Adomnáin* or 'Life of Adomnán'. Among them was the little verse in which Adomnán is said to speak about his own death on Iona.[21]

> If on Iona death should come,
> That merciful end would be welcome.
> No place under all the sky,
> Would be better than, for there, to die.

The ecclesiastical settlement at Kells had been developing by this stage for a hundred and fifty years, but not just as a monastery. It would continue to do so for another two centuries. Without excavation it has not been possible to identify the great subcircular enclosure – revealed in the present street pattern – with any particular phase in its earlier history (or, for that matter, pre-history), other than in a general sense. Likewise, it is still difficult to give precise dates for the high-crosses and early ecclesiastical buildings there. It is likely that the imposing Cross of Patrick and Columba (also known as the Tower or South Cross) at Kells is a monument to the linking of the two monastic communities associated with those saints in the person of Máel Brigte. This and other evidence would date it to the early tenth century, possibly making it contemporary with the Market Cross. The other crosses, however, could date to the previous century. Ann Hamlin has suggested that the Columban churches such as Iona and Kells were pioneers in 'the

[21] Herbert and Ó Riain, *Betha Adamnáin*, 60–1, on which the rhyming version here is based.

development of free-standing stone crosses in the late 8th and 9th centuries'. A bell tower is mentioned in Kells in 1076, which is probably identifiable as the surviving ruined Round Tower. However, we cannot assign close dates to the small shrine-chapel known as Saint Columb's House, although Tomás Ó Carragáin has argued recently that it 'was probably built in the late eleventh century to replace the reliquary church referred to in the Irish Life of Adomnáin written at Kells in the tenth century'.[22]

In 904 Kells was 'profaned' when the Clann Cholmáin king of Tara Flann son of Máel Sechnaill attacked his own son Donnchad there and 'many were beheaded around the oratory'. Donnchad, who would himself become king of Tara, seems to have been using Kells as a base from which to carry on a dispute with his father. In 920 Kells was attacked again – this time by the Vikings: 'the stone church was damaged … and a large number suffered violent death in it'. In 951 Kells was attacked by the Norse from Dublin led by Gothfrith son of Sitriuc. The annals say, in what looks like gross exaggeration, that 'three thousand men or more were taken captive and a great spoil of cattle and horses and gold and silver was taken away'. Then for a short period those 'foreigners' based themselves in Kells, moving out from there to plunder other church settlements in the vicinity. Even if there is an element of exaggeration in this account, it is clear that Kells was a wealthy and busy settlement. It was attacked again in 969 and in 970. On the second occasion a large herd of cattle was captured. On both occasions the raiding Vikings were assisted by groups of the native Irish from Leinster.

The abbot Robartach, who had succeeded Dubthach and was also accorded the title of Successor of Colum Cille and Adomnán, died in 954. He was succeeded by Dub-dúin of the Cenél nÉogain whose family origins seem to have made his a somewhat unusual appointment. However, as Máire Herbert points out, the genealogists – almost certainly tongue-in-cheek – defended his eligibility for the office with the explanation that his ancestors had built a currach for Colum Cille. He died in 959.

Around that time the *Betha Adomnáin* or Life of Adomnán was written in the Irish language. The modern editors of the Life, Máire Herbert and Pádraig Ó Riain, have shown that the work was composed at the monastery of Kells between the years 956 and 964.[23] Although it may contain some basic material that relates to its seventh-century subject, the *Betha* is in effect a *roman-à-clef* in which its author 'was presenting the events of his own time in terms of that of Adomnán'. In barely concealed historical fiction the activities of Congalach son of Maíle Mithig, who became king of Tara in 944 and was assassinated in 956, are discussed and criticised. The stories told about the seventh century

[22] Ó Carragáin, 'The Architectural Setting', 136 and 153.

[23] Herbert and Ó Riain, *Betha Adamnáin*, 8. See also ch. 13 in Herbert, *Iona*.

are structured to parallel the events of the author's own lifetime. The hidden agenda of the Life appears to be the retribution that will be suffered by any king who does not support the community of Colum Cille.

> [The] king of Tara ordered that the lands of Colum Cille should be on the same footing as the lands of [Saints] Patrick, Finnian and Ciarán as regards freedom from imposition. This, in effect, meant the [Columban] lands were declared subject to tribute. The matter was related to Adomnán who thought it unjust, for the men of Ireland had granted freedom of his lands to Colum Cille because he was of more noble descent than any other saint in Ireland. Adomnán said: 'Short will be the life of the king who gave the order. He will be killed by his own kin, none of his race will ever be ruler, and no one of his name will ever [again] be king of Tara.' And all *of* this came to pass.[24]

The anonymous author of the *Betha* was familiar with both secular and religious sources including the annals and the genealogies, and he (the reasonable assumption is that it was a he) makes considerable use as a model of the *Vita Martini* by Sulpicius Severus, just as Adomnán himself had done when writing his *Vita Columbae.* The Life is in the form of a homily for preaching on Adomnán's feast day, 23 September. It may be that visiting kings and their supporters were obliged to listen to it, sitting or standing captive in a church congregation at the solemn liturgies for that occasion. The underlying message of the Life is that kings would disregard the saint and his community at their peril, and that the alleged family connections of their founder Colum Cille entitled his community to unquestioning support, particularly from the Uí Néill.

In 964 Mugrón succeeded as *comarba* of Colum Cille in Kells. He became well known as a writer of verse.[25] A number of surviving works are attributed to him, among them a litany addressed to each of the three persons of the Holy Trinity, as well as a traditional *lorica* or 'shield-poem' in which Christ's cross is invoked for protection.

> Cross of Christ over this face
> And thus over my ear.
> Cross of Christ over this eye.
> Cross of Christ over this nose …
>
> Cross of Christ over my community.
> Cross of Christ over my church
> Cross of Christ in the next world.
> Cross of Christ in this world.

[24] Herbert & Ó Riain, *Betha Adamnáin*, 51.

[25] Kenny, 'Sources', 726–7.

From the top of my head
To the nail of my foot,
O Christ, against every danger
I trust in the protection of thy cross.[26]

That poem is also sometimes attributed – almost certainly inaccurately, to Colum Cille himself. Another of Mugrón's works is a short poem in honour of the sixth-century saint whose 'successor' he had become. On his death in 980 the Annals of Ulster described Mugrón as the 'successor of Colum Cille both in Ireland and Scotland' and added that he 'ended a happy life'. A little verse about him, *comarba cadhlai Colaim*, 'Graceful heir of Colm', is attached in the margin of the manuscript.

Since God's son was born from heaven,
Nine hundred years and eighty
To the death of verse-praised Mugrón,
Graceful heir of Colm.

In the year 989, 'Dub dá Leithe, successor of Patrick [since 965], took the successorship of Colum Cille by the counsel of the men of Ireland and Scotland.' The abbacies of Armagh and Kells were thus formally joined together again for the second time. Dub dá Leithe was about seventy-four years of age at the time, accordingly his appointment has been interpreted by some authors as a semi-retirement from the Armagh position which, effectively, had made him head of the church in Ireland. Máire Herbert has noted that the collection of writings known as the Irish *Liber Hymnorum* is a 'product of learned collaboration between the *literati* of the communities of Patrick and of Colum Cille in the period of monastic amalgamation', following the assumption of the role of *comarba* of Colum Cille by Dub dá Leithe.[27] The *Liber Hymnorum* is an important anthology of early poems many of which have Columban associations, such as the *Noli Pater Indulgere* and the *Amrae Coluimb Chille*. The poems are supported by later explanatory material that purports to outline the circumstances – almost certainly in most cases fictionally – that had given rise to the original compositions: the *locus* or place, the *tempus* or time and the *causa* or reason.

Dub dá Leithe died early in the month of June 998 and was succeeded by Muiredach son of Críchan who had previously been a lector in Armagh. Muiredach's appointment definitely indicates some kind of continuing link between the monastery of Kells and the church of Armagh although the precise nature of that connection is not very clear. We know that the *familia*

[26] Quoted by Fisher, *Early Medieval Sculpture*, xiv.
[27] Herbert, Preface, 68.

of Colum Cille was not a closed, separate institution in the sense of the religious orders of the later Middle Ages. Many of its officials in Kells and elsewhere also held joint positions in churches that were not closely or previously associated with the Columban confederation. Muiredach held his post till 1007 when he retired, apparently – as the annals suggest – in order to lead a more contemplative life. He died in 1011 and is given an elaborate death notice in the Annals of the Four Masters:

> Muiredach, son of Crichan, successor of Colum Cille and Adomnán, a learned man, bishop, and virgin, Lector of Armagh, and intended successor of Patrick, died after the seventy-fourth year of his age [the Annals of Ulster says eighty-fourth], on the fifth of the Kalends of January [28 December], on Saturday night precisely; and he was buried with great honour and veneration in the great church of Armagh, before the altar.

In the year that Muiredach retired 'for the sake of God' the Clann Cholmáin king of Tara Máel Sechnaill reconvened the Fair of Tailtiu. The holding of that fair was one of the ancient privileges of the king of Tara although it had been in abeyance for nearly a century. Despite the antiquity and prestige of the kingship of Tara, a new all-Ireland power had arisen in the person of the Munster king Brian Boru. Brian had cultivated relations with the leading church in the country, Armagh, as part of his strategy to gain national political power. Máel Sechnaill was forced to counteract the influence of Brian. At the Tailtiu assembly Ferdomnach was installed as the *comarba* of Colum Cille. Whether or not Muiredach was, as it were, turned out of office in order to accommodate Ferdomnach, Máire Herbert believes that Máel Sechnaill was almost certainly acting deliberately to separate Kells from the influence of Armagh and its new patron, Brian.

Ferdomnach lived for only one more year but his appointment in 1007 had signalled the renewal of the former alliance between the southern Uí Néill and the *familia* of Colum Cille. Also in 1007, a year that saw several major changes in Kells, the 'Great Gospel of Colum Cille' – no doubt the Book of Kells,

> was wickedly stolen by night from the western sacristy in the great stone church of Kells. It was the most precious object of the western world on account of its human ornamentation.[28]

The book was found two months later hidden under a sod but its gold decorations, probably mounted on its *cumhdach* or shrine-box, had been removed.

[28] Annals of Ulster 1007, 11.

Kells was raided again in 1018, this time by Sitric and the Dublin Norse. The Annals of the Four Masters says that they 'carried off innumerable spoils and prisoners, and slew many persons in the middle of the church'. Notwithstanding this attack, the settlement survived. From 1009 when Ferdomnach died until 1040 the office of *comarba* was held by members of the Uí Uchtáin family. They also provided *fir léiginn* or 'lectors' to the monastery – an earlier one of whom may have been the anonymous author of the *Betha Adomnáin.* From around this time our sources of knowledge about the settlement become more detailed. Shortly before 1040 what are known as the 'Kells charters' began to be recorded and were subsequently transcribed on to blank spaces in the Book of Kells. These are mainly notes about the granting and transfer of land. They specify the names of many of the officials of the monastery and also demonstrate the ongoing relations with many of the secular rulers of the time, including the local Uí Máel Sechnaill kings and later the O'Rourkes from the kingdom of Breifne. The latter began to extend their influence to the Kells area from about 1117 onwards.

The annals continue to record the deaths of the *comarbadh* as well as incidents of more local interest. Burnings in Kells are recorded throughout the eleventh century. In 1060 the annals tell us that the settlement 'was completely burned, including its stone church'. It was burned again 'with its churches' in 1095. Many of these incidents, such as that in 1099 when it 'was destroyed by fire', were probably the result of nothing more sinister than the sort of accidents which were commonplace in the mainly wood-built towns and settlements all over medieval Europe. But there were deliberate acts of violence by local lay people also. In 1076 Murchadh son of Flann ua Máel Sechlainn, who had been king of Tara for only three nights, was killed in the tower at Kells.

Máire Herbert has drawn up lists of the occupants of the various offices of the monastery as recorded in the annals and the 'charters'.[29] Besides the *comarba* who was the abbot as well as the president of the federation of Columban churches, those offices included: lectors, priests, resident superior or administrator, porter or sacristan, head of the hermitage, superior of the students, chief celebrant of the canonical hours, superior of the guest house, and prior. Occasionally there is a mention of a bishop. A group of *Céile Dé* or monks attached to the monastery who followed a stricter religious discipline were also present in Kells. These were housed in the *dísert* and had their own separate superior.

Several of these offices were in effect secularised, hereditary and dominated by particular families. Many of the office-holders were involved in business and property transactions in which payments were made in gold and silver.

[29] Herbert, *Iona*, ch. 8.

In one case there is a record of a priest acquiring property for his sons. There was a market and families of tradesmen. Kells also had a high reputation as a centre of learning. When Máelán the *Fer Léiginn* died in 1050 he was described as 'the most learned of all the Irish'.

By that stage the settlement had developed into a lot more than just a monastery.[30] It was effectively a 'township' which also had outlying agricultural estates. It had its own political life and was obliged to accommodate itself to external political upheavals, particularly in the first half of the twelfth century. Kells was at the centre of the political struggles in the Irish midlands and the east in the first half of the twelfth century – the time of the so-called 'high-kings with opposition' – when a number of individuals and dynasties from different parts of the country were attempting to establish a monarchy over all of Ireland. During these struggles Kells was attacked and burnt on many occasions: in 1135, 1143, and three times in 1144.

Domnall mac Robartaig who succeeded to the abbacy in 1062 was almost certainly a son of a previous *comarba,* Robartach who had died in 1057, and a grandson of another *comarba,* Ferdomnach who had died in 1009. It seems clear that by then there was a strong hereditary element in the succession to that office, just as there was with similar offices in other monasteries throughout the country. The extent to which any of these individuals was actually in clerical orders has to be questioned; certainly they do not appear to have been constrained to any degree by the discipline of clerical celibacy.

It was Domnall mac Robartaig who was involved in the making of the great Columban treasure later known as the shrine of the *Cathach.* In 1090 the Annals of Tigernach records that

> Colum Cille's reliquaries, that is, the Bell of the Kings and the *Cuilebad* [the fan or *flabellum*] and the two Gospels, were brought out of *Tír Conaill* [Donegal], together with seven score ounces of silver. And it was Óengus Ua Domnallán that brought them from the north.

Óengus is described in one of the Kells charters as 'the chief *anmchara* ['soul-friend' or 'confessor'] of the community of Colum Cille'. He brought these precious items to the craft workshops of the Mac Áeda family in Kells to have them enshrined. The accompanying *largesse* of silver was almost certainly a gift from the Donegal king Cathbarr Ua Domnaill, or at least payment for the job.

The 'Bell of the Kings' is not easily identified although some authors have suggested that it is the 'Bell of the Will/Testament' or Saint Patrick's bell which had its shrine made at the behest of Domnall Ua Lochlainn who died in Derry in 1121. Another suggestion is that it is the bell now known as the Bell of

[30] See D.L. Swan, 'Kells and its Book', in O'Mahony, *Book of Kells,* 48–59.

Saint Mura, associated with the monastery of Fahan about ten miles north of Derry. Although the latter bell is not known to have had any connection with the cult of Colum Cille, it is decorated in a style so close to that of the shrine of the *Cathach* and also to the decoration on a similar object known as the *Misach* – which also had a Derry connection, that the work was almost certainly carried out by the same craftsmen or in the same 'school'.

In 1034 Maicnia ua hUchtáin whose family held various positions of importance at the monastery of Kells was drowned while crossing from Scotland to Ireland with the *Cuilebad* of Colum Cille, which the annals say was lost also on the occasion. The *Cuilebad* seems to have been a *flabellum* or liturgical fan which was believed to be a relic of the saint. Either it was recovered or a believable substitute provided because it too is listed among the items taken to Kells from *Tír Chonaill* in 1090. The *Cuilebad* is mentioned in a version of the tale known as *Immram Snedgusa ocus Maic Ríagla* – 'the voyage of Snedgus and Mac Ríagal'. The tale occurs in various forms of differing dates in both prose and verse versions. The fullest version is to be found with the title *Sechrán clérech Choluim Cille* – 'the wanderings of Colum Cille's clerics' in Manus O'Donnell's sixteenth-century *Betha Colaim Chille.* There is another version dating to the eleventh century that purports to explain how the object came to be in Kells.

A local problem had arisen and an Irish king sent a request to Colum Cille asking for a judgement on the matter. The two monks Snedgus and Mac Ríagal were dispatched from Iona with the saint's decision. On their way home the wind blew them way out into the open ocean and, as in other early Irish voyage tales, they visited many islands and encountered various wonders. On one island they came across a beautiful tree.

> And the bird gave a leaf of the leaves of that tree to the clerics, which was as large as the hide of a great ox; and told the clerics to take it with them, and place it on the altar of Colum Cille. And that is the *Cuilebad* of Colm Cille at this day. And it is at Kells that it is.[31]

The *Cuilebad* does not survive and we have no exact idea of what it looked like. However, as Raghnall Ó Floinn suggests, some of the decoration on the early inscribed stone slabs in *Gleann Cholm Cille* or on the so-called 'Marigold Stone' in Carndonagh, Co. Donegal, may be based on similar types of liturgical instruments.[32] A depiction of a flabellum being used to cool the

[31] Quoted in Reeves, *Columba*, 323, from TCD Ms H.2.16.

[32] Ó Floinn, 'Sandhills', 131–2. Lacy, *Archaeological Survey*, esp. 250 and 291–4. Raghnall Ó Floinn, 'Schools of Metalworking in Eleventh- and Twelfth-Century Ireland', in M. Ryan (ed.), *Ireland and Insular Art – A.D. 500–1200* (Dublin 1987), 179–87. C. Newman & N. Walsh, 'Iconographical analysis of the Marigold Stone, Carndonagh, Inishowen, Co. Donegal', in R. Moss (ed.), *Making and meaning in Insular art* (Dublin 2007), 167–83.

fourth-century Christian Roman emperor Constantine, which is decorated almost identically to the Carndonagh 'Marigold Stone', occurs in a mid-fourteenth-century fresco in the Capella di San Silvestro in the inner courtyard of the church of Santi Quattro Coronati in Rome.[33]

One of the 'Gospels' mentioned in the 1090 list was almost certainly the *Cathach* – actually not a gospel at all but a copy of the Psalms – and the other may well have been the *Misach.* Although the *Misach* manuscript does not survive, the decoration of the shrine-box made for it is very similar in style to that of the *Cathach.* The *Misach* was originally associated with the cult of Saint Cairnech of Dulane in County Meath. However, a medieval text, *Aided Muirchertaigh Meic Erca* – 'the death of Muircertach Mac Ercae [a sixth century king of the Cenél nÉogain]' parts of which may date to the eleventh century, says that the *Misach* along with the *Cathach* and the 'Bell of the Will/Testament' (better known as Saint Patrick's Bell) were given by Saint Cairnech to the Cenél Conaill and the Cenél nÉogain.[34]

The *Misach* was definitely in the Derry area in the middle of the twelfth century. We only have the vaguest outline of the process by which this came about. The Uí Uchtáin family who had held the abbacy of Kells from 1009 to 1040 had many connections with the monastery of Dulane. Presumably, in some way they transferred the *Misach* from Dulane to the cult of Colum Cille at Kells and from there it was transferred to the northwest of Ireland – almost certainly to Derry – before the composition of the *Aided.* In the later Middle Ages the *Misach* was preserved by the O'Morrison family at Clonmany in Inishowen, County Donegal. It is now owned by the National Museum of Ireland which acquired it by sale only a few years ago, appropriately, from Saint Columba's Church of Ireland College in Rathfarnham, County Dublin.

The shrine of the *Cathach* consists of a small, hinged wooden box covered in decorated metal plates. As we have it now, some of the surface decoration dates to the fourteenth century and later but the back of the shrine – which features an openwork pattern of crosses – and the cast silver plates along the narrow sides seem to be original. An inscription in Irish which runs around three sides of the box tells us about the making of the shrine.

> Pray for Cathbarr Ua Domnaill for whom this shrine was made and for Sitric son of Mac Áed who made it and for Domnall son of Robartach for whom it was made.

Cathbarr Ua Domnall was a Síl Lugdach king from Donegal. From him would descend the O'Donnell chieftains of the later Middle Ages. The lands of the Síl Lugdach were located originally in the Cloghaneely and Tory Island

---

[33] Lacey, *Cenél Conaill*, 287.
[34] See Ó Floinn, 'Sandhills', 126–31.

area of northwest Donegal but in the eighth and ninth centuries they had expanded to include the territories in which Gartan, Kilmacrenan and Templedouglas, as well as several other minor sites said to be associated with Colum Cille, were located. Almost certainly as a result of tuition by the monks of Kilmacrenan, the Síl Lugdach became very conscious of the Columban heritage that formed part of their intellectual patrimony. They had provided an abbot to Iona in the ninth century and around the same time they may have had connections with Derry. In fact it could be that the legend of Colum Cille's foundation of the monastery of Derry, as seemingly first outlined in the preface to the poem *Noli Pater Indulgere* dating to the tenth or early eleventh centuries, derived from a Síl Lugdach source.[35]

Sitric the maker of the shrine of the *Cathach* belonged to a family which is recorded elsewhere as having provided craftsmen in Kells. The Scandinavian origin of his first name is not too surprising. The foliage and zoomorphic motifs used to decorate the objects that have been identified as his or his associate's work show strong Scandinavian influences and parallels, particularly with artwork recovered from the Norse period excavations in the centre of Dublin.[36]

Domnal mac Robartaig retired as *comarba Coluim Cille* sometime before 1094 and died in 1098. Perhaps – as Máire Herbert supposed – he had travelled back to the northwest of Ireland from Kells with the various enshrined Columban relics, including the *Cathach*. The history of that object in the twelfth century is somewhat obscure but it may have been one of the chief treasures kept in the monastery of Derry, although if so not with that name. The Mac Robartaigh family, at least in later times, had lands close to Derry. There was another Mac Robartaigh family in south Donegal who were the keepers of the *Cathach* in later medieval times but we do not know what relationship, if any, existed between the two families. Neither do we know if there was any connection with the Ó Robhartaigh family who were associated in later medieval times with the Cloghaneely area of Donegal and nearby Tory Island, although such a relationship is likely given the Columban links of all these places.

In 1117 the abbot of Kells Máel Brigte son of Rónán was slain along with other members of his community by Áed Ua Ruairc and the Uí Briúin of Breifne on the eve of the festival known as *Crom Duban* Sunday, at the end of July or beginning of August. The chronicler whose record is preserved in the Annals of Ulster was so appalled by this incident that he quoted Psalm 37 verse 17: 'The face of the Lord be against those committing these wickednesses, that he may wipe out their memory from the earth.' Áed's son, the famous Tigernán

[35] Lacey, 'Columba, founder ... of Derry', 45.

[36] Ó Floinn, 'Schools of Metalworking', 179–87.

O'Rourke, came to power shortly afterwards. He is mentioned a number of times in the Kells 'charters': twice as a witness to the transactions of others and twice more as a granter of land himself. He continued as an influential force in Irish affairs generally until his death in 1172. By that time, however, the kingdom of Meath had disintegrated and the prestigious position of *comarba Coluim Cille*, and with it the leadership of all the Columban churches in Ireland, had been transferred from Kells to Derry.

Other Columban Monasteries in Ireland

Three hundred churches he founded;
One hundred were close by the sea;
And Colum – as well as the churches,
Three hundred good books, wrote he.

Manus O'Donnell,
Betha Colaim Chille (1532)

Throughout the eighth, ninth, tenth and eleventh centuries there continue to be reports in the annals about several of the other Irish monasteries associated with the traditions and *familia* of Saint Colum Cille. In addition to the more important centres there were, undoubtedly, many lesser churches and places that were connected in a looser way with the cult, not to mention a wide variety of holy wells and landscape features scattered all over Ireland that were part of the devotion to the saint. Among the most unusual examples of the latter, for example, is the oddly shaped boulder on the Connemara shore of County Galway which is still known locally as Saint Colum Cille's boat and which, it is said, was used for transporting the saint to and from the Aran Islands. In Scotland legends claimed that the saint used a lighter form of transport – a cloud!

Many of the places mentioned in the medieval sources have survived in some form or another with their Columban associations preserved right down to the present day. Writing one hundred and fifty years ago William Reeves listed thirty-seven *Sancti Columbae Ecclesiae Hibernicae* or 'Irish churches of Saint Colum Cille'.[1] The twelfth-century Middle Irish Life of Colum Cille lists a small number of those places as churches founded by the saint in the course of a fictional journey he is said to have made around the country.

[1] Reeves, *Columba*, 276–98.

Durrow

There can be little doubt that the monastery of Durrow now in County Offaly was, at least originally, the most important Columban foundation in Ireland. In fact it is the only monastery in Ireland that Adomnán explicitly claims to have been founded by the saint himself:

> At one time, when for some months the blessed man remained in the midland district of Ireland, while by God's will founding the monastery that is called in Irish Dairmag [Durrow] ...

We have seen above also that Laisrén, a contemporary of Columba and his second successor in the abbacy of Iona, was for a while almost certainly the *praepositus* or prior at Durrow. That monastery seems to have been linked, at least in the eighth century, with and supported by the rising local dynasty of the Clann Cholmáin Mór. In 763 a member of that dynasty, Domnall Mide, died after twenty years as king of Tara. During his reign he had many connections with the *familia* of Colum Cille. He was buried according to the Annals of the Four Masters in the monastery of Durrow 'with honour and veneration'.

Interestingly among the first references in the Annals of Ulster to Durrow are mentions of the involvement of the community there in battles. In 764 a battle was fought at the unidentified *Argaman* between the community of Clonmacnoise and the community of Durrow. In 776 the community of Durrow were the allies of the Clann Cholmáin Mór in a battle against the Munstermen. On that occasion, unlike the first, they were on the victorious side. The battles, of course, were probably fought by the lay monastic tenants rather than by the monks themselves.

In 833 Durrow was burned 'to the very door of [its] church' by the powerful king of Cashel Feidlimid son of Crimthann who had previously attacked and burned Clonmacnoise. In 836 'Durrow of the Britons' as it was called (presumably on account of the numbers of students from Britain there at some point in its history) was plundered by the Vikings and many were killed. Many others were taken away as captives. Sporadic references to the monastery continue through the ninth and into the tenth centuries. In 973 the superior of Durrow, Máel Muire, was drowned while crossing the River Erne at Assaroe near present-day Ballyshannon. Presumably he was either coming from or going to the old homeland of Colum Cille in *Tír Chonaill*, probably on some kind of monastic business.

The deaths of several other officers of the monastery are mentioned in the annals from the ninth to the twelfth centuries including: superiors (abbots), scribes (in the sense of ecclesiastical judges rather than mere scriveners), a bishop and a lector. There are also several references to the involvement of the settlement in the complicated local secular affairs. In 1019 the stone church of Durrow was 'broken down' by Muircertach ua Carraig in his pursuit of Máel Muad, the king of the midland territory of Fir Chell. Máel Muad was forcibly taken from the church and put to death. In 1095 Durrow 'with its books' was burned. The Leinstermen, under their famous king Díarmait mac Máel na mBó, were defeated at Durrow in 1059 'through the miracles of God and Colum Cille'. In 1068, when Donnchad son of Brian Boru was slain by the men of Tethba – roughly, modern County Longford – in revenge for their having been plundered and preyed, 'his head was taken to Clonmacnoise and his body to Durrow'. In 1137 there was another O'Brien connection: Mór, the daughter of Muircertach O'Brien – the wife of the Ua Máelsechnaill chieftain – 'died in Durrow of Colum Cille after penance'. Murchadh Ua Máelsechnaill himself died in Durrow in 1153.

A finely carved Scripture Cross dating to the ninth or tenth century survives at Durrow together with a fragment of a second cross decorated with interlace, as also five early Christian grave-slabs. There may have been a third stone cross there also. The present much later church at the site may incorporate fragments of an early Christian period building and, close by, is the 'Headache Stone' (actually the base of a high cross). Nearby is 'Colum Cille's Well'. After a successful campaign led by the Dublin archaeologist Dr Elizabeth O'Brien to preserve the monastic precinct from development, the site of the ancient monastery – which previously had been difficult to access – has been acquired by the state and can now be visited easily by the public.

Raphoe

County Donegal has lots of ancient monuments, folk sites and place names associated with the cult of Colum Cille. One of the principal Columban churches in Donegal was said to have been *Ráith Both* (Raphoe), where the cult of Adomnán along with that of Colum Cille was especially honoured. We have no genuine information about the foundation of that monastery; in fact our understanding of the origins of the church of *Ráith Both* is clouded in considerable confusion. It is common to attribute its foundation to Colum Cille but to qualify that by claiming that Adomnán was also associated as 'patron' from his time onwards.[2] William Reeves pointed out in 1857 that the matter was further confused by a late tradition of a separate, second Adomnán (known locally in an anglicised form of his name, as Eunan) who was believed to have been the founding bishop of that church.

[2] See for example A. Gwynn and R.N. Hadcock, *Medieval Religious Houses: Ireland* (Dublin 1988), 94.

> [W]hen Raphoe became an Episcopal see [in the 12th century] but under its old patronage, after-ages, supposing that a bishop's see must originate with a bishop, took advantage of Adamnan's (*sic*) phonetic name *Eunan*, and created a bishop *Eunan* patron of the diocese, moving his festival a fortnight back in the month, and leaving *Adamnan* to enjoy his old abbatial honours on the 23rd [September]. Pope Clement XII approved of a mass for Bishop Eunan's festival on the 7th of September, which was printed in Paris in 1734. Accordingly the Bollandists place the commemoration of 'S. Eunanus Episcopus, Confessor, Raphoae in Hibernia,' at Sept. vii, in a short notice edited by Joannes Stiltingus. Alban Butler, following this authority, repeats the error at the same day; and in the Irish Calendar appended to the Dublin edition of his valuable book, the same fictitious patron intrudes on another saint's day.[3]

The latter confusion was clarified somewhat in the 1860s by the removal of this second Saint Eunan from the calendar of saints.[4] Surprisingly, if the better-known Adomnán who was ninth abbot of Iona did have genuine connections with Raphoe there is no mention of this in his hagiographical Life, *Betha Adamnáin*. However, as we have seen above, the editors of that text have shown that it was composed in the monastery of Kells (County Meath) between 961 and 964, and that it is a sort of *roman-à-clef*:

> while purporting to be a life of a saint who died in 704, … [it] in fact deals with the relationship between his successor at Kells and the secular power in Ireland at a very much later period … the second half of the tenth century.[5]

Nevertheless, the absence of any mention of Raphoe in the *Betha Adamnáin* is striking and merits at least some consideration.

The earliest alleged narrative description of the foundation of Raphoe occurs in the Middle Irish Life of Colum Cille dating to the middle of the twelfth century or a little later.

> Afterwards Colum Cille founded Raphoe. It was there that he revived the carpenter who had been drowned in the mill-pond. In Raphoe, also, when his community lacked a ploughshare, he blessed the hands of the little lad who was beside him. The latter, who was named Fergna, made the ploughshare, and was an expert smith from that time onwards because of Colum Cille's blessing.[6]

We have no idea what the references to the 'carpenter' and Fergna in this quotation actually mean; they probably derived from some sort of local

[3] Reeves, *Columba*, lxi–lxii; see also 256–8.
[4] J. Silke, *Two Abbots* (Letterkenny 1997), 63.
[5] Herbert & Ó Riain, *Betha Adamnáin*, 41.
[6] Herbert, *Iona*, 257.

folktale. Clearly, little or no reliance can be placed on this account. For example, the same Life gives Colum Cille the role of founder of the monastery of Derry although as we have seen above such historical evidence as we have is contradictory on that point. Somewhat more ambiguously the Life also involves the saint in the establishment of the monastery at Kells discussed above although we know from the annals that this was not founded until the years 804 to 807. There is, in fact, no evidence that the monastery of Raphoe had been founded as early as the dates of either Colum Cille or Adomnán although that in itself cannot be taken as proof that it did not exist during the lifetime of either of them. The 630 'battle of *Both*' between the victorious Suibne Menn son of Fiachna – allegedly of the Cenél nÉogain of Inishowen – and the defeated Domnall son of Áed of the Cenél Conaill may have been fought in the vicinity of Raphoe. Raphoe would have been an appropriate location for an encounter between these two opposing groups but there is no indication from the annalistic entries about the battle that a church existed there at the time.[7]

However, by 817, when it is mentioned unambiguously for the first time in the annals, Raphoe was definitely associated in some way with the Columban federation of churches:

> Máel Dúin son of Cenn Fáelad, superior (*princeps*) of *Ráith Both*, a member of Colum Cille's community (*de familia Columbe*), was killed.[8]

The notice of Máel Dúin's death has been taken as being linked to the entry which immediately follows it: 'Colum Cille's community (*muinnter*) went to Tara to excommunicate Áed.' The implication is that this Áed was involved in the killing of the abbot of Raphoe. The subject of the excommunication was the Cenél nÉogain king of Tara Áed Ingor ['the undutiful'] who himself died two years later, although why he should have been involved in the killing of Máel Dúin is not clear. However, it may have had something to do with the abbot of Raphoe propagating the cult of Colum Cille in County Donegal. Áed, was also a Donegal man (from Inishowen) but he seems to have been a supporter more of the cult of Saint Patrick associated with the church of Armagh rather than of the cult of Colum Cille.

Raphoe, as mentioned above, is situated in land that probably in the sixth century was the homeland of the Cenél nÉnnai. Originally their territory had stretched almost certainly as far north as (and included) Derry.[9] The Cenél nÉnnai, unlike the Cenél Conaill and the Cenél nÉogain, failed to establish themselves in power and quickly faded as an influential force on the history

[7] Lacey, *Cenél Conaill*, 220–1 and 243–9.
[8] Annals of Ulster, 817.7.
[9] Lacey, *Cenél Conaill*, 120–31.

of the northwest of Ireland. Consequently control of their lands was much fought over. Indeed, *Ráith Both* (Raphoe) may have been in origin a Cenél nÉnnai secular hillfort-type monument that was later handed over to the church by the Cenél nÉogain in order to neutralise it when the Cenél Conaill were driven out of this area after the battle of *Clóitech* in 789. However, while there is no evidence for a church there before 817 neither is there any hard evidence for a 'hillfort' – except, perhaps, the place name.

As we have seen, at one time there were actually traditions of two different Adomnáns connected with the church of Raphoe. The feast day of one of these (the one said to have been a bishop) occurred on 7 September. However, despite the alleged connections of the other Adomnán (the abbot of Iona) with the church of Raphoe, the only person with a similar name of whom we have any genuine historical evidence in this part of Donegal is the early eighth-century Adamnán (*sic*) bishop of *Ráith Maige Enaig*, who has been mentioned above also.[10] The church of *Ráith Maige Enaig*, which was associated with the very early saint Brugach mac Dega, was almost certainly at or near a place now known as Rateen, about five miles northeast of Raphoe.[11] It is probably relevant that references to *Ráith Maige Enaig* in the annals disappear about the same time that references to Raphoe begin to occur. It seems strongly possible that genuine traditions of a cleric called Adamnán associated with *Ráith Maige Enaig* somehow became mixed up (either accidentally or more likely deliberately) with Adomnán of Iona and were transferred from the church of *Ráith Maige Enaig* to the newly-founded church at Raphoe. It is quite probable that it was the Adamnán of *Ráith Maige Enaig* who definitely was a bishop according to the annals, whose feast day occurred on 7 September. That coincidence of names was either exploited deliberately to create a new legend for Raphoe (fictionally linking it with Adomnán of Iona), or else a genuine historical memory had become so corrupted (or forgotten) that it facilitated the same end.

As a member of the Cenél Conaill with a mother who almost certainly belonged to the Cenél nÉnnai, there is a strong possibility that Adomnán of Iona was born and grew up in the area of east Donegal close to Raphoe. However there is absolutely no evidence of his connection with the establishment of a church there which, possibly, was not founded until about a century after his death.

Apart from the notice of Máel Dúin's death in 817, the only other entry in the annals that explicitly relates to Raphoe prior to the twelfth century occurs in 959 when the Annals of Ulster records the death of Aengus ua Lapán. The Annals of the Four Masters noting the same event, but at the year

[10] Annals of Ulster, 731.8.

[11] Brian Lacey, 'The church of Ráith Maige Oenaig and the Donegal Cenél nÉnnai', in Condit & Corlett, *Above and Beyond* (Dublin 2005), 213–18.

957, identifies Aengus as *epscop Ratha both* – 'the bishop of Raphoe'. The killing of another Aengus ua Lappan, described in a secondary hand as 'king of Cenél Énna', is recorded in the Annals of Ulster at 1011. The Ua Lapán family was connected with Lough Lapán (a lake now greatly reduced in size and known as 'Portlough') which is just five and a half miles west of Derry. They possibly had a crannog or lake-dwelling there.

As we have seen above, the annals record the death in 938 of Dubthach, 'the successor (*comarba*) of Colum Cille and Adamnán'. Dubhtach's title – as also that of his successor Robartach who died in 954 – has often been taken by commentators such as William Reeves to mean that he had some particular connection with 'Adamnán's church' at Raphoe and that he may have been the abbot there. Dubthach seems to have taken up this position in 927 on the death of his relative Máel Brigte son of Tornán. However, as has been described above, Máire Herbert has shown that Dubthach and Robartach were both abbots of Kells while also accepting that 'the possibility cannot be discounted that Dubthach, first holder of the title ['*comarba* of Colum Cille and Adomnán'], held the abbacy of Raphoe, or of another church associated with Adomnán, at some time previous to his appointment as *comarba*'.[12] This may well be the case. Dubthach definitely did have an association with ecclesiastical matters in the northwest of the country. He seems to have belonged to the Cenél mBógaine whose territory lay in the southwest part of County Donegal – the area where *Gleann Cholm Cille* is located.

Significantly his uncle, Caencomhrac son of Maeluidir who died about ten years earlier than Dubthach, seems to have held the senior post in the monastery of Derry, and was himself particularly involved with the cult of Adomnán. He is described in the Annals of the Four Masters as the *maor cána Adomnáin*, that is, 'the steward of the Law of Adomnán'. That title presumably gave him the right to collect the fines that were imposed for any breach of the law in question. A later relative of his, Máel Eoin Ua Tornán, would die as abbot (*comarba*) of Derry in 1025. More importantly, as mentioned before, Dubthach was a relative of Máel Brigte son of Tornán the Cenél mBógaine *comarba* of Patrick who, unprecedentedly and in a revolutionary manner, had also become *comarba* of Colum Cille in 891. In fact, at his death on 22 February 927 Máel Brigte is styled Comarba of Patrick, Colum Cille and Adomnán as well as 'head of the piety of all Ireland, and the greater part of Europe'.[13] Máire Herbert has written: 'Whatever the circumstances of his appointment, ... Máel Brigte's tenure of office as *comarba* of Colum Cille may be seen to mark an important departure in the history of the saint's community.'[14]

[12] Herbert, *Iona*, 80.
[13] Annals of the Four Masters, under the year 925.
[14] Herbert, *Iona*, 75.

Apart from the absence of historical records there are also very few physical reminders of what the monastery of Raphoe may have been like. Two fragments of a Romanesque period (12th century?) lintel-stone, depicting scenes from Christ's passion and crucifixion, are located at the present but partly late medieval Church of Ireland cathedral, which is likely to have been built on the site of the original monastic enclosure.[15] A Round Tower survived there until the early seventeenth century when it was removed by the Protestant bishop John Leslie for the construction of his new fortified palace close by. Interestingly, Bishop Leslie, like his predecessor, had previously been Bishop of the Isles – the Scottish diocese that included the island of Iona. In 1635, King Charles I wrote to Bishop Leslie at Raphoe concerning a matter which, originally, had been the business of his predecessor.

> Reverend Father in God: Whereas we are informed that Andrew late Bishop of Raphoe at his transportation from the Bishopric of the Isles did without just cause or any warrant from our late royal father [James I of England, VI of Scotland] or us, carry with him two of the principal bells that were in Icolmkill [Iona] and place them in some of the churches of Raphoe; To which purpose we do remember that at the time of your being Bishop of the Isles you were a suitor to us for effectuating that thing at your predecessor the Bishop of Raphoe's hands which we now require of you: Therefore and in regard we have given order to the present Bishop of the Isles for repairing the cathedral church of that bishopric [on Iona], and that it is fit for such things as do properly belong thereunto be restored; it is our pleasure that you cause deliver unto the said bishop these two bells for use of the said cathedral church with such timely convenience as may be; Which we will acknowledge as acceptable service done unto us.
>
> Whitehall, 14 March 1635

It is not clear if the bells in question were ever returned to Iona.

Kilmacrenan

The origins of the church of Kilmacrenan or *Cill mac nEnáin* (modern *Cill Mhic Réanáin*) are also obscure. It is not mentioned in the surviving annals until 1129, but that absence is unlikely to be a reflection of its true age or of its importance in the early medieval period. We know that as well as a number of literary and genealogical sources a chronicle associated with that church did exist.[16] It does not survive and it does not seem to have been available to

[15] Peter Harbison, 'The Biblical Iconography of Irish Romanesque Architectural Sculpture', in Bourke, *Isles*, 271–80. See also Lacy, *Archaeological Survey*, 284–6.

[16] W.M. Hennessy & D.H. Kelly, *Book of Fenagh* (Dublin 1875), 346–7 and 352–5; Lacey, *Lugs forgotten Donegal kingdoms*, ch. 4.

the annalists of the fifteenth, sixteenth or early seventeenth centuries whose work has been preserved down to our day. A number of modern general commentaries state that Kilmacrenan is where Colum Cille received his earliest education and fosterage with a priest called Cruithnecán, and that later as an adult he returned to found a church there. While Adomnán in the *Vita Columbae* of *c.*700 does confirm that a priest called Cruithnecán was the saint's foster-father (*nutritor*), he does not name the location of the latter's church as Kilmacrenan or, indeed, give any information that can lead to the identification of the place in question. However, later tradition associates Kilmacrenan with Colum Cille's fosterage and, under the apparently older version of its name – *Doire Eithne*, with the homeplace of his mother. William Reeves cited references in some of the medieval poems about Colum Cille contained in the manuscript Laud Misc. 615 as proof that *Doire Eithne* and Kilmacrenan were the same place,[17] and in his *Betha Colaim Chille* of 1532 Manus O'Donnell also confirms that understanding. Somewhat surprisingly, the mid-twelfth-century Middle Irish Life of Colum Cille, which makes a point of listing the principal churches in Ireland associated with the saint, seems to deliberately ignore Kilmacrenan which, whatever about the past, was by then undoubtedly associated with the saint's *familia*. The reason for that avoidance is not obvious but most probably had something to do with the fact that the Life is a Derry propaganda text and its authors may have wanted for contemporary political reasons to play down the role of Kilmacrenan in the saint's life.

Although composed perhaps a thousand years or so after the establishment of its church, Manus O'Donnell's *Betha Colaim Chille* contains what, in some respects at least, is a foundation legend for Kilmacrenan. Needless to remark there is no contemporary historical evidence to support any of this narrative and the historicity of some aspects of the story seems extremely doubtful. Nevertheless the account clearly reflects late medieval belief in Donegal:

> Colum Cille's father, took the kingship of Ulster and, after he had been king a long time and old-age and great feebleness came on him, he relinquished his kingdom and divided it between his brothers … Brendan, Ninnid, Fiacha, Fidruidh, Cathrand, Loarn, and Sédna, the youngest of them. A great feast was held by them in the place called Both Brain in today's Tír Fergna in the district of Kilmacrenan …
>
> Colum Cille then went to Both Brain … he met Sédna first … who made him very welcome. Colum Cille asked if he and his brothers had shared out the land.
>
> 'We have,' said Sédna.

[17] Reeves, *The Life of St Columba*, 281.

> 'Have tithes for the church been set aside by you,' said Colum Cille.
>
> 'They have not,' said Sédna.
>
> 'It is my choice if it is God's,' said Colum Cille, 'that this division should not be approved or prosperous until tithes are set aside.'
>
> 'Cleric, you will have your tithe,' said Sédna, 'for a piece of the portion which I got will be given to you as tithes.'
>
> That is the Termon of Kilmacrenan today ...[18]

The text does not claim that Colum Cille founded a church at Kilmacrenan – or, indeed, that a church was founded there at all – but it does seek to explain how the associated *termon* (the protected area in which the church would have been located) became part of the Columban patrimony through the agency of Sédna (Sétna), Colum Cille's uncle.

Notwithstanding the need for historical scepticism about many of the legends concerning him, there are strong indications that Colum Cille was born and spent the earliest years of his life in the general Kilmacrenan and Gartan area which was said to be originally the homeland of his mother and her people, the Corpraige.[19] However, from about 650 the area was taken over as part of the territory of his father's people, Cenél Conaill, and by *c.*800 it had been taken over again, this time by the Síl Lugdach.[20]

There seems to be at least one genuine if indirect sixth-century link between Columba and Kilmacrenan. According to a list of the saint's relatives attached to the so-called B-manuscripts of Adomnán's *Vita Columbae* one of Columba's sisters called Mincoleth was said to be the mother of the sons of Enán (their father's name) after whom the church of Kilmacrenan was allegedly named.[21] If this was so then Enán too presumably belonged to the Corpraige. Prof. Richard Sharpe accepts that this list almost certainly dates to roughly about the same time as the composition originally of the *Vitae Columbae*, *c.*700.[22] While it is not at all definite that the reference to Enán's sons was indeed the origin of the name Kilmacrenan – *Cill mac nEnáin*, that has been the general understanding for a very long time. William Reeves attributed that identification to the seventeenth-century writer from Donegal, John Colgan.[23] If the reference to the sons of Enán (who were also sons of

[18] Lacey, *The Life of Colum Cille*, 55–6.

[19] Gartan is usually understood as a district rather than as a specific place, but the area is at most about 5 miles from Kilmacrenan.

[20] Lacey, *Cenél Conaill*, 102–3.

[21] The list occurs in the late twelfth- to fifteenth-century copies in the British Library which ultimately derive from the medieval library at Durham Cathedral. See A.O. and M.O. Anderson, *Adomnán's Life of Columba* (1961), 546–9.

[22] R. Sharpe, *Adomnán of Iona* (1995), 354.

[23] Reeves, *The Life of St Columba*, 247; J. Colgan, *Triadis Thaumaturgae* (1647), 469b, n. 86, 479b, no. 17.

Columba's sister Mincoleth) was historically true then it would appear to be the earliest actual documentary evidence linking the saint (albeit indirectly through his nephews) with that part of Donegal, the area where his mother is said to have come from and where he was said to have been born, baptised, fostered and reared.

Although the Middle Irish Life of Colm Cille also says that he was born in Gartan,[24] the highly detailed information (allegedly) for the earliest events in the saint's life is found for the first time in Manus O'Donnell's *Betha Colaim Chille* of 1532. However the information outlined there is so comprehensive and precise that it must have been based on sophisticated existing accounts – whether oral or written – which were preserved in the general vicinity. Although Manus does not claim it, the various tales he tells seem to indicate that – at least in his time – there was a 'circular' pilgrimage route in honour of Colum Cille which started and ended at Kilmacrenan, winding its way around a number of specific locations – 'stations' – the legends connected with which, as it were, narrated the story of the saint's birth and first years.[25] Whatever the age of those monuments or the suggested pilgrimage around them, the tales which gave them 'authenticity' must surely have been preserved and cultivated by eminent local 'historians' such as the clerics who compiled the Kilmacrenan texts referred to above.

O'Donnell gives us very precise details about those sites as they were known to him in the early sixteenth century, seemingly depicting an integrated landscape that, itself, effectively narrated the story of the saint's birth and young life – its set-piece monuments laid out, as it were, in geographical and chronological order. A short *turas*, 'prayer round', or 'pilgrimage' in honour of the saint is marked out and still practiced in the local graveyard at Churchtown, however it seems as if there was a much longer pilgrimage route around all the sites listed here in medieval times, or at least in the time of Manus O'Donnell. That *turas* seems to have begun and ended at Kilmacrenan, the saint's mother's place. The other 'stations' seem to have included the following:

1. The semi-secret location where Eithne is said to have first experienced the labour pains of Colum Cille's birth and where the allegedly efficacious Gartan Clay is found.
2. The birth site at *Ráith Cnó* – actually two conflicting sites, as there seems to have been some late medieval confusion between sites at both Lacknacoo and Churchtown.[26]

[24] Herbert, *Iona, Kells and Derry*, 225 and 253.
[25] B. Lacey, 'Medieval Columban Pilgrimages in Derry and Donegal' (2009), 14–19.
[26] See P. Ó Gallachair, 'Where was St Colmcille born', *Donegal Annual* (1963).

3. The island in Lough Akibbon where Colum Cille played as a child and where the *Leac na Geanmnaidheachta* ['Stone of Chastity'] was located.[27]
4. Colum Cille's baptismal site at Templedouglas.
5. The *Cédimthecht Choluim Cille* ['First Walk of Colum Cille'], where the saint took his first steps as a baby.

There were a number of other minor or associated sites as well. But where did those stories come from and by what agency were they preserved from whenever they were devised down to the sixteenth century when Manus O'Donnell recorded them? The most likely candidates have to have been the learned clerical 'historians' associated with the church of Kilmacrenan. Manus himself seems to have been involved in an attempted renaissance in Kilmacrenan. As we saw above, he is credited with building a friary there for the Franciscans.

Gleann Cholm Cille

The most obvious place in Donegal associated with the saint is the remote valley in the southwest of the county that still bears his name – *Gleann Cholm Cille*. There are various ecclesiastical monuments from the early Christian period onwards in the valley, including a set of decorated stone slabs, which probably date from the early- to mid-ninth century.[28] These slabs and a number of associated sites of a more varied nature form the 'stations' of a *turas* or traditional pilgrimage route that is still made around the valley, particularly on the saint's feast day, 9 June.

The older name for this valley was *Senglenn* – 'the old glen', and no Columban associations are recorded about it until the stories told in Manus O'Donnell's sixteenth-century *Betha Colaim Chille*.[29] During Colum Cille's lifetime the valley lay in the territory of the Cenél mBógaine. This was probably not brought under the control of the saint's own people, the Cenél Conaill, until the early seventh century in the time of Máel Coba and Domnall who were sons of the important king Áed mac Ainmirech.[30]

[27] *Ibid.*

[28] P. Harbison, 'A group of Early Christian Carved Stone Monuments in County Donegal', in J. Higgitt (ed.), *Early Medieval Sculpture in Britain and Ireland*, BAR British Series 152 (Oxford 1986), 49–85; Lacy, *Archaeological Survey*. See also M. Herity, *Glencolumbkille* (Gleann Cholm Cille 1971). There have been many subsequent reprints and later editions of this booklet, both in English and Irish.

[29] Lacey, *Manus O'Donnell*, 25, 75–6. At a conference in Dublin in April 2006 Prof. Máire Herbert suggested that some of the poems about the glen in the sixteenth-century MS Laud Misc. 615 may be somewhat older.

[30] Lacey, *Cenél Conaill*, 76–84.

However this general area clearly had a reputation as a place of spiritual retreat and must have been considered as a space of ancient ritual and 'sanctity'. Apart from its remoteness and dramatic physical beauty, the valley and the surrounding area have some of the most important prehistoric megalithic monuments in the country; *Senglenn* was aptly named. In addition, the names of at least two other early saints who allegedly found refuge in that vicinity are recorded: Áed mac Bricc – whose cult is otherwise associated with the Irish midlands – and Assicus. The late seventh-century writer, Tírechán, says that 'Assicus the holy bishop was a coppersmith in the service of [Saint] Patrick, and he made altar-plates and square casks for the patens ...' Tírechán says that he died 'in the solitude of the mountains' of that district and was buried in another part of Donegal. It is certainly not impossible that Colum Cille spent some time in retreat there but, if he did, no trace of that has been left in the historical record.[31]

There is another *Gleann Choluimb Chille* on the Burren in County Clare. The earliest attestation of that name, however, does not occur until about 1600 and it is not clear what the connection with the Donegal saint actually was. Colum Cille is linked in legend with *Inis Mór* in the Aran Islands at the entrance to Galway Bay and, as we have seen, with the nearby coast of Connemara. The Aran Islands are relatively close to the Burren and Connemara is just across on the other side of Galway Bay.

Other sites in Donegal

Objections of various kinds can be made to the alleged links between Colum Cille and a number of the other religious centres in the Donegal area. Adomnán tells us that 'other monks of Saint Columba' were buried at the monastery of *Druim Tuama* in south Donegal but he does not claim that the church there was founded by his saintly predecessor. *Druim Tuama* – 'Ridge of the tomb' – was probably a pre-Christian site of some kind and it can probably also be identified with the alleged Patrician foundation of Sirdruimm.[32] It probably did not come within the sphere of Cenél Conaill political control or the ecclesiastical control of the Columban *familia* until around the end of the sixth century when, almost certainly, the area was conquered by the king Áed mac Ainmirech.

As outlined above, there are also late traditions about Colum Cille converting the local population and founding a church on Tory Island nine

[31] For a discussion of additional early ecclesiastical connections with this area of Donegal, see Einar Ólafur Sveinsson, *Camchuairt ar Éirinn, Ferdapaettir frá Írlandi, Impressions of Ireland* (Dublin 2005).
[32] Lacey, 'Tírechán's Sirdruimm'.

miles off the northwest coast of Donegal. The earliest attestation of those traditions occurs in the Middle Irish life of the saint, composed in Derry in the second half of the twelfth century. The Life claims that: 'He [Colum Cille] founded Tory and left a venerable man of his *familia* there, namely Ernaíne.'[33] However, Ernaíne belonged to the Cenél nÉogain as distinct from Colum Cille's own people, the Cenél Conaill, as did the only other two persons that we can connect at this early date with that island church: Damongóc Ailithir ('pilgrim') and Énna Toraid.[34] In fact, no one connected with the early medieval traditions of Tory (with the exception of the late retrospective traditions concerning Colum Cille) belonged to the Cenél Conaill and it is much more likely that its first church was founded in different circumstances.[35]

Drumcliff

The church at Drumcliff, now in County Sligo, was located in a strategic border location on the frontier between the territories of the Cenél Conaill and Cenél Cairbre and the kingdoms of Connacht. Apart from the battle of *Cúl Dreimne* in the sixth century which was mentioned above, two other important confrontations are recorded as having taken place in that classically border region. The first of these was the battle of *Corann* in 703 when the king of Tara Loingsech mac Óengusa was killed. Loingsech was a relative of Adomnán and the premier guarantor of the *Cáin Adomnáin*.

F.J. Byrne drew attention to the unusual precision with which the annalists on Iona noted that event. We are told that it occurred on 'Saturday, the fourth of the Ides [12 July] of July'. Even the time the battle commenced seems to have been recorded although inaccuracy crept into the transmission of the record and the separate sets of later annals actually give different times. The Annals of Tigernach says that it started at the third hour – 9.00 a.m.; *Chronicum Scotorum* says the fifth hour – 11.00 a.m.; while the Annals of Ulster says the sixth hour – noon. This confusion arises from the later copying and recopying of the original record; we can be fairly confident that the contemporary chroniclers on Iona knew exactly what time the battle commenced. Several historians have pointed out that, 'between the lines' of the annal entries about that battle we can almost read the despair the monks on Iona must have felt when they learned of the defeat and death of king Loingsech who had been one of their greatest patrons.

33 Herbert, *Iona*, 260.

34 Ó Riain, *Corpus*, 5:16; 8:40; 71:538; Lacey, *Cenél Conaill*, 89–91.

35 For an explanation of how Tory may have acquired its Columban associations see now Lacey, *Lug's forgotten Donegal kingdom*, 118–19.

Another battle is recorded as having taken place in roughly the same area in 1012 but, as it was a well-known frontier zone, there were probably many more that were not recorded.

Drumcliff, which was probably in origin the chief church of the Cenél Cairbre Mór, is mentioned in the Annals of the Four Masters in 871. According to an attached verse, the lord of that kingdom was buried there 'under hazel crosses …'. The place is mentioned again in the Annals of Ulster in 923 when its superior, who was also head of the church of Ardstraw – now in County Tyrone, died. As with the other Columban churches there are further casual references to Drumcliff over the centuries.

However, it has been shown that Drumcliff probably did not acquire its Columban identity any earlier than the eighth century.[36] My own suspicion is that this did not happen until a lot later, possibly not until the reign of the Cenél Conaill king Máelruanaidh Ó Máeldoraid who died in 1027 'on his pilgrimage'.[37] Máelruanaid had been very active in extending Cenél Conaill influence south of the Erne into north Connacht. The earliest ostensible Columban connection at Drumcliff seems to be the unique Irish carving of the Virgin and Child on a high cross there.[38] This rare motif occurs on St Martin's and St Oran's crosses on Iona – dated to the late eighth century, and on folio 7v of the Book of Kells which also is understood to have Iona as well as general Columban associations. The cross at Drumcliff is usually dated to the early 11th century (although alternative dates have been proposed),[39] which fits broadly with the dates and involvement of Máelruanaidh Ó Máeldoraid.

The main road from the west of Ireland to Donegal (both in ancient as well as modern times) passes through the middle of the ancient enclosure at Drumcliff. A stump of a round tower is preserved there as well as the shaft of a second tall, plain stone cross. Two fragments of a third cross from Drumcliff are now in the National Museum of Ireland.

---

[36] A. Candon, Drumcliff, County Sligo, in M. Meek (ed.), *The Modern Traveller to our Past: festschrift in honour of Ann Hamlin* (Belfast 2006), 70–7. As an aside, the grandfather of W.B. Yeats was vicar at the church there. Appropriately, the eminent poet is buried in the graveyard which occupies part of the area of the ancient monastery which was dedicated to 'the poet saint', Colum Cille.

[37] Annals of the Four Masters. According to the Annals of Inisfallen (1026) that pilgrimage had taken him first to Clonfert, then to Iona, then onward to Rome.

[38] See Dorothy Kelly, 'The Virgin and Child in Irish Sculpture', in Bourke, *From the Isles of the North*, 197–204.

[39] P. Harbison, 'Animals Date the Drumcliff Cross', in M. Timoney (ed.), *Dedicated To Sligo: Thirty-four Essays on Sligo Antiquarian and Related Topics*, forthcoming.

Brega and Leinster

There are a number of connections between Saint Colum Cille and churches and monasteries in the ancient kingdom of *Brega*.[40] *Brega* was the extremely important kingdom along the east coast north of Dublin, in which Tara was situated. As we will see below, most of those Columban associations may have come about quite late, perhaps only in the tenth century when they arose from the interests of the Norse king of Dublin, Amlaíb Cuarán, who clearly had a devotion of some sort to the saint of Iona.

The monastery of *Rechru* – almost certainly on Lambay Island as has been argued above – had been founded in the early seventh century by Ségéne, the fifth abbot of Iona. There are sporadic references in the annals to that monastery throughout the eighth century. Tuathal son of Feradach was captured during a Viking attack on the island in 832 but survived.[41] He may have been the son of the abbot Feradach son Ségéne who had died in 799. Tuathal himself died in 850 when he is described in the annals as the abbot of Lambay and Durrow, both of them Columban churches. There are other references to *Rechru* – such as the burning in 795 when 'its shrines were broken and plundered' – but it is difficult to distinguish these from references to Rathlin Island which as we have seen above had the same name in Irish. There could also have been some confusion with the Donegal island of Rathlin O'Birne.

The monastery of *Sord Choluim Chille* (now Swords, County Dublin) is first mentioned in the regular annals in 965 when Ailill son of Maenach, bishop of Swords and Lusk, died. Edel Bhreathnach has suggested that Ailill might have been related to Donnchad mac meic Maenaig the later abbot of Iona who died in 1099.[42] The word *Sord* means something like 'a pure spring well'. References to two Viking raids on Swords in the 840s, although occurring in a later text, may be genuine.[43] The legend of the foundation of that church by the saint occurs briefly in the Middle Irish Life where it is claimed that Colum Cille left one of his monastic community – Finán Lobur there along with one of his own Gospel books. However, it is also obvious from the same text that the cult of Saint Brigid was established in that vicinity prior to the arrival of the Columban influences.[44]

There are many references in the annals to 'burnings' in Swords and to the deaths of its officials throughout the eleventh and twelfth centuries. It was to Swords – then as until recently on the main road to the north of Ireland

---

[40] See Bhreathnach, Columban churches.

[41] Annals of Ulster, 832.5. The annal entry is a bit ambiguous and it is possible that Tuathal was elsewhere at the time.

[42] Bhreathnach, 'Columban churches', 13.

[43] *Ibid.*, 7.

[44] *Ibid.*

from Dublin – that Brian Boru's body was taken after he had been slain following the famous Battle of Clontarf in 1014.

> Mael Muire son of Eochaid, successor of Patrick, with his venerable clerics and relics, came moreover to Swords of Colum Cille, and brought away the body of Brian, king of Ireland, and the body of his son Murchad, and the head of Conaing [heir designate of Munster] and the head of Mothla [king of the Déisi of Munster], and buried them in Armagh in a new tomb. For twelve nights the community of Patrick waked the bodies in honour of the dead king.[45]

In 1035 the church at Ardbraccan in County Meath was plundered by the Dublin Norse under their leader Sitric son of Olaf. The monastery of Swords was plundered and burned in revenge by the Ua Máelsechnaill chieftain. Clearly Swords was thought of at that time as belonging to the Norse kingdom of Dublin.[46] It might be remembered in this context that Lambay Island (the later name of *Rechru* and in that form derived from Viking influences) was about ten miles from Swords, just off the coast. In 1042, Eochagán, described as the superior of Slane and the Lector of Swords and as 'a distinguished scribe,' died. A student was killed by lightning in Swords in 1056. In 1130 Swords was burned again and many relics were destroyed. The only remains of the monastery that survives to the present is the Round Tower with its pre-Romanesque doorway. In 1193 John, Lord of Ireland (later King John) granted to John the archbishop of Dublin 'the right to hold a fair once a year at Swords for eight days at the feast of Saint Columkill [9 June]'.[47]

Another Columban church in *Brega* was *Scrín Choluim Chille* – now Skreen in County Meath, although it is not mentioned in the list of the saint's churches in the Middle Irish Life. That church is of special importance due to its location on a hill just to the east of, and across the Gabhra valley from, the exceptionally important Hill of Tara. The earliest reference to Skreen and its association with Colum Cille occurs only in 976 when it was plundered by Muircertach the son of the powerful king Domnall úa Néill from the north of Ireland. The church may not have been established much earlier than that date and Edel Bhreathnach has suggested that it may have been the Norse king of Dublin Amlaíb Cuarán who founded it. Indeed Dr Bhreathnach has suggested that:

> Amlaíb Cuarán may have endowed Skreen, as its name suggests, to house a Columban relic particularly associated with the Norse and their conversion through the *familia* of Columba.[48]

[45] Annals of Ulster, 1014.2.
[46] Herbert, *Iona*, 90; Bhreathnach, *op. cit.*
[47] *Ibid.*, 15.
[48] *Ibid.*, 11.

Several authors have noted that the Columban churches in general and particularly the monastery on Iona may have played a major role in the conversion of the Norse settlers in the western parts and islands of Scotland. This missionary activity may have extended also to the related Norse kingdom around Dublin. It is suggested that the Dublin medieval church named after the Norman Saint Audoen – squeezed between the original High Street of the Norse city and the later city walls – may have been the site of a church originally dedicated to Saint Colum Cille.[49]

Amlaíb Cuarán eventually retired to Iona and died there in 980. This has led one scholar to suggest that the monastery there was at the time under Scandinavian rather than Irish or Scottish patronage.[50] A number of poems by the 'Chief poet of Ireland', Cináed ua hArtacáin, links the hill of *Acall* – as Skreen was previously called, with his contemporary the Norse king Amlaíb Cuarán. One poem possibly (but not certainly) written by Cináed specifically claims that Colum Cille had founded the church on *Acall*.[51]

> There came to Tara of the kings,
> Colum Cille without much fear;
> And on that hill where *Acall* lies,
> A church, by him, was founded there.

The abbot of Iona Fiachra Ua hArtacáin, who died in 976, was probably another link between Iona, Skreen, Colum Cille, Cináed and Amlaíb; Fiachra and Cináed were almost certainly relatives as Charles Doherty has pointed out. There are also other contemporary links that do not need to be outlined further here. In 1188 Pope Clement III confirmed the grant of the *ecclesiae sancti Columbe de Scrinio* to St Mary's Abbey. The latter church on the north side of the Liffey is now in the centre of modern Dublin, but in the twelfth century it was a suburb of the medieval city which itself lay on the southern side of the river.[52]

Moone, now in County Kildare, was another Columban church of some significance if the magnificent seventeen feet tall Scripture Cross there is any indication of its status. For many people this unusually slender sculpture is one of the most attractive stone crosses of the whole of the Irish series. Its naive but precise animal and human figures, depicting scenes from both the Old and New Testament, are frequently reproduced in modern artworks. The cross possibly dates to the ninth century. Fragments of a second cross are

---

[49] *Ibid.*, 6 notes 14 and 15; see also H.B. Clarke, *Irish Historic Towns Atlas No. 11: Dublin, part I, to 1610* (Dublin 2002), esp. p. 17.
[50] Smyth, *Warlords*, 171–2, 174 and 210–13.
[51] Quoted in Doherty, a Review, 298, on which this rhyming version is based.
[52] Bhreathnach, 'Columban churches', 15.

preserved on the site also. There are early references to a *Eó Mugna,* said to have been a great miraculous tree which grew nearby and which was later given a Christian symbolism.[53]

> Mughna a great sacred tree, and its top was as broad as the whole plain. Thrice a year did it bear fruit: it remained hidden from the time of the Deluge [at the time of Noah] until the night on which Conn of the Hundred Battles was born, and then it was made manifest.[54]

Máire Herbert has pointed out that the earliest reference to the monastery as *Móin Choluim* occurs in a gloss in the *Vita Tripartita* of Saint Patrick.[55] Edel Bhreathnach has suggested that Moone may originally have been a church dedicated to Saint Patrick which in the second half of the tenth century was re-dedicated to Colum Cille by the Norse king Amlaíb Cuarán.[56] Despite its obvious importance, there are only a few perfunctory references in the annals to the monastery at Moone.

In the Middle Irish Life of Colum Cille one of the churches said to have been founded by the saint was at a place called *Druim Monach* in Leinster. That place has yet to be identified but Máire Herbert has suggested that any one of the places dedicated to the saint in Leinster might originally have been called *Druim Monach.* She cites, for example: Kilcolumb and Columkille in County Kilkenny and Ardcolum in County Wexford.[57]

There are many other notices in medieval documents to churches and sites with Columban associations. In addition a large body of literary texts, most of which seem to date to the eleventh or twelfth centuries, mention Colum Cille and the places in Ireland connected with him. In 1041 Soerghus the lector and *airchinneach* ('monastic steward') of Tory died. The Shrine of Colum Cille was stolen by the Norse of Dublin in 1127 but 'was restored again to its house at the end of a month'. The 'house' in question may have been the church of *Scrín Choluim Chille* opposite the Hill of Tara mentioned above. Another 'house of Colum Cille' – this time at Kilmacrenan in County Donegal, was taken by Ua Tairchert from Áed son of Cathbarr Ua Domhnaill in 1129 and 'burned over him'. Áed's father was the Cathbarr Ua Domhnaill responsible for the making of the shrine of the *Cathach.*

---

[53] Mary Low, *Celtic Christianity and Nature: Early Irish and Hebridean Traditions* (Edinburgh 1996), 90.

[54] W. Stokes, *Félire Óengussa Céli Dé: The Martyrology of Óengus the Culdee* (London 1905, reprinted Dublin 1984), 259.

[55] Herbert, *Iona,* 282; Bhreathnach, 'Columban churches', 14.

[56] Bhreathnach, 'Columban churches', 11–12.

[57] Herbert, *Iona,* 282, note 378.

Iona

The monastery of Iona also continued to function throughout this period, with its abbot – at least intermittently – apparently retaining the title of *comarba Coluim Cille* until the beginning of the tenth century. The monastery suffered several attacks during the first phase of the Viking raids and there were a number of similar incidents much later. However, as the Norse colonists began to settle in the Hebrides – *na hInnse Gall* ('the islands of the foreigners' as they are still known in Gàidhlig) – they increasingly came under the influence of Christianity and the monastery on Iona. The Vikings are even said to have taken certain Columban traditions with them when they went to settle in Iceland.[58] Alfred Smyth points out that the *Landnámabók* claims that in the late ninth century Orlygur Hrappsson took the cult of Saint Colum Cille with him to western Iceland. At Esjuberg near Reykjavik, Orlygur kept a promise to the Hebridean bishop Patrick and built a church dedicated to Colum Cille [Kolumkilli] with timber he had brought specially for that purpose from the Hebrides.[59]

However, Iona – what Máire Herbert called the 'umbilical symbol' of the unity of the Columban churches in Britain and Ireland – was progressively marginalised from an Irish point of view.[60] The actions of Cinaed mac Ailpín in the middle of the ninth century had a similar effect from a Scottish perspective.

Despite this, Iona remained the burial place of Scottish kings as well as other aristocrats. As we've seen, Amlaíb Cuarán the king of the Norse of Dublin – who had formerly been king of York also – retired to Iona and died there about 980. At the end of the eleventh century Queen Margaret (herself later venerated as a saint) – the wife of the king of Scotland, Malcolm III – is believed to have endowed the monastery, although neither she nor her husband were buried there. In 1097 the island was visited by the king of Norway, Magnus Barelegs. The *Heimskringla* saga gives a short account of that visit:

> King Magnus came with all his company to the holy island ... Men say that he asked to open the small church of Colum Cille [the small shrine-chapel over the alleged site of the saint's burial]; he did not go in but closed the door again immediately and locked it, and said that none should be so bold as to enter that church.

Throughout the twelfth century there are sporadic references to Iona indicating the continuation of an Irish-style monastery there despite the upheavals in the Columban world elsewhere.

[58] RCAHMS, *Iona*, 48.
[59] Smyth, *Warlords*, 171.
[60] Herbert, *Iona*, 124.

Derry and the End of the Columban familia

The reason I love Derry is,
Its quietness, its purity;
For full of angels white it is
From one end to the other.

Attributed to Colum Cille
(11th or 12th century)

Since 1922 Derry has been a border city, located on the international frontier between Northern Ireland in the United Kingdom and the Republic of Ireland. In some ways, however, for much of the time since we've had records about it Derry has been a border place, even an important 'boundary marker'. Appropriately perhaps, Colum Cille – whose name and cult is closely associated with the city and its hinterland – can be seen as an iconic figure who is said to have crossed many of the boundaries of his time, boundaries that still unfortunately require some effort to cross in the twenty-first century: political, religious, linguistic and cultural borders.

Strictly speaking, Derry appears for the first time in the records in 619 with the death of Fiachra son of Ciarán who is described in some sources as having been its 'other' founder. We now know that the allegedly earlier references which purport to record its foundation by Saint Colum Cille – in the Annals of the Four Masters at 535 and the Annals of Ulster at 545 – are in fact late retrospective propagandistic inserts. There is no contemporary evidence that Colum Cille founded the monastery of Derry; the accounts that tell us that he did are all legends of a much later period. However, circumstantial evidence allows us to take the story of Derry back a little earlier than 619.

The earliest name by which the place is known to us is *Daire Calgaich*, meaning something like 'the oakwood of Calgach'. Derry is a very common place name in Ireland and the townland index records more than one thousand instances throughout the country. Some of those places – such as the sites at and near Derrynaflan in County Tipperary (where a magnificent set of early medieval, decorated metal liturgical objects was found) – are now 'islands' of higher dry land rising out of the surrounding 'seas' of peat bogs. To some extent 'Derry of Colum Cille' must have been just such an 'island'. Indeed, that is how the Elizabethans described it when they came to conquer it at the end of the sixteenth century: 'in manner of an Iland'.

Derry is an oval-shaped hill that rises up to about 120 feet in height and is about 200 acres in extent.[1] The River Foyle, which flows around the eastern half of that oval, is still tidal and fast-flowing at that point. It is about 40 feet in depth at high water and about 1,000 feet wide. The river, across which prior to the late eighteenth century there was no bridge, could only be crossed by ferry in ancient times. It was thus a formidable physical barrier and in the medieval period it formed a substantial political boundary. It was also, of course, simultaneously a considerably important water highway. The western side of the hill of Derry is defined by a relatively steep-sided valley, which in glacial times had been a channel of the River Foyle also. By the time that the monastery was established there in the late sixth century, the river had withdrawn from that valley leaving behind a strip of marshy boggy wetland – 'the Bogside' – by which name the area became famous in the late 1960s. The boggy strip itself could only be crossed easily in medieval times by one or two causeways. To the north of the Hill of Derry was another strip of bogland (also a former major river channel of glacial times) which crossed the isthmus at the base of the Inishowen peninsula. That too could only be crossed by a limited number of causeways in pre-modern times. Until the end of the eighth century, the latter bog formed the northern border of the kingdom of Columba's people, the Cenél Conaill. To the north was the territory of their neighbours and frequent enemies, the Cenél nÉogain.

We cannot be sure who the Calgach was who gave his name to the 'island' of Derry. Some nineteenth-century writers – almost certainly mistakenly – attempted to identify him with the southern Scottish (actually British 'Celtic') warrior who fiercely opposed the Roman military leader Agricola in the first century AD.[2] However, the Iona chroniclers recorded the death in 595 of a

[1] For a detailed description of the historical geography of Derry and its monastery during early medieval times see B. Lacy, 'The Development of Derry *c.*600 to 1600', in G. Mac Niocaill and P. Wallace (eds) *Keimelia: Studies in Memory of Tom Delaney* (Galway 1988), 378–96. See also Lacey, *Columba, founder of… Derry*, and Lacey, *Cenél Conaill*, 128–30. See also map of medieval Derry by John Bryson (forthcoming). Also B. Lacey, *Medieval and Monastic Derry* (forthcoming).
[2] See for instance J.K. O'Doherty, Derry Calgach, in *Derriana: Essays and Occasional Verses, Chiefly relating to the Diocese of Derry* (Dublin 1902), 1–12.

man called Tipraite son of Calgach, which suggests that they had some particular interest in him. There is some evidence to suggest that Tipraite's father may have been the Calgach of Derry[3] but we have no further information about him. Up to shortly before that time Derry had almost certainly been a secular fortification belonging to the Cenél nÉnnai; Tipraite and perhaps his father Calgach may have been the kings of those people. Probably under the powerful king Áed mac Ainmirech, Columba's own people, the Cenél Conaill, conquered the territory of the Cenél nÉnnai and handed over the Hill of Derry to the church, in part to 'fix' it as their new boundary marker. Almost certainly also it was Áed's nephew Fiachra son of Ciarán who then founded the monastery there, perhaps with Columba's blessing or involvement in some other secondary role. This seems to have happened around 578 or 579.[4]

Apart from the reference to Fiachra, there is no further mention of Derry in the sources until Adomnán refers to it in the *Vita Columbae* written around 700. He mentions the church there and its burial ground and refers to the port as a normal place of embarkation and disembarkation for people journeying to and from Britain, including to and from Iona. In 724, Caech Scuili, the *Scriba* of Derry, died. He was almost certainly a senior Columban church official – a Scribe in the biblical sense of an ecclesiastical judge rather than an ordinary copyist of manuscripts. As we have seen above, Caech Scuili was alive at the time of the composition of the influential *Collectio Canonum Hibernenses* which had several Columban connections. It is certainly possible that Caech Scuili might have had some involvement with that work.

These few references to Derry in the annals for the seventh and eighth centuries are just sufficient to let us know that throughout that period the monastery continued to survive there, most likely as a quiet relatively unimportant Columban church located on the northern boundary of Cenél Conaill territory which, in a secondary way, it was there to mark.

The only other reference to Derry in the sources for the eighth century is in 788 when it was burned. The circumstances of that conflagration are not further elucidated in the annals but it is very likely that it was connected with the contemporary campaign of attack by the Cenél nÉogain on the Cenél Conaill, which would culminate in the battle of *Clóitech* (Clady on the River Finn, now in County Tyrone) in the following year, 789. That battle would see the Cenél Conaill defeated and driven out of their homeland north of the Barnesmore Gap and deprived of any further role (with very few exceptions) in the overkingship of Donegal, as well as in the kingship of Tara. The burning of the Columban (for which read, 'Cenél Conaill') monastery of Derry in 788 was most probably part of that campaign. Apart from an incident in 833

[3] Lacey, *Cenél Conaill*, 128–9.
[4] *Ibid.*, 128–31.

when, interestingly, the Cenél nÉogain defeated the Vikings at Derry, we have no more references to Derry for about a century. It may be that the fire of 788 effectively destroyed the settlement there. But by the end of the ninth century when we begin to have references to it again it is clear that Derry had become part of the Cenél nÉogain world.[5]

In 921 there is a record of the death of Cináed son of Domnall who is described as 'superior' [*princeps*] of Derry and Drumhome 'and chief counsellor [*cenn adchamairc*] of Cenél Conaill of the North'. Cináed was clearly a very important person in his day. Besides a full reference to him in the annals, unusually his personal pedigree is specifically recorded in the secular genealogies.[6] The pedigree claims that he was a direct descendant of Áed mac Ainmirech, the sixth-century Cenél Conaill king who is said to have given Derry to the church. If anyone wanted to embroider the story of Áed granting Derry to Colum Cille, Cináed is a very likely candidate. The earliest surviving version of this 'official' account of the foundation of Derry is to be found in the prefatory material to the poem *Noli Pater Indulgere* in the *Liber Hymnorum.* The date of this material is generally reckoned to be about the tenth or early eleventh century. However, it is at least possible that the story belonged originally to the period around 921 when the grandiose title outlined above was claimed for Cináed.

In fact, it is very unlikely that Cináed was an official (senior or otherwise) in the monastery of Derry in any sense. For about a century and a half prior to his death, his people, the Cenél Conaill, had been excluded from the area in which Derry was situated and almost certainly from any office in that monastery itself. Cináed's title is probably no more than a nostalgic and outrageously propagandistic but anachronistic claim. By that stage it can hardly have been even a realistic aspiration. It may be that Cináed from his base in Drumhome was one of the first to argue – for propagandistic purposes – the theory of the foundation of the monastery of Derry by the Cenél Conaill's most important saint, Colum Cille.

Around the same time, Caencomhrac son of Maeluidhir who died in 929 was described as abbot and bishop of the monastery of Derry and steward of the Law of Adomnán. The death of the abbot (*comharba*) of Derry, Adhlann son of Eichneach, son of Dálach, was recorded in 952. Adhlann belonged to the Síl Lugdach, the west Donegal people who had moved into some of the territory previously occupied by the Cenél Conaill and who had taken on many of the characteristics of the latter, including a profound interest in the cult of Colum Cille. Adhlann is described in the Annals of the Four Masters

[5] B. Lacey, 'Derry, the Cenél Conaill and Cenél nEógain', in Meek, *The Modern traveler ....*

[6] M.A. O'Brien, *Corpus Genealogiarum Hiberniae*, Vol. I (Dublin 1962, reprinted 1976), 164: 144f18.

as the 'Guaire Aidhne of the clergy of Ireland'. Guaire Aidhne was a seventh-century king of Connacht who was considered to be an exemplar of princely generosity; the comparison with him was obviously a great compliment. Significantly this is also the earliest use in the Annals of the Four Masters of the anachronistic name for Derry, *Doire Choluim Cille*, rather than the older name *Doire* [or *Daire*] *Calgaich*.[7] Does this imply that Adhlann himself had some heightened consciousness of the Columban connections? From at least the beginning of the ninth century onward the Síl Lugdach to which he belonged controlled the area of northwest Donegal in which there was a plethora of sites associated with the birth and early life of Colum Cille. Just as with Cináed son of Domnall of a generation earlier, Adhlann would have had special but different reasons for fostering the cult of Colum Cille in Derry.

However, there is one problematic possibility that we cannot overlook in this context. Derry and the important Columban church at Kilmacrenan which was also known as *Daire Eithne* shared the element *Daire* or *Doire* in their names. Other evidence suggests that this occasionally lead to confusion – or even to deliberate distortion – regarding the two places in the medieval sources, particularly when the shortened forms of their names were used without further identification. It is quite probable that some incidents and stories connected in the literature with Derry should actually have been assigned to Kilmacrenan. This may well have been the case with regard to Adhlann (and maybe even to Caencomhrac son of Maeluidhir). By the tenth century Kilmacrenan was at the centre of Síl Lugdach territory.

As we have seen, the monastery of Derry had been founded – probably in the last quarter of the sixth century – by and on behalf of the Cenél Conaill; it retained that association until the late eighth century when the rival Cenél nÉogain secured control of all the territory around the settlement. As argued above, Derry may have been destroyed in 788 in the course of that conflict and, when we begin to get references to it again around the end of the ninth century, it is clear that it had passed in the meantime into Cenél nÉogain control. One cannot help thinking that the cultivation (and perhaps even the invention) of the legend that Colum Cille had founded Derry was designed, at least in part, as a propaganda bulwark by the Cenél Conaill against this takeover of their ancient church by the Cenél nÉogain. If that was so then it seems possible that the Síl Lugdach also had an interest in developing that legend. It would have tied in nicely with their own separate legends, which were connected with the sites associated with the saint in their expanded territory.

In 1100 the Norse fleet from Dublin attacked Inishowen and Derry. They were defeated by the ambitious Cenél nÉogain king Domnall Ua Lochlainn.

[7] The Annals of the Four Masters were, of course, compiled in the early seventeenth century but it does seem significant, whatever the reason, that the term is introduced here.

The reference in the annals clearly indicates that Derry was then definitely in the latter's hands; in fact, Derry had become, in effect, the capital of the Cenél nÉogain.

On 10 February 1121 Domnall died; he was one of the most powerful men in the Ireland of his day. The Annals of Ulster has the following obituary for him:

> Domnall son of Ardgar son of Lochlainn, over-king of Ireland, preeminent among the Irish in form and lineage, in sense and valour, in happiness and prosperity, in giving valuables and food, died in *Doire Coluim Cille* in the thirty-eighth year of his reign, the seventy-third year of his age, on Wednesday night, the fourth of the Ides [9] of February and the eighteenth [day of the moon], the feast of Mo Chuaróc the wise.

Domnall seems to have been living in Derry for much of his later years. We first hear of his association with Derry during the incident in 1100 mentioned above when he defeated the Dublin expedition that had actually come as allies of his arch-enemy and rival for the high-kingship of Ireland, Muircertach O'Brien. Muircertach himself came to the vicinity of Derry in the following year and allegedly destroyed the great hilltop monument known as the Grianán of Aileach a few miles away. The Grianán had been the symbolic headquarters of Domnall's people the Cenél nÉogain, probably for the previous three hundred years.

Those events must have been connected with Domnall's actual move into Derry. From early in the twelfth century we can see members of the king's extended dynastic line – the Cenél nÉogain – being appointed to the various offices of the monastery there. Domnall had come to power amongst his own people in 1083. He was an extraordinarily dynamic chieftain who set about expanding his power base; intruding himself and his appointees wherever and whenever the opportunity arose. He was too much interested in contemporary power to be overly concerned about the any ancient Cenél Conaill traditions associated with the monastery of Derry. As part of his campaign to secure the high-kingship of Ireland, Domnall set about reorganising the affairs of Derry. He appointed his own people to the senior positions there such as Congalach the son of Mac Conchaill – the *airchinneach* or 'monastic steward', who died at ninety-four years of age in 1112. In 1134 Bebhinn, a close relative of Congalach – probably his daughter, died with the title *banairchinneach* or 'female monastic steward'. She is the first named woman in the almost six hundred years of Derry's history and one of the first women whose name we know of to be mentioned in connection with any of the Columban sites, either in Ireland or Britain.

The entry in the Annals of Ulster announcing the death of Domnall Ua Lochlainn says that he died in *Doire Coluim Cille*, 'Derry of Colum Cille'. This is the first contemporary use in these annals of that name, although it may have appeared previously in some more literary sources. Its use here, rather than as a straightforward place name, also has a literary or cultic character to it; in some ways it is analogous to the way we would now talk about Joycean Dublin or Dickensian London. Around the eleventh and twelfth centuries a large collection of texts purporting to have been written by or about Colum Cille came into circulation. Many of these have a Derry theme: arguing that Derry was Colum Cille's first church, the one most loved by him, the one he was saddest to leave when the time came for him to go to Iona. Words are put into the mouth of the saint in verses that are blatantly propagandistic on behalf of the Columban monastery of Derry.

> And, oh! were the tributes of Alba mine,
> From shore unto centre, from centre to sea,
> The site of one house, to be marked by a line,
> In the midst of fair Derry were dearer to me.
>
> That spot is the dearest on Erin's ground,
> For its peace and its beauty I gave it my love;
> Each leaf of the oaks around Derry is found
> To be crowded with angels from heaven above.
>
> My Derry, my Derry, my little oak grove,
> My dwelling, my home, and my own little cell;
> May God the Eternal, in heaven above,
> Send woe to the foes and defend thee well.[8]

Since at least the tenth century when the *Liber Hymnorum* preface to the poem *Noli Pater Indulgere* had been composed, the belief that Colum Cille had been the original ecclesiastical founder of the monastery of Derry had been propagated and cultivated. As we have seen, the impetus for the elaboration of that claim may have been paradoxically part of Cenél Conaill propaganda in opposition to the new Cenél nÉogain rulers of Derry. By asserting that Derry had been founded back in the sixth century by the most important of their saints, the Cenél Conaill could justifiably claim that it still belonged by right to them in the tenth, eleventh and twelfth centuries – even if that claim was contradicted by contemporary realpolitik. However, if this is even part of the explanation for the explosion of Columban literature in Derry around this time, it backfired. It was the latter day rulers – the Cenél nÉogain – rather than the ancient owners – the Cenél Conaill – who fully developed the Columban legend and made the most use of it.

[8] Translation by Douglas Hyde. Alba, of course, refers to Scotland.

Derry had developed into a busy settlement by this period, with an obvious secular as well as monastic life. On 30 March 1135, Derry 'with its churches and houses was burned'. We know very little about the physical layout of the settlement[9] but there are a few references in the annals to the destruction of the oak trees that gave the place its name. Some of the stories about these trees show that they were protected by ancient taboos that had probably originated in pre-Christian times. In legend, Colum Cille is supposed to have said from Iona:

> Though truly I'm afraid
> Of death itself and Hell,
> I'm frankly more afraid
> Of an axe-sound, back in Derry.[10]

In 1137, Gelasius (or Gilla Mac Liag as he was known in Irish) who had been abbot of Derry for the previous sixteen years, transferred to Armagh to become the *comarba* or 'successor' of Patrick. That was the most senior position in the medieval Irish church. Gelasius had been strongly connected with the ecclesiastical reform movement that had been developing in the Irish church since the beginning of the twelfth century.[11]

In the year 1150 there was another major change in the monastery of Derry; the *airchinnech* Máelisa Ua Branain died and was replaced by Flaithbertach Ó Brolcháin who was a senior Cenél nÉogain ecclesiastic. Flaithbertach was probably the son of Máel Coluim Ó Brolcháin, the Armagh bishop who died while on pilgrimage to the 'hermitage' in Derry in the year 1122. Unexpectedly Flaithbertach was not accorded the title *airchinnech* like his predecessor; instead he would be known by the much more prestigious title of *comarba* of Colum Cille. For nearly one hundred and twenty years previously that title and the authority over the Columban *familia* in Ireland that went with it, had been the prerogative of the abbot of Kells. By the middle of the twelfth century, however, the influence of Kells and of the kingdom of Meath surrounding it were both in decline for political reasons; an opportunity existed for Derry to take over the leadership role from the midland monastery.[12]

We do not know how or why the decision to transfer this power from Kells to Derry came about. If there had been a general council or meeting of the

[9] For what we do know see Lacey, 'The development'.

[10] Lacey, *Manus O'Donnell*, 54.

[11] For the twelfth-century reforms see K. Hughes, *The Church in Early Irish Society* (London 1966), ch. 24; M.T. Flanagan, *The Transformation of the Irish Church in the Twelfth Century* (Woodbridge 2010).

[12] Herbert, *Iona*, chs 8 and 9.

Columban churches to arrive at a decision by consensus, then we have no record of it. On the other hand, a unilateral move by the authorities in Derry would have been supported by the Derry-based high-king Muirchertach Ua Lochlainn, while the leading churchman in the country – Gilla Mac Liag – must have been also well disposed to his former monastic *alma mater.* However the change came about, in 1158 at the synod of *Brí Mic Thaidg* – a place now in County Meath – Flaithbertach's position was given formal recognition and his status as the equivalent of a bishop was proclaimed.

> There were present twenty-five bishops with the legate of the successor of Peter [the papal legate], to ordain rules and good morals. It was on this occasion the clergy of Ireland, with the successor of Patrick, ordered a chair, the same as every bishop for the successor of Colum Cille, Flaithbertach Ó Brolcháin, and the chief abbacy over all the churches [of Colum Cille] throughout Ireland.[13]

In 1161 a synod under the patronage of Muirchertach Ua Lochlainn proclaimed that Flaithbertach was to receive all the tribute and jurisdiction of the Columban churches in Meath and Leinster which previously had been under the control of the local lay magnates. Flaithbertach was quick to collect whatever was 'owed to Colum Cille'. Immediately on taking up office he made a *cuairt* or official visitation throughout the territories controlled by the Cenél nÉogain in mid-Ulster.

> And he obtained a horse from every chieftain, a cow from every two *biatachs* [big farmers], a cow from every three freeholders, and a cow from every four *díomhaoin* [tenant farmers?], and twenty cows from the king himself [plus] a gold ring of five ounces, his horse and his battle-dress.[14]

He made a similar tour through Síl Cathasaigh in mid-Antrim the following year when he got 'a horse from every chieftain, a sheep from every hearth [house], and his horse, battle-dress and a ring of gold (in which were two ounces) from their lord'.[15] Two years later he visited the Dál Coirpre and the Uí Echach Ulad in what is now County Down. Again he received a horse from each chieftain and a sheep from each house, a *screaball* [a unit of precious metal], a horse and five cows from the lord – Ua Duinnsleibhe – and an ounce of gold from his wife.[16] In 1161 he went on a visitation to the territory of the *Osraige* [effectively, modern County Kilkenny]. The tribute due to him 'was seven score oxen: but it is their value that was presented there – namely, four

[13] Annals of Ulster, 1158.
[14] Annals of the Four Masters, 1150.
[15] Annals of the Four Masters, 1151.
[16] Annals of the Four Masters, 1153.

hundred and twenty ounces of pure silver: to wit three ounces for every ox'.[17] Charles Doherty has drawn attention to this particular visitation, with its similarity to the claims made on the king of *Osraige* by Colum Cille himself in the late fictional account of the Convention of *Druim Cett* which is found in the introduction to the *Amrae Coluimb Chille.*[18]

Flaithbertach seems to have undertaken a radical reorganisation of the physical layout of the monastery and the surrounding secular settlement shortly after becoming *comarba* in Derry, no doubt using the various tributes to Colum Cille which he was so assiduous in collecting. He commenced a number of building and monument projects. As early as 1155 he had had a 'door' made for the *Tempall.* The recording of this event suggests that it must refer to the insertion of a monumental doorway – possibly in the latest Hiberno–Romanesque style and perhaps similar to the roughly contemporary doorway inserted into Saint Oran's chapel on Iona.[19] The most significant of these projects seems to have occurred in 1162 when Flaithbertach with the help of 'the king of Ireland' Muirchertach Ua Lochlainn separated the ecclesiastical precincts from the secular areas of the township that had grown up around the ancient monastery. He had to demolish over eighty houses in the process. He then constructed a stone wall around the monastery and declared a malediction on anyone who would violate it.

His most important building achievement in conjunction with the same king was the construction of the *Tempull Mór* or 'great church' which was completed in 1164. This would become one of the most famous churches in the northwest of Ireland and in the following century it would be rededicated as the cathedral of the Diocese of Derry.

Flaithbertach's obvious success in reorganising the affairs of the Columban churches in Ireland generally was noticed in some unexpected quarters. This created something of a dilemma for him, as indicated in the annals in the same year that the *Tempull Mór* was finished:

> the leading members of the monastery of Iona, i.e. Augustin, the 'high' priest, and Dubhsidhe the Lector, and the head of the anchorites, Mac Gilladuff, and the head of the *Céile Dé*, Mac Forcellaigh, and the seniors of the monastery in general, came to meet the *comarba* of Colum Cille, Flaithbertach Ó Brolcháin, [to invite him] to take the abbacy of Iona, with the consent of Somerled [Lord of Argyll] and the men of Argyll and the Hebrides; but the *comarba* of Patrick [Gilla mac Liag] and the King of Ireland, [Muirchertach] Ua Lochlainn, and the chiefs of Cenél nÉogain prevented it.[20]

[17] Annals of Ulster, 1161.

[18] C. Doherty, 'Some Aspects of Hagiography as a Source for Irish Economic History', *Peritia* 1 (1982), 300–28.

[19] I. Fisher, 'The Heirs of Somerled', in R. Oram and G. Stell, *Lordship and Architecture in Medieval and Renaissance Scotland* (Edinburgh 2005), 85–97, p 85.

[20] Annals of Ulster, 1164.

About the same time that Derry was being reorganised physically and institutionally its 'historians' set about recreating the intellectual framework against which its monastery could be seen as the most important of the Columban churches in Ireland. Máire Herbert has shown that between 1150 and 1182 – and almost certainly before the 'Norman Invasion of Ireland' in 1169 – the text known as the Middle Irish Life of Colum Cille was written in Derry.[21] Although various versions of the life of the saint had been composed since Adomnán wrote his work in the late seventh century, those were all based on abridgements of the latter. The Middle Irish Life, containing slightly different material – although clearly heavily dependent on Adomnán's work, is nevertheless 'a new literary creation'. It was written as a homily to be preached on the occasion of the saint's feast day, 9 June.

> Christians celebrate the festival and commemoration of Colum Cille's death on the fifth of the Ides [9] of June as to the day of the month every year, (which is) on this day today … At that time every year, Irish scholars give a brief account of the holy Colum Cille's nobility of kin and ancestry, and furthermore of the wonders and innumerable miracles which the Lord performed for him here in this world, and of the culmination and excellent ending with which he finally crowned his victorious career, attaining his real home and his true native land, the abode of Paradise in the presence of God for ever.

One of the most important theses in the Life is that Derry was the first monastery founded by Colum Cille and, therefore, the one most loved by him. If that premise was accepted there could be little or no objection to Derry assuming the leadership of the confederation of churches associated with the saint. The Life clearly sets out the story of the foundation of Derry by Colum Cille, but it also claims that he was involved in the foundation of Kells although there is no doubt that that monastery was not established until the years 804 to 807. The story of the Columban foundation of Derry is no more reliable; its purpose was to bolster the new role of leadership of the Columban *familia* for the monastery there.

The Life is laid out with a clear biographical structure. The anonymous author uses the older Latin Life by Adomnán but, unlike that text, it reshapes its material into a linear chronological narrative. It gathers relevant information together from the more scattered approach of Adomnán and creates a continuous story, highlighting some of Adomnán's episodes, simplifying and clarifying others, deliberately leaving some out, supplementing others and transferring the locations of some events from

[21] Herbert, *Iona,* where there is a full text, translation, notes and discussion. See also J. Bannerman, 'Comarba Coluim Chille and the Relics of Columba', *The Innes Review*, Vol. XLIV, No. 1 (Spring 1993), 14–47, p 41, where the author argues for an Armagh provenance. However, that suggestion has not been accepted widely.

Scotland to Ireland. Kathleen Hughes, for example, said of the Middle Irish Life's simpler and more direct treatment of the story of the white horse that comes to sympathise with Colum Cille shortly before his death, 'it is all in Adamnán [*sic*], but muffled in words'.[22]

The Middle Irish Life, as is appropriate for the story of an exile, takes as its opening Biblical text the Lord's advice to Abraham: 'Leave your country and your land, your kindred and your own patrimony for my sake, and go into the country which I shall reveal to you' (Genesis 12:1). There follows the story of the saint's birth and early life, and then an outline of his career as a founder of monasteries in Ireland is set out in the form of a journey around the country. Colum Cille is said to have founded many monasteries but just twelve are named: Derry, Raphoe, Durrow, Kells, Clonmore (County Louth), Lambay, Swords, the unidentified *Druim Monach*, Moone, Assylin (County Roscommon), Drumcliff and Tory. There is also a suggestion of his involvement in the foundation of the famous monastery at Monasterboice in County Louth, otherwise connected with Saint Buite. That story is quite unhistorical but it undoubtedly reflects connections of some sort between Monasterboice and the *familia* of Colum Cille in the eleventh and twelfth centuries. However, the two saints were linked, at least in legend: Buite was said to have died on the same day that Colum Cille was born.

Colum Cille is depicted throughout as a spiritual model for his followers. Máire Herbert says of the Life that 'it caters for the demands of biography and edification, while also presenting twelfth-century aspirations in terms of the sixth-century lifetime of Colum Cille'. A story in the Life sets out to explain how one of the greatest treasures of Derry, the *Soiscél Martain,* came to be there in the middle of the twelfth century:

> On a further occasion [Colum Cille] went from Derry to Martin's city of Tours, and brought back the Gospel which had been on Martin's breast in the grave for a hundred years, and he left it in Derry.

Saint Martin, the fourth-century bishop of Tours in northern France, was noted in the early Christian period because of his reputation for introducing monasticism into western Christianity. The Irish church had a particular monastic character so Saint Martin's cult was widespread in Ireland, not least in the churches associated with Colum Cille. The Life of Martin by Sulpicius Severus was widely read and had been used as a model by Adomnán as well as by other Columban writers. One of the high crosses on Iona was named after Saint Martin, and in Derry there was a graveyard and a holy well dedicated to him. We might presume that some of the clearly fictional

[22] K. Hughes, *Early Christian Ireland: Introduction to the Sources* (London 1972), 236.

traditions associating Colum Cille and Tours might well derive from traditional stories associating him with Tory Island. The rendering of the name Tours in Irish as *Toirinis* looks suspiciously like the similar name of Tory and could easily have been the cause of confusion, not to mention facilitating the deliberate exercise of poetic license.

The *Soiscél Martain* was lost in the year 1182 when it was taken by 'foreigners' at the battle of Dunbo in north County Derry. It seems to have been in use then as a battle talisman in much the same manner that the *Cathach* was used in later times. This has led to a recent suggestion that the *Soiscél Martain* and the *Cathach* were one and the same manuscript.[23] The leading ecclesiastical family on Tory Island were the Ó Robhartaighs who may have been connected to the similarly-named Mac Robartaigh family to be found later in charge of the ancient site of *Rath Cunga* in south Donegal (where the *Cathach* was kept in the later Middle Ages), as well as their namesakes at Ballymagrorty just outside Derry. That the honor of being 'keeper' of that shrine was not without its own dangers is indicated by the events at the battle of *Belach Buidhe* in 1497. The Mac Robarthaigh *maor* or steward of the *Cathach,* who had accompanied the O'Donnells against the Mac Dermotts, was slain and the shrine was confiscated. It was returned two years later. In 1567, at the famous battle fought between the O'Donnells and the O'Neills at *Fearsat Mór* near Letterkenny, County Donegal, the Mac Robhartaigh *maor* was slain. Manus O'Donnell outlines the proper protocol for using the *Cathach* as a talisman:

> And to open it is not lawful. And if it is borne thrice right-hand wise around the host of the Cenél Conaill when they go into battle, they come back safe in triumph. And it is on the bosom of a successor or a cleric, that is so far as may be without mortal sin, that the *Cathach* should be borne around the host.

A number of other 'relics' or objects associated with Colum Cille were used in a comparable talismanic way. Mention has already been made above of the *Cathbuaidh.* The *Brecbennoch* or Monymusk Reliquary, which was also associated with the cult of Colum Cille, is a small church-shaped shrine-box that was carried by the Scots at the battle of Bannockburn in 1314.

Flaithbertach Ó Brolcháin died in 1175. Clearly he had been embarked on creating a new institutional future for the Columban *familia,* with Derry as its spiritual and – in his mind – historically appropriate headquarters. But he was too late. In 1169 one of the most momentous events in the history of Ireland had occurred, the arrival of the Normans in Leinster. Among other things, that event was to have profound implications for the *familia* of Colum

[23] Ó Floinn, 'Sandhills', 125.

Cille because many of the most important Columban churches were located in areas that quickly came under the control of the 'invaders'. Together with the great twelfth-century ecclesiastical reforms – such as the changeover to a formal diocesan system, the impact of the Normans dealt a final blow to the possibility of the Columban confederation reorganising along the lines of the continental religious orders like the Augustinians or the Cistercians, if that is what Flaithbertach had intended. In 1176 Kells was destroyed. In 1179 control of the monastery on Lambay was transferred to the canons of the church of Dublin. Swords was also transferred to the control of the Archbishop of Dublin while Moone became part of the possessions of the Bishop of Glendalough. Durrow also quickly came within the Norman sphere of influence. Raphoe changed, when it became the seat of the Diocese of Cenél Conaill. In 1175, when Gilla Mac Liac Ua Branain succeeded Flaithbertach as *comarb* on the latter's death, his title indicated little more than that he was abbot of the monastery of Derry.

It was the ultimate paradox. For some time Derry had been attempting to cultivate a reputation of pre-eminence among the Columban monasteries. In the first half of the twelfth century it had been at the forefront of moves to bring the Irish church fully into line with the rest of Christendom, drawing it away from the more exotic eccentricities of 'Celtic' monasticism – some of which may have been set in train by Colum Cille himself. Just at the point when Derry's claims to primacy were recognised, the world it sought to lead collapsed about it – partly from the forces which it itself had set in motion.

There was one final show of strength. About the year 1200 Reginald son of Somerled of the Isles founded a Benedictine Abbey and Augustinian Nunnery on Iona. Bethoc – Somerled's daughter – became prioress of the nunnery which possibly had connections with similar institutions in Ireland; some of the architectural details on the surviving early parts of the building are comparable with contemporary buildings in Ireland.[24] In December 1203 a letter from Pope Innocent III to Abbot Celestinus took the newly established Benedictine Abbey under papal protection. Unlike the nunnery however, which is located at some distance south of the main monastic complex, a huge new abbey building in the contemporary European style was commenced on the site of the ancient monastery itself. There was fury in Ireland, as recorded in the annals for the following year.

> A monastery was made by Ceallach [Celestinus] in the middle of the [original] enclosure of Iona, without any legal right and in violation of the community of Iona, and considerable damage was done to the [ancient] settlement. The clergy of the north of Ireland assembled to travel to Iona, namely: Florence

---

[24] Fisher, 'The Heirs', 87.

> O'Carolan, bishop of *Tír Eoghain*; Máeliosa O'Deery, bishop of *Tír Conaill*; and the abbot of the monastery of Peter and Paul in Armagh; Amhalgaidh Ua Ferghail, abbot of the monastery of Derry, with Ainmire O'Coffey and many of the community of Derry, as well as a great number of the clergy of the north. They went over to Iona and in accordance with the laws of the church they demolished the monastery, and the previously mentioned Amhalgaidh was ordained into the abbacy of Iona by the choice of the foreigners [the Norse of the Hebrides] and the Gaels.[25]

However, this proved to be no more than a futile attempt to stop the development of the new monastery and the restoration of the ancient connection with the northwest of Ireland. Amhalgaidh Ua Ferghail's authority could not have lasted for long, if at all; there is no further mention of it in the records. The Benedictine Abbey was completed shortly afterwards and expanded greatly over time, particularly in the fifteenth century. It still stands as the main architectural feature on the island, largely obliterating – as 'the clergy of the north of Ireland' had feared – almost all of the remains of the early Christian monastery.[26]

The account of the expedition to stop the building of the new abbey is the last mention of Iona in the Irish annals, except for one passing reference in 1249. Peculiarly, although there is no apparent reason for it to be mentioned, that reference simply notes that: 'twelve years and seven hundred years [have elapsed] since Colum Cille went to Iona to this year'. There continued to be some contacts with Ireland, of which one of the most intriguing is the fifteenth-century inscription recording the work of 'Donald Ó Brolcháin' on one of the pillar capitals in the Iona Abbey church. There has been considerable discussion about Donald's identity and about possible parallels with work in the northwest of Ireland.[27]

After 1220 there are no further references in the annals to the *comarba* of Colum Cille in connection with Derry. In 1397, when it was visited by the Archbishop of Armagh John Colton, we hear of the 'monastery of the Canons Regular, called the Black Abbey of Derry'.[28] At some stage in the late twelfth or early thirteenth century, like many similar ancient Irish churches, the Columban community of Derry had adopted the rule of Saint Augustine. It became a house of Augustinian canons of Arrouaise, subject to the Abbey of Saints Peter and Paul in Armagh. It survived in that fashion throughout the later Middle Ages, until the English conquest of Ulster and the dissolution of the monasteries in the Gaelic areas in the late sixteenth century.

---

25 Annals of Ulster, 1204.
26 For full description see RCAHMS, *Iona*.
27 *Ibid.*, 107 and 144.
28 Reeves, *Acts of Archbishop Colton.*

The formal position of the *comarba Coluim Cille* as leader of the saint's *familia* was ended with the end of the *familia* itself. When we next hear of this title it is being used more generically, in connection with several of the other old Columban churches. The *comarba* of Colum Cille at Drumcliff who died in 1252 was 'the richest and most prosperous man of his time in Ireland and the most esteemed, most charitable and most generous'. When Manus O'Donnell was 'enkinged' in 1537 it was 'by permission and advice of the Cenél Conaill and the *comarbadh* [successors] of Colum Cille'. These were almost certainly the clergy of Kilmacrenan, perhaps supported by ecclesiastics from other older Columban churches.

Colum Cille, from the Middle Ages to the Present

> Hail Columba, most holy of saints, from the stock of the king, celebrated islander … Father Columba, glory of our tradition, accept the prayers of your servants; save this choir that is praising you from attack by the English and assault by rivals.
>
> Medieval Scottish prayer to Saint Columba[1]

Of course Columban traditions of one kind and another continued in Scotland and, apparently, even in the North of England and on the continent as well as in Ireland throughout the later Middle Ages. As we have seen above, in England Durham cathedral played an important role in transmitting Adomnán's *Vita Columbae* as well as other unique information about the saint. It also preserved relics of the saint into the later Middle Ages, as did the church at Leominster in Herefordshire.[2] A fourteenth-century manuscript now in Edinburgh preserves the music and words for a service of lauds for the Feast of Saint Columba from the Augustinian Abbey of Inchcolm, in the Firth of Forth opposite the city. Parts of the music are said to date back possibly to the twelfth century or even earlier.[3] Other medieval musical works associated with the saint (who himself was occasionally known as *Colum Cille ceolach* – 'the musical Colum Cille') have also survived.[4]

A later Scottish work known as the *Breviary of Aberdeen* also contains much material of Columban interest.[5] It was compiled for William Elphinstone who

[1] Edinburgh University Library, Ms. 211. iv.

[2] Ó Floinn, 'Insignia Columbae', 144.

[3] Introductory notes by Isobel Woods Preece to CD album, *Scottish Medieval Plainchant: Columba, Most Holy of Saints.*

[4] Ann Buckley, 'Music in prehistoric and medieval Ireland', in D. Ó Cróinín (ed.), *A New History of Ireland: I Prehistoric and Early Ireland* (Oxford 2005) 744–813, pp 791–4 and 796.

[5] A. Macquarrie (ed.) with Rachel Butter & contributions by Simon Taylor, *Legends of Scottish saints: Readings, hymns and prayers for commemorations of Scottish saints in the Breviary of Aberdeen* (Dublin 2012).

was bishop of Aberdeen from 1483 to the time of his death in 1514. Elphinstone is one of the most interesting individuals in the whole cast of characters associated with the memory of Saint Colum Cille – and that's saying a lot. He was born in Glasgow in 1431 but his mother died when he was a child; he is said to have been brought up, to a large extent, by the clergy of the cathedral nearby to where he lived. He later studied at the universities of Glasgow (where he was ordained a priest) and Paris. He had many connections with France throughout his life and occasionally served as an ambassador from the Scottish king to that country as well as to England, in Germany and the Netherlands. He was a member of the Scottish parliament and held several senior public offices, among them Lord High Chancellor and Keeper of the Privy Seal. He was, effectively, the founder of Aberdeen University which he modelled on his *alma mater* in Paris.

As bishop in Aberdeen he was actively involved in the rebuilding of parts of the ancient cathedral dedicated to Saint Machar – a name that, as we have seen above, probably conceals that of Colum Cille – as well as a bridge over the River Dee. He is credited with being at least partly responsible for the introduction of printing to Scotland about 1507. One of the first such publications was the *Breviary of Aberdeen* which Elphinstone had caused to be assembled. It was printed in Edinburgh about 1510 and parts of it may have been written by Elphinstone himself. As well as much non-Columban matter the book includes, for example, material drawn from the *Vita Columbae* and rare information on both Finán and Colmán, the seventh-century Irish bishops of the Columban monastery at Lindisfarne. The *Breviary* also includes an 'office' – consisting of nine short lessons – for reading on the feast day of Saint Adomnán on 23 September. This bears a striking similarity to parts of the tenth-century text from Kells in Ireland, the *Betha Adomnáin.* There is still debate among scholars about whether or not both of those works are based on an original Iona composition that is now lost or – as Padraig Ó Riain has argued – the Aberdeen text was based on the *Betha Adomnáin.*[6]

The greatest of all the works compiled about Colum Cille in pre-modern times was completed by the Donegal aristocrat Manus O'Donnell in 1532. Manus succeeded to the chieftainship of the O'Donnells on his father's death in 1537 but he had been a leading figure in Donegal public life since at least 1511 when he deputised for the chieftain who was away on a pilgrimage to Rome. Manus continued to play an active political role from that time onwards; indeed, it seems strongly possible that one or two of the impressions that his father brought back with him from Rome may have found some expression in Manus's various projects relating to Saint Colum Cille.

[6] Herbert & Ó Riain, *Betha Adamnáin*, 36–41. See also Herbert, *Iona*, 170–4.

In a provocative study of his career, Brendan Bradshaw described him as 'Manus the Magnificent', suggesting that he was a Gaelic Irish version of the Renaissance prince Lorenzo de Medici.[7] Manus certainly made an impression on his contemporaries. There is a description of him by the English Lord Deputy St Leger who, when he met him in 1541, was surprised to find that, rather than the uncouth provincial he had expected to find, Manus was dressed instead in

> a coat of crimson velvet with aglets of gold, twenty or thirty pair, over that a great double cloak of right crimson satin, girded with black velvet [and] a bonnet with a feather, set full of aglets of gold.

His servants and attendants were equally well turned out.

Manus like his grandfather Aodh Ruadh O'Donnell was a great builder. He was responsible for the foundation of the Franciscan Third Order Regular Friary at Kilmacrenan in County Donegal.[8] The Kilmacrenan Friary was at or near the site of the old church of *Doire Eithne* where Colum Cille was said to have been fostered as a child around a thousand years earlier. Indeed the Friary may have been intended as a sort of millennial monument to the events that were believed to have happened at that very place. Precisely when the abbey was founded is not clear but it is not necessary – as some have argued – that it had to await Manus's succession to the chieftainship. He had completed the construction of his castle at *Port na trí namat* by 1527, as the Annals of the Four Masters put it 'despite Ó Neill and the Cenél nEoghain'. That castle was built in or near the present town of Lifford, located beside the point where the Rivers Finn and Mourne join to become the Foyle. The three rivers are said to be the *trí namat* – 'three enemies' of the place name. As it happens, the rivers could indeed be said to 'fight' each other at the junction, particularly when the tide is at its highest on the Foyle. Although usually said to have been located in what is now the urban area of Lifford, the castle may actually have been built on the County Tyrone side of the river, as its main function was to act as a spearhead in the almost continuous warfare between the O'Donnells and the O'Neills.[9]

[7] 'Manus the Magnificent: O'Donnell as Renaissance Prince', in A. Cosgrove and D. McCartney (eds), *Studies in Irish History* (Dublin 1979), 15–36. For additional biographical information about Manus, see D. Mac Eiteagáin, 'The Renaissance and the Late Medieval Lordship of Tír Conaill; 1461–1555', in W. Nolan, L. Ronayne and M. Dunlevy (eds), *Donegal History and Society* (Dublin 1995), 203–28; also Lacey, *Manus O'Donnell*, 7–15.

[8] The O'Donnells were great patrons of the Franciscans in Donegal. A tiny depiction of Saint Francis can be found incised below a fuller repoussé image of Colum Cille on the front face of the *Cathach* shrine-box – see, C. Hourihane, *Gothic Art in Ireland 1169–1550* (New Haven and London 2003), 121.

[9] Local tradition assumes that the castle was in what is now Lifford but there is an area called 'Castletown' on the Tyrone side of the river and the use of the word 'despite' is suggestive of a more forward position.

Manus may also have been involved in the construction of the castle built by the O'Doherty's (for their overlords the O'Donnells) in Derry, probably around the beginning of the early sixteenth century. If he was the type of modernising aristocrat that Brendan Bradshaw suggested, he may even have contemplated a Renaissance of sorts for that settlement – *Doire Choluim Cille* – which was connected in ancient tradition with his great patron saint. The account in the *Betha Colaim Chille* of the *oilithre* or pilgrimage in Derry in honour of the saint is the only description we have of that allegedly traditional devotional custom.[10] Manus might have included it in an attempt to boost the reputation and economy of the settlement through pilgrimage – the medieval equivalent of tourism. Other aspects of the *Betha* seem to show that Manus was – as we might expect – fully familiar with the layout of the settlement of Derry in the early sixteenth-century.

It was at the castle of *Port na trí namat* that Manus completed the *Betha Colaim Chille* or 'Life of Colum Cille' in 1532. The book is a huge compendium – an encyclopaedia – of everything that was known or believed about Colum Cille at the time that it was written. For Brendan Bradshaw its composition bears 'characteristic marks of the Renaissance spirit'. Manus is said to have written other material. A number of satirical verses as well as love poems alleged to have been composed by him survive. The love poems – in the contemporary *amour courtois* style – include two works written after his first wife Siobhán, Con O'Neill's daughter, had died in August 1535.[11]

Strictly-speaking, Manus did not actually write the *Betha Colaim Chille* himself although he was particular, in a clear departure from medieval practice, to assert his role as its 'author'. Instead, he brought together a team who collected and assembled material 'that was scattered throughout the ancient books of Ireland'. The preface states that he 'ordered the part of this Life that was in Latin to be put into Gaelic, and the part that was in hard Gaelic [Old and Middle Irish] to be made easy, so that it might be clear and simple to understand by all'. He dictated the Life 'with his own lips' to a scribe and he did that 'having conceived an affection and brotherly love for his high-saint and kinsman in blood, and for his own dear patron to whom he was fervently devoted'. Manus believed, almost certainly incorrectly, that as an O'Donnell he belonged to the ancient line of the Cenél Conaill, the kin group to which Colum Cille himself had belonged a thousand years earlier. In fact, the main impetus to write the Life may have been suggested by whatever celebrations (if any) were organised to mark the one-thousandth anniversary

[10] Lacey, 'A Lost Columban Turas in Derry', *Donegal Annual* (1997), No. 49, 39–41.

[11] For Manus's satirical poems see C. MagCraith (ed.), *Dán na mBráthar Mionúr* (Dublin 1967), 375–6, numbers 114-16. For the love poems attributed to him see T.F. O'Rahilly (ed.), *Dánta Gradha* (Dublin 1926), nums 49–53.

of the saint's birth. According to Manus's own calculations – and, despite alternative traditions, he was almost certainly correct – that event would have fallen in the year 1520.

Interestingly no copy of the full text of Adomnán's *Vita Columbae* could be found in Ireland for Manus but the Derry Middle Irish Life was available as was a whole host of other pieces of Columban literature, including a number of texts which are referred to but which are not known to survive to the present. The best-known manuscript of the text, Rawlinson B 514 in the Bodleian Library in Oxford, consists of sixty vellum folios, each page 17 inches by 11½ inches, followed by eighteen folios of poems on the O'Donnells. There is a picture of the saint in the robes of a mitred abbot on the second folio and some authors have suggested that the model for the face might actually have been Manus himself. However, there is some confusion about the date of this manuscript. Some authors suggest that it derives from the end of the sixteenth century while others suggest that it is nearer to the date of the original composition of the text.[12] The manuscript is bound in 'a furry sealskin'.

A metal image of the saint, somewhat similar to that in the Bodleian manuscript, occurs on the late fifteenth- or early sixteenth-century front face of the *Cathach* shrine-box. Broadly similar images, also interpreted as depictions of Colum Cille, can be found on the face of two other shrine-boxes: the *Misach* (1534) and the *Domnach Airgid* (15th c.).[13]

There is a second sixteenth-century vellum manuscript of the *Betha* in the collections of the Irish Franciscans which have recently been transferred to the library of University College Dublin. That manuscript was made in the 1530s or 1540s for the Tyrone aristocrat Niall Óg Ó Néill by the scribe Eoghan Carrach Ó Siaghail. Niall Óg was also known as Niall Conallach on account of his connections with *Tír Chonaill* or Donegal; he was married to a sister of Manus O'Donnell. A third version, but written on paper, was made in 1608 by a scribe called Brian Mac Niallghais from an original – the date of which is not known – made by a member of the famous Donegal Ó Cléirigh learned family, Giolla Riabach Mór. The Mac Niallghais family had long held hereditary ecclesiastical rights in *Gleann Colm Chille.*

---

[12] See P. Walsh, 'The Life of Columcille by Maghnus Ó Domhnaill', in N. Ó Muraíle, *Irish Leaders and Learning through the Ages: Paul Walsh* (Dublin 2003), 407–11; P. Ó Fiannachta, 'Betha Choluimb Chille', in *Léachtaí Cholm Cille* XV (1985), 11–33, pp 11 and 13; F. Henry & G. Marsh-Micheli, 'Manuscripts and Illuminations', in A. Cosgrove, *A New History of Ireland* (Oxford 1993), 781–815, pp 807–9 and T. O'Neill, *The Irish Hand; scribes and their manuscripts from the earliest times to the seventeenth century, with an exemplar of Irish scripts* (Portlaoise/Mountrath 1984), 85.

[13] Hourihane, *Gothic Art*, 121, 124 and 130.

One of the points frequently made about the *Betha Colaim Chille* is that it seems to have been composed in a context in which Manus O'Donnell was familiar with that most recent innovation of his time – the printed book. Some authors have suggested that the appearance of the Rawlinson B 514 text is based on the layout of printed books.[14] It has been speculated, without of course any specific evidence to support the view, that Manus himself may have intended or at least hoped that the work would be printed. Already Lives of the two other patron saints of medieval Ireland had been printed – Cogitosus' Life of Brigid in Milan in 1486 and Jocelin's Life of Patrick in Antwerp in 1514,[15] and William Elphinstone had printed much of Columban interest in Edinburgh about 1510. However, we have no specific evidence that O'Donnell was aware of the existence of any of these publications. The O'Donnell text was not printed in any form until 1647 when John Colgan gave a Latin translation of it as his *Quinta Vita* of the saint in his *Triadis Thaumaturgae seu Divorum Patricii, Columbae, et Brigidae ... Acta.* Colgan's source seems to have been the manuscript A 19, the copy made by Brian Mac Niallghais in 1608.[16]

Manus tells us in the preface that his reasons for compiling the work were '[God's] honour and the raising-up of [Colum Cille's] name, and ... the good of the people who read and listen to it, and ... the good of [his] own soul and body, and ... the Devil's dishonour and great hurt.' The Life is laid out in the normal chronological and biographical manner and is written for the most part in Irish. It is extraordinarily detailed, with 'events' – especially events in Ireland – specifically localised to places and landscape features that were clearly known to Manus himself or which could be corroborated in his own time. Some of the stories he tells have what might be described as a characteristically Irish twist to them.

> Another time when Colum Cille was in Derry, a gambler and a poor man came to him. And he gave a *bonn* [a coin] to the gambler and a penny to the poor man. And it seemed strange to all that he should give more to the gambler than to the poor man. God revealed to Colum Cille that everyone was amazed at this, but he said to some of them that were present that they should follow the gambler and the poor man to see what each would do with the money he had given them. And they found the gambler in a tavern drinking the value of the *bonn* and sharing it with every needy person who came to him. And this was the way that they found the poor man: dead on

[14] D. Mac Eiteagáin, 'The Renaissance and ... Lordship of Tír Chonaill', 219, quoting from T. O'Neill, *The Irish hand* (Portlaoise 1984), 84–5.
[15] R. Sharpe, *Medieval Irish Saints' Lives: An Introduction to Vitae Sanctorum Hiberniae* (Oxford 1991), 38.
[16] Ó Fiannachta, 'Betha Choluimb Chille', 11 and 13.

> the road and the penny that Colum Cille had given him sewn into his clothes along with five marks. They returned to Colum Cille with the news.
>
> Then Colum Cille said: 'God let me know that the poor man had only a short time to live but even if it had been longer he wouldn't have used for himself, or anyone else, what he'd been given but hoard it as he did with the five marks. And although the gambler was a bad man, he didn't hoard what he got but, to the value of the *bonn*, he satisfied himself and the others that were in need. That's why I gave him more than the poor man.'

The wonder-working saint of recent folklore is already fully apparent in this text. As well as the mystic youth painted onto stained-glass windows or the larger than life character encapsulated in plaster and stone statues, that figure would continue to develop into a wish-fulfilling 'magician'. He appears as such in the traditional Irish language song – *Colum Cille na Féile* – from Aranmore Island off the coast of County Donegal, where he operates on no higher a spiritual level than that of helping a young man find his true-love. However, Colum Cille was not always believed to have such benign characteristics.

In the Autumn of 1566, during the course of the Elizabethan conquest of Gaelic Ulster, an English garrison set up a base in Derry, including, it is believed, in the twelfth-century *Tempull Mór* cathedral church. The following April a fire broke out and spread to the ammunition store causing an explosion that killed at least thirty people. The near contemporary commentator Philip O'Sullivan Beare, in his highly partisan *History of Catholic Ireland*, claimed that the English soldiers were heard to cry out 'The Irish *god* Columba killed us all.' Death 'through the miracles of God and Colum Cille' had frequently been reported in the sources throughout the Middle Ages.[17] In 1542 the Annals of the Four Masters records a similar incident:

> Brian Dorcha Mac Conmhidhe, son of Sólaimh, a man skilled in poetry and literature, a rich and affluent man who kept a house of general hospitality for all, died about the feast day of Colum Cille through a miracle of God and Colum Cille and the curse of Ó Robhartaigh because he had profaned and dishonoured the Great Cross, for he had struck it before that time.

This great jewelled cross, which was mentioned in other contemporary sources, was preserved as a relic of the saint by the Ó Robhartaigh family on Tory Island.[18] Probably what was another jewelled cross associated with the saint is mentioned in 1584. The English Lord Deputy in Ireland Sir John Perrot sent William Cecil – Queen Elizabeth's Chief Secretary of State – a relic of Colum Cille which he had acquired as booty from Dunluce castle on

---

[17] For a discussion of some of those instances, see D. Mac Giolla Easpaig, *Breccán Cathe*, a forgotten Derry Saint, *Ainm* vol. vii (1996–1997), 75–88, esp. pp 75–7.

[18] Ó Floinn, 'Sandhills', 132–3.

the Antrim coast during his campaigns against Sorleyboy MacDonald. Perrot was quite sarcastic about the beliefs that the native Irish are said to have had in the efficacy of the cross.

> And for a token I have sent you holy Colum Cille's Cross, a *god* of great veneration with Sorleyboy and all Ulster, for so great was his grace that happy the man thought himself who could get a kiss of the said cross. I send him [the cross/god] unto you that, when you have made some sacrifice unto him, according to the disposition you bear unto idolatry, you may, if you please, bestow him upon my good Lady Walsingham, or my Lady Sydney, to wear as a jewell of weight and bigness, and not of price or goodness, upon some feast or triumph day at Court.[19]

When the English under Sir Henry Dowcra captured Derry again in 1600, according to the contemporary author of the *Life of Red Hugh O'Donnell*:

> they tore down the monastery and the church, and they showed neither honour nor respect to the great Saint [Colum Cille], for they destroyed all the ecclesiastical edifices in the place, and made rooms and sleeping apartments of them, and used some of them to eat in.

But not everything could have been destroyed. When Sir Cahir O'Doherty attacked the English settlement in Derry in 1608, according to Thomas Ridgeway writing to Lord Salisbury, the old abbey church, the *Dub Regles* – believed to have been the very church founded by Colum Cille:

> whose timber work, either in respect of the height or in devotion to their solemn Colum Cille, the patron of that place, and whose name they use as their word of privity and distinction in all their wicked and treacherous attempts, was not fired.[20]

The events of the late sixteenth and early seventeenth centuries – when Ulster was conquered by the forces of Queen Elizabeth and, under the Scottish king James VI and I, was colonised by loyal English and Scottish settlers – finally broke up the social and religious systems that had preserved the cult of Colum Cille as part of the everyday dominant culture in the northwest of Ireland for the previous thousand years. The introduction of Protestantism and the Post-Reformation responses of the Roman Catholic church brought an end to many of the traditional forms of Christianity which, at least in some respects, must have dated back to the time of the saint himself.

Richard Sharpe has pointed out that Scotsman Roderick MacLean (bishop of the Isles), who obviously had access to a full text, published a paraphrase

[19] *Calendar of State Papers Ireland 1574–85*, 20 October 1584, 530.
[20] *Calendar of State Papers Ireland 1606–8*, 3 July 1608, 606.

in Latin verse of two of the books of Adomnán's *Vita Columbae.*[21] This was printed in Rome in 1549. The first time that any of the actual texts of the earlier Lives of Colum Cille themselves appeared in print was in 1604 at Ingolstadt, now in Germany, when H. Canisius published, in volume 5 of his *Antiquae lectionis*, the short version of Adomnán's *Vita Columbae.* That version had been made originally in the monastery of Sankt Gallen in Switzerland in the middle of the ninth century.

In 1621 an Irish Jesuit priest called Stephen White[22] rediscovered Dorbéne's full text at the monastery of Reichenau in Lake Constance. White was allowed to borrow the manuscript and bring it to Dillingen in Germany where he then worked: coincidentally, he had previously held a professorship at Ingolstadt. He made a copy of Dorbéne's text which, through the Irish Franciscans in Louvain, became the basis for the version published by John Colgan in 1647. Simultaneously, Colgan also published a Latin translation of Manus O'Donnell's Life of the saint along with a dossier of many other important and relevant texts. White's copies also became available to a number of other individuals and institutions such as the Bollandists who were researching the Lives of the Saints generally on behalf of the Catholic church. A copy was also made available to the great Irish Protestant scholar and Archbishop of Armagh, James Ussher.

The memory of Colum Cille was also preserved and advanced in the various writings of the seventeenth-century Donegal authors known as the Four Masters, such as the exceptionally long entry in the Martyrology of Donegal.[23] However, the bulk of the saint's relics and other 'treasures' associated with his cult – detached now from the contexts that had given them their original religious meaning – were removed from their traditional locations and scattered as 'antiquities' to Dublin, Britain and the continent.

The 'Plantations in Ulster' introduced a totally new way of living and believing which was at variance with the ancient faiths and social customs of the native inhabitants. Perhaps surprisingly the great new Protestant cathedral in the colonial city of Londonderry – constructed between 1628 and 1633 – was dedicated to Saint Columb when we might have expected its London builders to have named it after a patron with whom they were more familiar – Saint Paul or Saint George for example. Something of the ancient traditions did survive, especially but not exclusively in the folk beliefs and practices of the descendants of the pre-Plantation inhabitants of Ulster – the *ab origines* as they are referred to in some nineteenth-century documents.

21 Sharpe, *Iona*, 92.

22 Sharpe, *Medieval … Lives*, 44–6, provides an excellent summary of Fr White's career.

23 J.H. Todd & W. Reeves (eds), *The Martyrology of Donegal: A calendar of the saints of Ireland*, (Dublin 1864), 9 June.

Columban traditions were also widespread among the Catholic and Protestant populations in the highlands and western isles of Scotland. Many of those were collected in the late nineteenth century and published by Alexander Carmichael in his enormous work *Carmina Gadelica* or *Ortha nan Gaidheal*.[24] Alexander Carmichael, or Alastair Mac Gille Mhícheil, was born on the island of Lismore in 1832. He came from a family that claimed links back to the monastery founded on Lismore by St Lugaid or Mo Luag in the late sixth century. He was educated in Greenock and Edinburgh and later joined the civil service as a customs and excise official. His work took him to various parts of the Gàidhlig-speaking western isles and mainland of Scotland. In the course of those travels he commenced his great collections, writing down the oral 'literature' of the ordinary people 'from Arran to Caithness, from Perth to St Kilda'. The first two volumes of his work were published in 1900, but he continued collecting up to around 1910 when he was already in his late seventies. He died in 1912. Carmichael's work among the crofters was not limited to intellectual matters and he is also credited with bringing about various social advances. Critics have pointed out that he seems to have 'improved' on at least some of the texts that he took down, but his defenders have pointed out that this was no more than the common practice of the times and that his work still carries a great deal of authenticity. In the introduction to this material Carmichael himself said:

> Whatever be the value of this work, it is genuine folklore, taken down from the lips of men and women, no part being copied from books. It is the product of faraway thinking, come down on the long stream of time. Who the thinkers and whence the stream, who can tell? Some of the hymns may have been composed within the cloistered cells of Derry and Iona, and some of the incantations among the cromlechs of Stonehenge and the standing stones of Callarnis [Callanish]. These poems were composed by the learned, but they have not come down through the learned, but through the unlearned – not through the lettered few, but the unlettered many – through the crofters and cottars, the herdsmen and shepherds, of the Highlands and Islands.

Carmichael's work was continued by his daughter Ella, his grandson James Carmichael Watson, as well as by other members of his family and later scholars. Three more volumes were published by 1954. The sixth volume – which included the indexes – was published in 1971, edited by Angus Matheson as was the fifth volume. A recent author has said of the material that:

> These religious texts with their strange blend of pagan and Christian imagery, witnesses to the spirituality of a vanished age, their complement of mysterious

[24] Much of what follows is drawn from J. MacInnes, Preface, in Moore, *Carmina Gadelica*, 7–18.

> words and phrases, apparently unknown outside this repository of incantations, and their dignified, almost liturgical, style, fascinate the reading public, Gaelic and English alike. Here it would seem was a lost lexicon of piety which almost miraculously had survived into modern times. It had been discovered on the verge of extinction, in remote places and in an obscure tongue; it was now, at the last possible moment, being revealed to the world at large. The publication of *Carmina Gadelica* was a signal triumph, an outstanding literary achievement, and an event of the greatest moment to the whole of Gaelic Scotland.[25]

Colum Cille is of course also widely represented in Irish folklore such as in the marvellous Schools Collection of the 1930s. A perusal of those records would lead you to believe that almost every parish (if not every townland) in the country has its own local story about the saint. Among the Irish folk survivals were the so-called 'prophecies' of Colum Cille. Edel Bhreathnach has drawn attention to the fact that references to these occur as far back as the late twelfth century.[26] In *Expugnatio Hibernica* the twelfth-century writer Giraldus Cambrensis talks about John de Courcy who came, as part of the Norman invasion of Ireland, to Downpatrick:

> The same seer [Colum Cille] wrote that a poor and needy man, a fugitive, so to speak, from other lands, was going to come to Down[Patrick] with a small force and take possession of the city without acknowledging the authority of any superior. He also foretold many battles and other events of various kinds, which were clearly fulfilled in the person of John de Courcy. John himself keeps this book of prophecies, which is written in Irish, by him as a kind of mirror of his own deeds.[27]

John O'Donovan in his early-nineteenth-century Ordnance Survey letters mentions a James O'Hood from around Maghera in County Derry 'a great Irish scholar, who lived about the period of the Siege of Derry (1689), [and] was the last person to understand Columbkill's prophecies'. Versions of these alleged predictions circulated widely, and a popular edition with 'literal translation and notes' was published by Nicholas O'Kearney in 1856. This was immensely popular reading throughout Ireland right into the twentieth century and there were many subsequent reprints of the work. O'Kearney came from near Dundalk and was himself a poet and a scribe in the Gaelic tradition. But his 'prophecies' amounted to little more than rewritings – probably mostly by himself – of some of the poems attributed to Colum Cille

[25] *Ibid.*, 7.
[26] Bhreathnach, 'Columban churches', 14–15.
[27] A.B. Scott & F.X. Martin (eds), *Expugnatio Hibernica. The Conquest of Ireland by Giraldus Cambrensis* (Dublin 1978), 176–7. Quoted by Bhreathnach *op. cit.*

that had been in existence from around the twelfth century. He gave colourful nationalist interpretations to many of the references in the poems. William Reeves, who at that time was working on his own monumental *Life of St Columba* which was published in 1857, rejected O'Kearney's work – denouncing one of the so-called prophecies as 'not as old as the [1851] Ecclesiastical Titles Bill!'

Reeves book, although bejeweled with a lot of extra information, is based on an annotated edition of the Dorbéne manuscript of Adomnán's *Vita Columbae.* This, as has been shown above, was rediscovered in 1621. However, it seems to have disappeared from view again for the rest of the seventeenth and much of the eighteenth century. By whatever means, it was transferred to the public library in the town of Schaffhausen in Switzerland before 1799 where, in 1845, it was found by Dr Ferdinand Keller, a student of Irish manuscripts.[28] Dr Keller says that he found it 'at the bottom of a high book-chest, where it lay pêle-mêle with some other MSS and old books totally neglected, bearing neither title nor number'. Dr Keller's facsimiles and collations with the printed sources were made available to William Reeves in 1851.

Richard Sharpe has drawn attention to the sectarian debates in the second half of the nineteenth century that followed the publication of Reeves' great work.[29] Just as with Saint Patrick, Roman Catholics and Protestants of separate traditions – in a multitude of publications produced both in Britain and Ireland – argued about the nature of Columban and 'Celtic' Christianity. Reeves – himself an extraordinary scholar – was certainly not to blame for this, but his encyclopaediac book was used as a quarry of ideas by the protagonists on the differing sides.

What was believed to have been the thirteen-hundredth anniversary of the saint's death in 1897 provided a major opportunity for such denominational display – not least in Derry where remarkable Catholic ceremonies were organised by Fr William Doherty, the administrator of Saint Columba's church.[30] Ten years later Fr Doherty embarked on an ambitious rebuilding programme at that church. Saint Columba's or, as it is better known in

[28] Reeves, *Columba*, xxiii–xxiv.

[29] Sharpe, *Adomnán*, 95–8.

[30] Excellent accounts of these events can be found in *Derry Columbkille: Souvenir of the Centenary Celebrations in Honour of St. Columba, in the Long Tower Church, Derry, 1897–99* (Derry 1899). The 'souvenir' is, in fact, a 200-page hardback book, edited (and presumably largely written) by Fr Doherty. A similar account of contemporary events in Donegal can be found in the book *'Cuímhne Coluimcille' or The Gartan Festival – being A Record of the Celebration held at Gartan on the 9th June, 1897 – The Thirteenth Centennial of St. Columba* (Dublin 1898). For a recent analysis of the surrounding events in Derry, see B. Lacey, 'Revival or Re-Invention: Columban Traditions in Nineteenth Century Derry', *Ulster Folklife*, Vol. 50 (2004), 27–50.

Derry, the 'Long Tower' – taking its name from the adjacent Round Tower of medieval times – was originally built in 1784; the first Roman Catholic church in Derry since the Plantation and the Reformation. It was erected outside the seventeenth-century city walls in an area that was increasingly turning into a Catholic ghetto. That area would become famous all over the world in the second half of the twentieth century as 'The Bogside'.

Most of the people who lived in that district in the nineteenth century had come into the city from neighbouring County Donegal, where many folk traditions about Colum Cille had survived from the Middle Ages at various popular levels. The Long Tower church had been built on or very close to the site of the great twelfth-century *Tempull Mór*, but tradition in Derry – especially that cultivated by Fr Doherty – claimed that it was the site of Colum Cille's own sixth-century church. Fr Doherty claimed that the rebuilding programme which went on between 1907 and 1909 gave him the opportunity to search for the site of the ancient monastery.

> The exact position of the Dub Regles was fixed beyond yea or nay by the discovery of foundations during excavations preparatory to the erection of the present church. Father William Doherty made a careful examination of the remains and, after comparing them with the seventeenth-century manuscript maps, and [Manus] O'Donnell's description, was able to define the original outline.[31]

Alleging apparent archaeological precision, the results of Fr Doherty's investigations were commemorated in a series of inscribed plaques inserted in the floor of the church and surrounding churchyard. Throughout the refurbished church elaborate and beautiful stained-glass windows, paintings, sculpture and mosaic were used to depict the familiar stories of the saint. The building became a translation of the ancient legend into art and architecture, a monument – in effect an 'interpretive centre' of its time – to Colum Cille and the traditional story of his foundation of the monastery of Derry.

Fr Doherty was almost certainly wrong about his identifications. Apart from the issue of the identity of the founder, the monastic church – as distinct from the *Tempull Mór* – was most probably on the site occupied then by the Church of Ireland Saint Augustine's chapel-of-ease. With hindsight, it is easy to be critical of the enthusiasms of this remarkable priest but, given the mutual political and sectarian hostility of the times, it would have to be said that at the beginning of the twentieth century Derry Catholics would have found it difficult to admit that the site of the original Columban monastery was in modern times occupied by a Protestant church.

[31] Anon., *The Story of the Long Tower 546–1946* (Derry 1946), 11.

The Columban churches and traditions in Scotland experienced parallel difficulties. Iona had various problems, not the least being the religious and political upheavals that swept these islands during the sixteenth and seventeenth centuries. The main abbey building on the island dates originally to the thirteenth century but it had had to be extensively rebuilt in the fifteenth century, after fifty years or so of neglect. That neglect is often blamed on the abbot Fingon Mackinnon. The restoration was carried out by Abbot Dominic who was in office between 1421 and 1465. There is an effigy of the last abbot of Iona, John Mackinnon, who died in 1499, in the choir at the east end of the Abbey church.

In act II, scene 4 of *Macbeth*, William Shakespeare refers to Iona as the burial place of Duncan who was murdered by Macbeth and:

> Carried to Colmes-kill,
> The sacred storehouse of his predecessors
> And guardian of their bones.

The real Macbeth himself is said to have been buried on Iona, as well as many other famous kings of Scotland. The island's traditions claim that as many as sixty kings – forty-eight of them Scottish, four of them Irish and eight of them Norwegian (more correctly, 'Norse') – were buried in its hallowed ground. In 1549 Donald Munro, dean of the Isles, described the *Relig Odhráin* as follows:

> Within this Isle of Colum Cille there is one sanctuary also, or churchyard, called in Irish *Relig Odhráin*. In it are three tombs of stone formed like little chapels … In the stone of one is written – *Tumulus Regum Scotiae*, that is, the Tomb of the Scots Kings – within this lie 48 crowned Scots Kings. The tomb on the south side has this description – *Tumulus Regum Hiberniae*, that is the Tomb of the Ireland Kings; there were four Ireland Kings in it. Upon the north side of our Scots tomb the inscription bears – *Tumulus Regum Norwegiae*, the tomb of the Kings of Norway. Within this sanctuary ly also the most part of the Lords of the Isles, with their lineage …

Notwithstanding such royal clientele, the Abbey gradually fell into ruins. As we have seen above in 1635 King Charles I ordered the Bishop of the Isles to repair the church which by then was the cathedral of the diocese of the Isles. However, it continued to deteriorate. In 1773 the great lexicographer Dr Samuel Johnson visited Iona as part of his *Journey to the Western Islands of Scotland.* He has left us the oft-quoted impression of his visit to Colum Cille's island.

> We were now treading that illustrious Island, which was once the luminary of the Caledonian regions, whence savage clans and roving barbarians derived the benefits of knowledge, and the blessings of religion. To abstract the mind

> from all local emotion would be impossible if it were endeavoured, and would be foolish if it were possible. Whatever withdraws us from the powers of our senses, whatever makes the past, the distant, or the future, predominate over the present, advances us in dignity of thinking beings. Far from me, and from my friends, be such frigid philosophy as may conduct us indifferent and unmoved over any ground which has been dignified by wisdom, bravery, or virtue. That man is little to be envied, whose patriotism would not gain force upon the plain of Marathon, or whose piety would not grow warmer among the ruins of Iona.

The poet John Keats (1795–1821) also famously visited Iona – 'the most holy ground of the north' – and was shown the graveyard,

> where they say 61 kings are buried – 48 Scotch from Fergus II to Macbeth, 8 Irish, 4 Norwegians and 1 French – they lie in rows compact ... many tombs of highland chieftains – their effigies in complete armour face upwards – black and moss covered – abbots and bishops of the island always of one of the chief clans. There were plenty Macleans and Macdonnels, among these the famous Macdonnel Lord of the Isles.

It was not until the late nineteenth century, however, that restoration of the medieval buildings got under way. The campaign – firstly at the Abbey church, the restoration of which was completed by 1914 – was led by George Douglas Campbell, eighth Duke of Argyll. This work was initially associated with the 1897 events commemorating the alleged 1300th anniversary of the death of the founding saint. In 1899 the Duke handed the Abbey over to the Church of Scotland, on condition that it would be made available to all denominations that requested use of it. A magnificent monument to the Duke and his wife (his second duchess) stands in the south transept of the Abbey church although the Duke himself is buried elsewhere.

The Iona Community, who are now the tenants of the fully restored Abbey, was established in 1938 by the Reverend George McCleod from Govan in Glasgow. The organisation was seen originally as a means of bringing young religious ministers and craftsmen together for the purpose of rebuilding the rest of the Abbey – both in its own right and as a symbol of the unity of 'work and worship'. Since then the Community has grown into an international fraternity whose members live in ordinary society but who have a common commitment to making Christianity relevant to the modern world.

A significant moment in the modern history of Columban scholarship was the publication in 1961 of the annotated edition and translation of Adomnán's *Vita Columbae* by Alan and Marjorie Anderson which spawned a whole series of specific studies as well as general commentaries on the early church in Ireland and Scotland.

In a striking harking back to the use of Iona as the burial place of the kings of Scotland, John Smith, the then Scottish-born leader of the British Labour Party, was buried on Iona following his sudden unexpected death on 12 May 1994. His grave is actually located where originally a large circular building dating to the very earliest phases of the monastery had once stood.[32] The grave is now visited by many of the pilgrims and tourists who go to the island. Shortly before his death Mr Smith was known to be speaking to political colleagues about the plans to celebrate what was understood to be the forthcoming fourteen-hundredth anniversary of the death of Saint Colum Cille in 1997.

There is a little medieval verse in Irish in which, fictionally, Colum Cille is said to have commented on the universal experience of death:[33]

> They speak in a proverb of three little sods,
> Impossible from which, anyone to save:
> The sod of his birth, the sod of his death,
> And lastly, of course, the sod of his grave.

As mentioned previously, in 1997 in what was then thought to be the fourteen-hundredth anniversary of the death of the saint, elaborate commemorative programmes were organised in most of the chief places associated with his name – both in Britain and Ireland as well as many places further afield. A huge amount of related scholarly work took place or was initiated, and in the United Kingdom the Royal Mail issued a beautiful stamp designed by the artist, Clare Melinsky. Many other commemorative plaques and works of art were commissioned – British Airways even repainted the livery and renamed some of their planes in honour of the saint.

In June 1997, the then Irish President Mary Robinson officially toured some of the relevant places in both countries. During her visit to the Isle of Skye, together with the British Minister of State for Education, Industry and Gàidhlig – the Scotsman Brian Wilson, she launched the joint governmental organisation known as *Iomairt Colm Cille.* Now retitled simply *Colmcille* with the motto: *Èirinn's Alba,* this is an initiative largely concerned with bringing the Gaelic language speaking communities in both Scotland and Ireland (north and south) – and more recently the Manx speakers from the Isle of Man – together for various mutual benefits and to foster an understanding of their related cultural experiences. A number of relevant conferences and seminars have been held as well as other inter-country events and projects. Recently a heritage trail *Slí Colmcille* or 'Colmcille's Path' – across Donegal, Northern Ireland and Scotland – has been placed on the internet.

[32] F. McCormick, 'Iona: the Archaeology', 53 note 4.
[33] Lacey, *Manus O'Donnell*, 62.

Throughout these islands in 1997 (and leading up to it) various associated ancient monuments were refurbished or made more accessible. A number of new museum exhibitions and various interpretive centres were also opened, including one at Fionnphort, the embarkation point on the Isle of Mull for people travelling onward to Iona. The name of Colum Cille was introduced to the digital age through various computerised projects, not the least of which was the CD-Rom of the *Cathach* issued by the Royal Irish Academy.

We now know that 1997 was unlikely to have been the correct anniversary year – it is more likely to have been 1993. However, as a result of the commemorations an impetus was given to a great deal of fresh scholarly enquiry into the subject. Many new professional and cultural ties were established across all the relevant boundaries, in a manner that almost certainly the real Colum Cille (or at least the version that has come down to us) might have approved.

As Columba, the 'dove' – the international symbol of peace, the saint has also been invoked appropriately in recent times in connection with the process of reconciliation in Northern Ireland, and between Ireland and Britain. The Prime Minister of the United Kingdom, David Cameron, on a visit to the Stormont assembly in Belfast in the summer of 2011 introduced his speech in the following manner.

> I know the calendar can have its own sensibilities in this part of the world, but it is an honour to address you on such an auspicious day, the ninth of June. This is the feast day of St. Columba, who very specially symbolises the historic linkages and deep bonds between Britain and Ireland.
>
> Born a Prince in Donegal, exiled in Iona, and honoured today in the Central Lobby of the Palace of Westminster ... his monks provided not just an Irish national treasure, the Book of Kells, but also a British national treasure, the Lindisfarne Gospels.

Perhaps the saint *is* still working miracles!

In all the ways described above, and in many other ways, the memory and maybe something of the spirit and ideals of that man, have survived from the sixth century to the present day. No matter what one believes, or whether one believes, we can still derive inspiration from the symbol that is Colum Cille.

Index